D0882104

The Jewish Challenge

Or the Vicissitudes of Judaism in the West

FREDERIC SEAGER

The Jewish Challenge

Or the Vicissitudes of Judaism in the West

PICARD • **Montreal**

ISBN 0-9681136-0-5

To my children,

Pierre and Anne-Marie,

and to their children.

Contents

PREFACE

ALL IS NOT WELL in contemporary Judaism. Despite general prosperity and increased social acceptance, Jews in the West are clearly perturbed. A glance at the Judaica section of any well-stocked bookstore, particularly in the United States, will provide ample evidence of this malaise. Along with volumes on lost Yiddishkeit can be found an increasing number devoted to the theme: why be Jewish? The answer to this question is implied in a steady stream of works dealing with the Holocaust, as the Nazi genocide is commonly called, and the State of Israel. The essence of being Jewish, it seems, is to remember the tragedy and to ensure that it will not recur by supporting the only country that will always accept Jewish refugees. Running through all popular Judaica nowadays is a sense of inadequacy, as if Jews were somehow not Jewish enough. The current wave of nostalgia over Yiddish culture bespeaks regret at having abandoned time-honoured traditions. Compounding this feeling is the realization that the Jews were totally ineffectual in opposing Hitler's evil designs. A largely secularized Jewish majority is absorbed in soul-searching as to what might have been done to prevent, or at least to mitigate, the catastrophe. Whatever their degree of religious observance, Jews tend to agree that self-awareness was lacking in that crucial period. Only a firm sense of identity, they believe, will enable them to recognize any new dangers that may await them.

Auschwitz remains at the core of the Jewish psyche, as Jews continue to berate themselves, or other Jews, for not having produced an adequate 'response' to the disaster. In immediate terms, the beneficiaries of this guilt complex are the secular and religious leaders of mainstream Judaism, whose appeals for solidarity serve to buttress their own position. Those who stand to gain the most, however, are the militants of the religious Right. Resurgent Orthodoxy owes much of its success to a myth, one that is widely accepted among Jews, even the non-observant. It holds that the tendency to assimilate into Gentile society was (is) a sign of weakness, which made the Jews an easy prey for the Nazis. A return to strict observance, so runs this argument, will enable Jews to resist assimilation and retain their Jewishness. Only then can they hope to face their ubiquitous enemies on anything approaching equal terms. In this view, every aspect of Jewish-Gentile relations becomes a test of strength; and the Jews must always prevail, lest they allow themselves to be drawn into yet another genocide. The ultimate test, the one on which all Jewish survival is seen to depend, is centred on the ancient land of the Bible. Should the State of Israel yield Judaea and Samaria to the Palestinian Arabs in order to placate the Christian West, all Jews would be defenceless before their foes. Jewish self-awareness is therefore concentrated on retaining the West Bank. In the mind of his assassin, Israeli prime minister Yitzhak Rabin was simply not Jewish enough.

Ever since Rabin was brutally gunned down at a peace rally in Tel Aviv on 4 November 1995, liberal Jews have been wringing their hands in dismay. They are aghast that a Jew should kill another Jew and tend to blame some lunatic fringe for that dreadful event. In fact, the Jewish opposition to Rabin's peace initiative is far more general than is commonly supposed. It is widely endorsed by the poorer elements of Diaspora Jewry who, for both religious and socioeconomic reasons, cannot share the liberals' close relationship to the Gentile majority. These people harbour deep resentment toward the mainstream Jewish leadership for neglecting their particular concerns. Among American Jews, the strife within the community is played out against a backdrop of Israeli politics. The Labour Party has the tacit support of liberal Jews, while the Orthodox favour Likud. Shortly before his death, Rabin had been denounced by Orthodox militants in Israel and the Diaspora as a Nazi and his government compared to a *Judenrat*—an allusion to the Jewish councils of wartime Europe which regularly selected new victims for the Nazi death camps. Former Premier Shamir warned his American supporters that Israel faced a Holocaust if the peace accords with the PLO were implemented. Other alarmists claimed that the Jewish state would be reduced to 'Auschwitz borders'.

The current psychosis has been building up for many years and can be traced to a spiritual and intellectual void, an inability to explain what caused the genocide and what its place in history might be. By avoiding this issue, mainstream Judaism leaves the field open to the right wing. For a time, some Hasidic rabbis claimed that the genocide was God's way of chastising the Jews for having been lured into Zionism. This is a providential view of history, in which everything happens because God wants it to. It has since been eclipsed by yet another, namely that the Jews were punished for the sin of assimilation. Either way, Auschwitz is attributed to Jewish moral failings, which other rabbis, even the most liberal, do not deny. The latter make no attempt to explain the tragedy; they merely refer to it occasionally with bowed heads. The synagogue prayers which recall the numerous examples of divine intervention to save the Jews from destruction are not modified, despite the obvious fact that God did not rescue the inmates of the death camps. The more sensitive rabbis are naturally upset over this absence, but prefer not to question the motives of the Almighty.

That rabbis have been unable to impart any meaning to Auschwitz is understandable in view of their particular training. Academic historians have no such excuse. Their role is to explain past events, in so far as is humanly possible, not merely to relate them. History used to be called the science of causality, but the senseless killing of the First World War and the atrocities of the Second seem to defy any causal explanation. It is often tempting to retreat into A. J. P. Taylor's adage that things happen because they happen. Yet, whether we like it or not, Auschwitz remains the central fact of the outgoing century. If academic historians refuse to seek any meaning to it, the untrained and the uneducated will eagerly fill the gap.

The wanton murder of six million European Jews came about not through any fault of their own, or because their brethren elsewhere were somehow inadequate, but because the society in which they lived had been educated in the belief that the Jews are

Christ-killers and that Judaism teaches vengeance. Christian teaching on the Jews and Judaism, exacerbated by fears of Bolshevism, nurtured the hatred that led to the massacre. Understandably, most Jews are loath to hold Christianity in any way responsible. They have polite, often amicable, relations with Christians and do not want to offend them. To seek the root cause of the tragedy should not, however, be construed as an accusation directed at individual Christians in our own day. Auschwitz must be dealt with as a historical, and not a current, issue. Otherwise, it will continue to be used by self-appointed Jewish spokespersons for their own political purposes.

Jewish reluctance to face the Christian problem goes back at least five centuries. Ever since the expulsion from Spain in 1492, Jews have tried to avoid Christianity in its various manifestations. Their abandonment, in the sixteenth century, of a mission to the Gentiles, was a concession to ecclesiastical pressure. As they retreated into mysticism, the Jews of Europe fell prey to Messianic movements in the seventeenth and eighteenth centuries. It was all a flight from reality. Some advanced thinkers of the Enlightenment proposed to solve the Jewish problem by incorporating Jews into society and treating religion as a private matter. The Jews of Western and Central Europe fairly jumped at the opportunity to become full-fledged citizens, but here too they encountered disappointments. Their newly-won civil rights were challenged by the anti-Semites. In a further attempt to efface all religious differences, many Jews turned to socialism. But their visible presence in the forefront of the Socialist International served only to arouse more anti-Jewish hatred, as they were accused of conspiring to dominate the world. The Russian pogroms and the rise of Nazism brought Zionism into prominence; but as the State of Israel has failed to normalize Jewish-Gentile relations, a rejuvenated Hasidic movement now promises the imminent coming of the Messiah.

Instead of continually fleeing from reality, Jews may some day prefer to confront it by dispelling the frightful misconceptions about themselves and their religion that have been engendered by Christianity. To do so, they will have to educate Christians in

Judaism and accept as proselytes those who request conversion. But proselytism finds few advocates among Jews, most of whom seem to be completely unaware that Judaism ever sought converts. Jews tend to view themselves as a community of suffering. They cannot understand why any Gentile should want to join it and often ridicule those who try. The few hardy souls who nonetheless succeed in converting to Judaism are soon made to feel that they have not suffered enough to be really Jewish. In fact, Jews are not suffering at present. They typically enjoy happier, healthier and more productive lives than most Gentiles. To the extent that they suffer as Jews, it is at the thought of what might have happened to them had they lived in Europe during the Second World War. Their lack of hospitality toward converts can be explained in part by the world's general indifference at that time to the Jewish victims of Nazi persecution, most of whom were denied refuge in Western democratic countries. As a result, there has been a tendency among Jews to view all Gentiles as being basically malevolent. Those who express a desire to adopt Judaism are presumed to have ulterior motives.

Sooner or later, Jews will have to recognize that proselytism is the most important question facing them today—if only because of intermarriage. In most cases, the Gentile spouses of Jews are accepted into Judaism as a last resort and without enthusiasm. Yet there are more positive reasons for Jews to proselytise. As Mr. Michael Lerner puts it somewhat off-handedly in his recent book, *Jewish Renewal*,[1] 'If you have something good, why not share it?' Indeed a persuasive case can be made for the proposition that Judaism is missionary in its very essence. Unless Jews actively seek converts, all attempts at Jewish renewal are likely to be short-lived. One cannot truly understand a subject until one explains it to others. This essential truth is manifest throughout Jewish history. Whether in the Hellenistic period, mediaeval Spain, pre-Hitler Germany or contemporary France, Judaism has been

---

[1] New York: Grosset/Putnem, 1994.

most vigorous when Jews presented their case, however obliquely, to Gentiles.

To do so in today's circumstances, they must first come to terms with their own history. The following pages offer the interpretation that the Jewish experience in the West has been shaped largely by the society in which Jews have lived, a society that for centuries has been essentially Christian. Adapting to a religion that has always pronounced Judaism to be null and void necessarily placed the Jews in a defensive position. They became increasingly withdrawn and ethnocentric. The emancipation of the eighteenth and nineteenth centuries allowed them to enter civil society only to the extent that they left their Judaism at home. In some cases, they were content to abandon it altogether.

Given the assimilationist tendencies of Western society, it is hardly surprising that religious Jews take a dim view of intermarriage, some calling it a 'soft genocide'. If Hitler could not finish off our people, they argue, then marriage to Gentiles surely will. Professor Norman Cantor, in his recently published survey of Jewish history entitled, *The Sacred Chain*,[2] accuses Jews who marry outside their community of committing what he calls 'ethnic suicide'. Perhaps they are, but since when was Judaism the sole preserve of an ethnic minority? That young people choose to marry at all in these uncertain times is remarkable in itself, a tribute to the resiliency of the human spirit. Judaism has always put a positive value on marriage, as a means both to attain personal happiness and to transmit Jewish values. By opposing mixed marriages, rabbis and other Jewish leaders seem to imply that Judaism is unable to compete for people's hearts and minds in a free society.

Actually, Judaism has much to attract converts, as Yossi Klein Halevy has discovered in his refreshingly frank *Memoirs of a Jewish Extremist*.[3] The son of a Holocaust survivor, Halevy was raised in the belief that all Gentiles are implacably hostile. He joins

---

[2] New York: Harper Collins, 1994.

[3] Boston: Little, Brown, 1995.

the Jewish Defence League, convinced that only direct—often violent—action can serve the Jewish cause. Then he marries a Gentile woman who not only adopts Judaism herself, but in effect converts him to Judaism. Through her, he discovers its inner beauty. At the close of his book, Halevy has made his peace with the world—which, after all, is God's creation. Although no two cases are alike, Halevy's spiritual journey shows that mixed marriages can be turned to Judaism's advantage.

In recent years, anti-Semitism has ceased to be a political issue, as people turn away from the notion that there ever was a Jewish conspiracy to dominate the world. To assert its own *raison d'être*, Christianity must continue to oppose Judaism; but individual Christians have shown themselves to be increasingly receptive to it. If Jews are ever to reach out to these righteous Gentiles, they must first exorcise the demons of the past. They will have to reject the myth that Jewish history is nothing more than a tedious chronicle of persecution. The sufferings of former years all had specific causes, which, once elucidated through critical study, can eventually be overcome. Then the Jews may join with their fellow human beings to abandon survival as an end in itself and get on with life.

Chapter I

A NEW WORLD-VIEW

HAS HISTORY A MEANING? Is the human adventure leading us anywhere? Or is it, in Shakespeare's words, merely 'a tale told by an idiot, full of sound and fury, signifying nothing'? Academic historians tend to avoid such philosophical questions, preferring instead to publish reams of learned monographs in a never-ending quest for research grants and promotions. During periods of great economic expansion, an occasional well-established professor, having won recognition through specialized research, will turn his gaze from the trees to the forest and seek some overall meaning to history. Thus Edward Hallett Carr, an authority on Soviet Russia, devoted a series of lectures to the question: *What Is History?*[1] His answer was that history records the progress of human society, both material and moral. But that was in 1961, as the West was still basking in the glow of the Eisenhower and Kennedy prosperity. Today, as human welfare—nay, human existence—appears increasingly threatened by disease, pollution, famine and the spread of nuclear weapons, the inevitability of progress is less discernible.

Consciously or not, Western intellectuals seem to have reverted to the conventional wisdom of the ancient Greeks and Romans, who saw human existence as repetitive—a continual series of rites and customs dictated by the seasons. The Roman calendar, dominated by the god Janus who is represented as facing both directions at once, symbolizes this belief: the year is a circle; it returns to where it originated. The new year was deemed to begin just after the winter solstice, when the period of daylight, at least in the northern hemisphere, is shortest, and everyone feels

---

[1]London: Macmillan, 1961.

rather depressed. Celebrations marking its arrival were typically accompanied by orgies of gluttony and drunkenness. Revelry, not rededication, was the order of the day. The New Year's eve parties of our own times, although usually more subdued, show the influence of that ancient pagan tradition.

Paganism was based on the assumption that the forces of nature had to be appeased, lest they destroy us all. It devised gods and goddesses for every conceivable natural phenomenon, the sun god being the most important. The sun was easily recognized as our main source of energy, giving warmth and causing plants to grow. Without it, there would be no life on earth; and maintaining life was the essential preoccupation of primitive society. Even today, people in certain parts of Africa greet each other with the question, 'How is your vital force?' The popular space drama, *Star Wars*, revived this tradition with the incantation, 'May the Force be with you.' In addition to worshipping the sun and rain gods, pagans engaged in periodic fertility rites as part of their efforts to continue the species.

Appeasing the forces of nature led to the veneration of power in all its forms, whether it be the sexual drive or political authority. Power-worship was carried to its logical conclusion toward the end of the ancient period, when Roman emperors assumed the title of gods and had temples erected in their honour. Ordinary mortals had to submit to forces beyond their control and could hope to influence them only through supplication. Considerations of justice, while not totally ignored, were always subordinate to those of material order. Such order was maintained throughout the ancient world largely because of paganism, which insisted on submission to established authority. The system worked; and thanks to the organizational skills of the Romans, ancient civilization attained a degree of general prosperity that would not be seen again until the eighteenth century.

The reverse side of the coin was that the ancient order was based largely on slavery. Slave labour was used to build the Roman roads, aquaducts, baths and other engineering marvels that contributed to the general well-being. The slaves themselves were part of the spoils of war, civilians captured by the victorious Roman armies. Thus ancient civilization, in its most glorious and enlightened form, depended on military victories for its sustenance. It was based on naked force: the power to kill.

Some two thousand years before ancient civilization, as exemplified by the Roman empire, reached its zenith, a small, almost insignificant, people first sounded a discordant note that was eventually to clash with the overall harmony of paganism. The Hebrews appeared on the scene while the civilization of the Middle East was still in its early youth. Their modest entry into history did not in any way prevent the ancient world from continuing on its chosen path. Nor did the Hebrews eschew pagan ways completely. They kept slaves, for example, while trying to ameliorate their condition. But in one fundamental respect, the Hebrews threw down a challenge to ancient civilization and its successors: they postulated the existence of a unique God who is the author of history. This signified that history had to have a meaning.

What that meaning is can already be discerned in the early books of the Bible. History is taken to begin with the expulsion of Adam and Eve from the Garden of Eden. It can end only when their descendants (i. e.: all of humanity) return to the God that gave them life, and do His bidding. Then, and only then, will oppression and injustice disappear from the face of the earth. When God called Abraham's grandson, Jacob—renamed Israel—into His service, Jacob and his offspring were entrusted with a mission: to lead struggling humanity to its final, golden age. Here, then, lies the true significance of the term, the chosen people. The expulsion from Eden may be seen as point A. The final stage of history, when all of God's creatures have learned to live in perfect harmony, is point B. The role of the Israelites (and their successors, the Jews) is to lead themselves and all other suffering mortals from point A to point B. Since we must assume that God knew what He was doing when He designated Jacob as His messenger, the role imposed on the Israelites has to be seen as the result of a conscious choice.

The Israelites' election to the status of holy people did not confer upon them any special privileges or mastery over other nations. 'The Lord did not set His heart upon you nor choose you because you were more numerous than any other people—for you were the fewest of all peoples' (Deut. 7.7). Rabbinical tradition holds that the last part need not be taken literally: it simply reminds Jews to be humble before God. It is certain, in any event, that they were not chosen to be an empire. The truth cannot be imposed by force; it will prevail only through teaching and example. Just what to teach and how to behave are laid out in the doctrine handed down to Moses at Sinai. If God revealed Himself to all of humanity through Adam, the Israelites alone were chosen to observe His commandments. This distinction confers upon them special responsibilities that they dare not avoid. 'You alone have I known of all the peoples of the earth; therefore I will punish you for all your iniquities' (Amos 3.2).

To fulfill their mission, they had to be released from slavery; only a free people can truly serve God. After their tribulations in Egypt, they needed a territorial base which would give them enough autonomy to order their own lives. Therefore God commanded the Israelites to disperse the native peoples living in the Promised Land and destroy their temples. But this was meant to give them dominion over one particular country, not over the entire world. Even at that, they did not in fact occupy completely the country that God had allocated to them: it was supposed to extend all the way to the Euphrates (Gen. 15.18), and the Israelites could not get that far. Nor were the native peoples totally dispersed; the Canaanites in particular stayed on (Joshua 17.13). The Israelites did not receive a country to settle in because of any virtues of their own. Moses painstakingly had to remind them of their earlier backsliding into idolatry, when they took to worshipping a Golden Calf (Deut. 9.5-7, 21-24). Clearly, they are unworthy of being the chosen people; but then again, anyone else would be equally unworthy.

From the very outset, the Israelitic faith (strictly speaking, one cannot refer to Judaism until Ezra's time) distanced itself from nature and nature-worship. As the great Salo W. Baron has explained in the preface to his magisterial *Social and Religious*

History of the Jews,[2] the practice of circumcision was already widespread among Semitic peoples. In this regard, the Israelites invented nothing new. What was novel, however, was the rule of having boys circumcised only a week after birth, rather than at puberty, as Muslims still do. Among the Jews, the rite of circumcision relates to the covenant (*brith* in Hebrew) that God made with Abraham, and not to incipient manhood. It commemorates a historical, rather than a natural, event. The dietary laws indicate that not all things found in nature may be eaten, even though they are often perfectly edible. Here again, nature is not a guide to religious practice. Finally, the Jewish New Year does not commemorate any natural occurrence, such as spring, the solstice or the fall harvest. A separate Jewish holiday, *Sukkoth,* is associated with the harvest. There is no Jewish holiday intended specifically to celebrate the arrival of spring, when life burgeons anew. Instead, the Jews, like their Israelite ancestors, commemorate the Exodus from Egypt. The only Jewish holiday that occurs in early winter is *Hannuka,* which recalls the revolt of the Maccabees and has nothing to do with seasonal change. The Jewish New Year is a very solemn festival, which begins the ten Days of Awe, culminating in the Day of Atonement. During this period, the faithful must individually review their conduct during the year just past and vow to improve themselves in the future. That such soul-searching occurs in late summer or early autumn is largely independent of the seasons.

Like religious practice, personal morality is not tied to nature. As the dietary laws suggest, one must discipline one's natural instincts. Sexual conduct is likewise subject to numerous rules and regulations. In Judaism, sex is not glorified as in pagan fertility rites, nor is it suppressed, as the Catholic clergy try to do. Rather, it is judiciously channeled toward marriage and the family, which are incumbent upon all Jews. In the thorny question of birth control, the Catholic church has made a distinction between natural and unnatural means of contraception. Not so the Hasidic Jews, who

---

[2]New York: Columbia University Press, 1952.

reject birth control in all its forms, raising large families that many pious Catholics would envy. Those Jews—the majority—who do practise birth control similarly make no distinction between so-called natural or unnatural means.

If nature is not a guide to morality, that is, to impressing some moral order on one's own existence and that of humanity, then what is? Any rabbi would quickly answer: the Torah, the body of statutes and ordinances which God gave to Moses at Sinai. The originality of this particular form of divine revelation is best understood by placing it in its historical context. Before the Israelites could receive God's instructions, they first had to experience the degradation of slavery in a country that had initially been hospitable to them. In the Bible, ancient Egypt represents pagan society *par excellence*, with all its good qualities and defects. Enslaving an entire people was an act of extreme brutality, an excellent example of political power that is allowed to run rampant. Consequently, the Israelites were admonished, in view of their own sufferings, not to oppress others. Nearly everyone is familiar with the commandment to love one's neighbour as one's self. Christian tradition mistakenly attributes its authorship to Jesus of Nazareth. Actually, it comes from the Hebrew Bible: specifically, Leviticus 19.18. The nineteenth-century English liberal philosopher John Stuart Mill was surprised to learn of the commandment's true origins, as indeed most of his compatriots probably would be today. Yet however noble loving one's neighbour may be, what follows a few verses further on is even more edifying. It commands the Israelites to love the stranger who settles among them for, as the Bible reminds us, 'you were strangers in the land of Egypt' (Lev. 19.34).

Such a proposition can be fully appreciated when compared to two moral maxims, one very famous and the other somewhat less so. The first is the 'Golden Rule' of Jesus: Do unto others as you would have them do unto you (Luke 6.31). The second originated with Hillel, the great rabbi who lived a hundred years before Jesus. A pagan once challenged Hillel to teach him Judaism while he stood on one foot. The rabbi replied, 'Whatever is hateful to you do not do unto your fellow human beings. That is the whole

Torah; the rest is commentary thereon. Go study the commentary'
(Shabbat 31 A). Christian and Jewish apologists have long argued
over which of these maxims is the nobler. The Christians, who
often seem to forget that Jesus was a Jew, point out that his
formulation is positive, while the so-called 'Silver Rule' of Hillel is
negative. The Jews reply that Hillel's maxim is applicable in all
cases, whereas that of Jesus is not.

Whichever formulation one may prefer, both are overshadowed by the text of Leviticus 19.33-34, because it is based on
historical experience. The Israelites are admonished to love the
stranger in their midst precisely because they were **not** always so
loved. Their sufferings as slaves in Egypt should make them more
sensitive to the feelings of others. The Pentateuch is replete with
references to the moral lesson to be derived from that difficult
period. Typical among them is this passage: 'You shall not oppress
a stranger, for you know the feelings of the stranger, having
yourselves been strangers in the land of Egypt' (Ex. 23.9).

The stranger referred to in this and other texts is clearly one
who dwells among the Israelites as a part of a small minority. The
native peoples who inhabited the Promised Land and whom God
commanded the Israelites to disperse obviously do not fall into this
category. No love is wasted on them. Although the slave people
that Moses led out of Egypt had not been tested in battle, the
statutes and ordinances handed down at Sinai are full of detailed
instructions on how to wage war. If the Israelites wanted a country
of their own, they would have to take it by brute force. Here is
posed for the first, but not the last, time the dilemma of how to love
others while looking out for one's vital interests. Judaism has long
recognized that the use of force, including deadly force, may be
necessary for self-preservation. One cannot do any good to one's
family or to society in general if one does not exist. To be truly free,
the former slaves will have to bear arms—and occasionally to use
them.

By defeating other nations and taking captives, the Israelites
run the risk of resembling the pagans whose religious customs God
told them to abhor. They lose their distinctiveness and often

relapse into idolatry. God is angry with them and delivers them to the Philistines, whose domination they must endure for forty years. The prophet Samuel saves his flock from utter annihilation by imploring God to intervene. Divine thunder throws the Philistine army into confusion, and the Israelite warriors carry the day. For many years, the community prospers under Samuel's benevolent guidance.

But the temptation to be like other peoples is too great for the Israelites. Once Samuel has grown very old, the elders of the community petition him to 'appoint a king for us, to govern us like all other nations' (I Samuel 8.5). This was a reasonable request, since God had already promised the Israelites that they could have a king of their own if they ever wanted one (Deut. 17.15). But a monarchy is not without disadvantages, as God pointedly tells Samuel. 'Heed the demand of the people in everything they say to you. For it is not you that they have rejected; it is I whom they have rejected as their king' (I Samuel 8.7). Then the prophet is told to warn the Israelites of the misfortunes that will befall them if they choose a king: crushing taxes, requisitions of animals and property, and forced labour will so oppress the people that they will call upon God to end this tyranny, but He will not answer them. The healthy distrust of political power that characterizes later Judaism has its origins in this Biblical passage.

As kings go, the early rulers of Israel were not all that bad; they were certainly more responsive to the wishes of their subjects than most pagan monarchs. Yet they were not paragons of virtue either. David, whose name in Hebrew means well-beloved, commissioned the writing of the Psalms; but he was also an adulterer and a murderer. Solomon, who wrote the book of Ecclesiastes and rendered wise judgments, had too many wives and too much gold, in direct violation of earlier, divinely-ordained limits on kingship (Deut. 17.17). Under the influence of his foreign wives, Solomon turned away from God late in his reign (I Kings 11.1-4). In time, the kingdom grew corrupt and split in two: Israel in the north and Judah in the south. The latter, whose capital was Jerusalem, had to endure a series of particularly incompetent monarchs. One of the worst was Manasseh, who, after ascending the throne at the tender age of twelve, restored idol-worship and often consulted ghosts (II Kings 21.1-6). Judah was eventually conquered by the army of Babylon, to which thousands of its citizens were sent as captives. The Babylonian captivity came as a shock to the Israelites. Had God abandoned His chosen people? It fell to the prophets to wrestle with this problem. Jeremiah had an apparently simple answer: 'Your conduct and your acts/Have brought this upon you' (Jer. 4,18). He quickly added, however, that it was not God's wish that they perish in exile. Instead, they should marry and have children, in order to make the best of their new condition. 'And seek the welfare of the city to which I have exiled you and pray to the Lord on its behalf; for in its prosperity you shall prosper' (Jer. 29.7).

The Jewish Mission

An even more positive note is sounded by Isaiah. Yes, the people Israel has suffered, but its sufferings are brought on largely by the sins of others, who are so blinded by idolatry and superstition that they oppress God's servant (Is. 53.6-7). God has not forsaken Zion, he reassures the people. 'Can a woman forget her baby,/Or disown the children of her womb?' (Is. 49.15). The exile has a holy purpose, for it will allow the descendants of Jacob to 'teach the true way to the nations' (Is. 42.1). Israel, says the prophet repeatedly, must be a 'light unto the nations' (Is. 42.6; 49.6). The notion that the Israelites have a mission to fulfill among the other peoples of the world was not totally new. The former slaves assembled at Sinai were told to observe the divinely ordained laws faithfully 'for that will be proof of your wisdom and discernment to other peoples...' (Deut. 4.6). But with the exile, and Isaiah's interpretation of it, the missionary ideal comes to fruition. 'For from where the sun rises to where it sets, My name is honoured among the nations, and everywhere incense and pure oblation are offered to My name' (Malachi 1.11). Gentiles who 'attach themselves to the Lord' are welcome members of the congregation. 'For My House shall be called/A house of prayer for all peoples' (Is. 56.6-7).

By accepting righteous Gentiles into their midst the Israelites can avoid falling into the rut of tribalism, which is not only sterile in itself, but unworthy of a people chosen to obey God's commandments. Here, Moses set the example by marrying not a Hebrew woman, but Zipporah, the daughter of Jethro, a Midianite priest. When Jethro acknowledged the supremacy of God and joined the Israelites (Ex. 18.10-12), he became, in effect, the first convert to their religion. Only through hospitality toward the stranger, with a view to educating him in the doctrine of truth and justice, can the Israelites fully justify the confidence that God has placed in them.

As it turned out, the exile was not mere punishment, but an opportunity. When Cyrus, the King of Persia, took Babylon and offered the Hebrews a chance to return to their former homeland, many of them—perhaps a majority—preferred to stay put. Babylon was, after all, a remarkably advanced society. In addition to accomplishing such engineering feats as the renowned Hanging Gardens, it was a world leader in banking and finance. The use of personal cheques for the payment of debts originated in Babylon. Jerusalem was, by comparison, a scientific and cultural backwater. Throughout the centuries, the Jews of Babylon thrived both materially and intellectually. Rabbinical academies were founded there and eventually produced the Babylonian Talmud, which is far more extensive than its Jerusalem counterpart. On the eve of the First World War, Jews constituted the largest ethnic group in modern-day Baghdad. The community continued to flourish until it was destroyed along with the Iraqi monarchy in 1958.

Even as returning exiles from Babylon rebuilt a state in what came to be known as Judaea (from which was derived the word, Jew) in 586 B.C.E., a Jewish *Diaspora,* or dispersion, spread throughout much of the Mediterranean basin. It was called into being by the expansion of maritime commerce which had originated with the Phoenicians (many of whom eventually adopted Judaism) and which continued throughout the Greek and Roman periods. The descendants of Jacob were no longer a compact community:

more of them spoke Greek than Aramaic, and most lived too far from Jerusalem to participate in official rites, particularly the sacrificial cult. Even in Judaea itself, where Ezra had restructured the religious practices of the returning exiles, thus laying the foundations for normative Judaism, Hellenistic influence was pervasive. Hellenism had much the same impact on ancient civilization before and during much of the Roman period as American culture has today. It was chic to speak Greek (or what passed for Greek hundreds of miles from Athens) and to imitate Greek ways.

The religious authorities in Jerusalem took a dim view of the Hellenistic vogue. They especially objected to the growing popularity of gymnastics, partly out of concern that it might encourage narcissism in young men. Swimming was deemed both proper and beneficial; in Judaism, fathers are duty-bound to teach it to their sons. But land exercises, done naked alongside Gentiles, tended to alienate Jewish athletes from their religion: many felt ashamed to be circumcised. The first Book of Maccabees (1.14-15) recounts that Hellenized Jews built a gymnasium in Jerusalem, in imitation of the Greeks, and 'fashioned foreskins for themselves'—that is, they underwent surgery to effect such an appearance.

Traditional Judaism, with its priestly cult of sacrifice, proved incapable of stemming the Hellenistic tide. It was too elitist, religious rites being confined to the *Kohanim* (the priestly caste) and the Levites. Some way had to be found to involve ordinary Jews whose education was limited and whose knowledge of Hebrew was slight. This task fell to a group of educators known as the Pharisees. They were not a sect, but a movement; and in no way did they resemble the caricature found in the Gospels. The Pharisees were religious reformers whose purpose was to infuse all aspects of daily life with holiness. Their reforms were based on what they called the oral Torah, those divinely ordained practices that do not appear in the Bible. The written word of God had, of course, been interpretated for generations, but no one had thought of giving such interpretation legal sanction. To justify the concept of an oral Torah, the Pharisees invented a charming bit of fiction.

Moses, they said, had dictated to scribes the revelation received at Sinai during the daylight hours only. After dusk, he continued to transmit the Torah orally. It was this oral tradition that the Pharisees claimed to be heirs to.

At the centre of Pharisaic Judaism was prayer. Inasmuch as most Jews lived too far from Jerusalem to participate regularly in the sacrificial cult, the Pharisees emphasized prayer, which they called 'the sacrifice of the heart'. The Hebrew prophets had often cast doubt on the moral value of animal sacrifice, as in Hosea (6.6): 'For I desire love, not sacrifice,/And the knowledge of God rather than burnt-offerings.' The Pharisees did not try to abolish sacrifice, but they considered prayer more important. Jews were encouraged—nay, commanded—to pray after getting up in the morning, before lying down at night, and at mealtimes. Washing one's hands before meals, though it does not appear anywhere in the Bible, became another practice incumbent upon all Jews. Its purpose was not primarily hygienic, although the Pharisees did recognize the importance of personal cleanliness. The Christian Bible pays oblique homage to their zeal in washing pots, pans, cups, etc., as well as market produce (Mark 7.3-4). What the Pharisees had in mind when prescribing such ablutions was mainly to perpetuate and popularize the custom of the High Priest, who regularly washed his hands before offering a sacrifice at the Temple. The ordinary Jew, as he was about to partake of his modest meal, thus became equal to the High Priest in holiness. Pharisaism was religious democracy.

It was not limited to the home. Faced with the danger of assimilation represented by Hellenism, the Pharisees created a network of schools, known in Hebrew as *Beit-Hamidrash* (house of learning) or *Beit-Haknesset* (house of assembly), and which the world calls by their Greek name of synagogue. The first synagogues had been founded in Ezra's time; under the Pharisees, they became the focal point of Jewish religious and communal life. The synagogue was a centre for continuing education, long before that term had ever been invented. Its leader was called a *rav*, or master. (In Hebrew, *rabbi* means simply, my master.) On the

Sabbath, the Jews gathered at the synagogue were led in prayer by the *hazan*, or cantor. Then the rabbi would instruct them in the meaning of Holy Writ, be it passages from the Pentateuch or selections from the prophetical writings. Unlike the Temple, which had to be located in Jerusalem, a synagogue could be built anywhere—usually as far from a pagan temple as possible A quorum of only ten adult Jewish males was required for a service. Synagogues sprung up throughout the Near East. Some were quite imposing: the Great Synagogue in Alexandria was so large that beadles had to wave flags in order to let the congregation know when to rise and when to be seated. The synagogue service soon attracted pagans in virtually every city and town of the Diaspora; they could not participate directly, but stood at the open door listening to the prayers and to the rabbi's commentary, which was given in the vernacular so that even the most uneducated Jew could understand.

As a further means of winning back Jews from Hellenistic values, it was decided to translate the Hebrew Bible into Greek. By the third pre-Christian century, more Jews could read Greek than Hebrew. So a Greek translation of the Bible would bring these culturally assimilated Jews closer to the source of their faith. According to legend, the task was undertaken by seventy rabbis, each representing one of the world's known languages. The legend probably has little basis in fact. The 'rabbis'—actually scribes—were all engaged in translating the Scriptures into one language, Greek; it hardly mattered just how many languages were known at the time or how many the translators could actually read. In the Talmud, the figure seventy is used to designate all the world's nations. Thus, the legend indicates that the Bible was consciously being offered to the whole of humanity. Henceforth, any person—Jew or Gentile—who read Greek could study Holy Writ. And there were far more Hellenized Gentiles than Hellenized Jews. The new translation of the Bible, called the Septuagint after the seventy scribes, did in fact serve to bring the many Greek-speaking Jews into closer contact with the basic tenets of their religion. But it went far beyond that: even more than the synagogue, the Scriptures made Judaism accessible to the entire civilized world.

The challenge of Hellenism had transformed the ancient Hebrew faith into a worldwide missionary religion. In fact, it was the first religion in history to break out of the bounds of ethnicity or political structure. Allusions to proselytism can be found in the Bible, albeit in a somewhat roundabout way. The Israelites were still wandering in the desert when they received instructions as to which foreigners could be admitted into the Assembly of the Lord. No Ammonite or Moabite would be allowed in—'even to the tenth generation'—because these nations did not answer the Israelites' call for food and water as they fled Egypt (Deut. 23.4-5). On the other hand, Egyptians could join the congregation in the third generation (Deut. 23-9). The hospitality granted to Egyptians is all the more remarkable since the Israelites had been slaves in Egypt. Presumably, all hard feelings between the two peoples would dissipate after two generations. Even the prohibition against the Moabites did not last forever. Ruth, the very personification of a foreign woman who enters Judaism through marriage, was herself a Moabite. The Bible reminds us, moreover, that she was the grandmother of King David, indicating that her conversion was serious.

The Pharisees, whose first task had been to educate ordinary Jews in the basic elements of their religion, now took up their mission to the Gentiles. With the new translation of the Bible tucked under their arms, they applied their pedagogical skills to any interested pagan who could read Greek. Having the Bible as its source, Judaism was a portable religion, unlike the various pagan cults which were tied to particular countries and temples. The latter gained foreign adherents primarily through military conquest. Even the Jews had, on at least two occasions, resorted to forced conversions in order to consolidate their hold on Judaea after the Maccabean revolt. But it was in the the Diaspora, where Jews were a minority, that the Jewish mission registered its most impressive gains. There the Pharisees made converts by reasoning with them, without having to rely on political authority or military might.

Further contributing to the spread of Judaism in the ancient world was a growing disenchantment with paganism. It is no coincidence that conversions to Judaism reached their peak during the reign of Augustus Caesar, when the general standard of living in the Mediterranean basin was higher than ever. The imperial order had fostered trade by virtually eliminating piracy. Roman aquaducts brought water to parched farmland and greatly improved overall hygiene. Paganism had originated in the belief that the forces of nature were uncontrollable and had to be appeased. Now, however, nature was no longer quite so fearsome; and people began to wonder if life had any purpose beyond the continual repetition of the seasons. The early Greek philosophers, in the relatively prosperous Athens of the fifth pre-Christian century, were among the first pagans to seek some direction to human existence. By the time of Augustus, their inquiry had been taken up in one way or another by almost everyone who could read. Judaism provided an answer in the form of historical monotheism, in which God is deemed to be the driving force of history.

In practical terms, Judaism had much to offer the many pagans who had outgrown their ancestral religion. Its most attractive feature was the Sabbath, which offered them a full day of rest each week. The respect shown to women was another: in the Augustan age, female converts to Judaism outnumbered males, who were often afraid to be circumcised. The most illustrious was Helene, head of the royal house of Adiabene, on the Tigris. Poppea, Nero's wife, was strongly attracted to Judaism and followed many Jewish practices, though she did not formally convert. Finally, there were economic and social advantages to becoming a Jew. A wealthy proselyte enjoyed the wide-ranging business contacts afforded by the Jewish community. A poor one could rely on a well-organized system of Jewish charities and relief organizations.

Not all pagans who stood at the synagogue door during the Sabbath service or who read the Bible in Greek converted to

Judaism. Many were deterred by the requirement of circumcision. Those pagan men who did formally adopt Judaism showed a remarkable degree of commitment. Their decision was a highly personal one which, once taken, could not easily be reversed. Ritual circumcision prevented Judaism from making mass conversions as its daughter religion, Christianity, later did through the baptism of whole crowds. Despite this seeming disadvantage, however, the Jewish mission was remarkably successful. During the reign of Augustus, the Roman empire numbered some eighty million inhabitants. An estimated eight million—ten percent of the total—were formally Jewish, but only three million of these were of Jewish ancestry. The rest were converts or the descendants of converts. Jewish proselytism was further aided by the official tolerance of pagan Rome. Because Judaism did not rely on any particular political system, it was not perceived as a threat to the empire. The imperial government granted it the status of *religio licita*, or authorized religion; only the official cult honouring the Roman gods enjoyed a similar distinction.

The growth of Jewish communities within the Roman empire provoked resentment and often enmity, as is only natural when one group increases in both numbers and property in relation to others. This was not anti-Semitism, however. The anti-Semite considers the Jews to be the embodiment of all evil and attributes supernatural powers to them. In the pagan Roman empire, the most common accusation leveled at the Jews was that of laziness, since they took one day a week off from work. Sexual jealousy, often an aspect of intergroup rivalry, was also present. The Roman historian Tacitus claimed that the Jews were prone to lust. A lesser writer, Meleager of Gadara, grieved at the loss of his mistress. 'If your lover is a Sabbath-keeper, no wonder. Love burns hot even on cold Sabbaths.' For the rest, anti-Jewish sentiment was similar to the hostility directed at any religious or ethnic minority in a multi-national political system.

Clearly, ancient civilization was ripe for a new, monotheistic faith. Many pagans who did not convert to Judaism continued to attend Sabbath services while standing respectfully at the synagogue entrance. They were called 'proselytes of the gate' or 'God-fearers' by the rabbis, and no attempt was made to disperse them. Yet despite its extraordinary success in attracting pagans, Judaism was not to become the majority religion of the Mediterranean world; it did not conquer Rome. The Pharisees were not interested in taking over an empire. They approached their mission to the Gentiles on an individual basis: education, not political power, was their aim. Although the Jews had grown in number since the writing of Deuteronomy 7.7, they had to remain a minority until, in the fullness of time, all of humanity could be enlightened by divine wisdom. Roman rule, even at its most civilized, was based on military conquest; and the Pharisees did not want to become heirs to that tradition. This was just as well. No one in the Augustan age could foresee that the superbly efficient Roman system would eventually crumble. Had Judaism become the dominant religion, its leaders would have had to preside over a decadent empire.

In more immediate terms, the failure of the Jewish mission to sweep everything before it cannot be attributed to any fundamental weakness in Judaism itself. Rather, it stems from the Jews' own ambivalent position toward Rome. Throughout the Diaspora, the Jews were loyal, often prosperous, subjects. Their situation in Judaea was quite different. Very few got rich in that country's agricultural economy, and nearly all resented having to pay taxes to a pagan emperor. Judaea had been conquered by Pompey in 63 B.C.E. and became a Roman protectorate. Its population did benefit materially from the conqueror's public works projects and general maintenance of order. But the presence of the imperial standard in the holy city of Jerusalem was an offence to the Judaeans. They sought deliverance in the form of a liberator who would set everything right, throwing off Roman rule and establishing peace and justice throughout the world. The very success of the Jewish mission to the Gentiles convinced many of them that the kingdom of heaven was about to be established on earth. In their prayers, they beseeched God to send speedily that liberator, whom they called *Mashiach:* the Messiah.

Chapter II

MESSIANISM

THAT THE FIRST WAVE of Messianic fervour should appear during the reign of Augustus is hardly surprising. For the Jews of Judaea, the contrast between the promise afforded by the flowering of ancient civilization and their own humiliation could not have been more striking. On the one hand, the material and intellectual advances of the age had led increasing numbers of pagans to Judaism. On the other, the Jewish state itself was subjugated by an empire of idol-worshippers and had to endure their military occupation. Only the Messiah, they believed, could resolve this contradiction by freeing Judaea and establishing peace throughout the world. The Messianic ideal finds its most noble expression in the vision of Isaiah, who prophesied that the peoples of the earth will 'beat their swords into plowshares/And their spears into pruning hooks:/Nation shall not take up/Sword against nation;/Nor shall they ever again know war' (Is. 2.4; also Micah 4.3). Then the entire world will be united under God. 'All flesh shall come to worship Me, said the Lord' (Is. 66.23).

The coming of the Messiah signifies not the end of the world—which may indeed destroy itself someday (Ps. 102. 25-26)—but the end of history. All history, we recall, is taken to begin with the expulsion of Adam and Eve from the Garden of Eden. Because they disobeyed God, they and their descendants must endure pain and suffering, injustice and oppression. Only by returning to God and obeying His laws can humanity redeem itself. From this standpoint, the entire human experience can be seen as a struggle between power and piety. Those who exploit power may seem to dominate for a while, but piety will eventually triumph. Such is the basic faith of Judaism. It holds that by following God's doctrine and teaching it to others, the pious will help make the world a better place. Human nature, which encourages all of us to seek an unfair advantage over others, will have been transformed in the fullness of time. The *Pax Romana* of the Augustan age showed that universal peace was possible. To fulfill the Messianic prophesy, however, it had to be established on a more enduring basis than mere military domination.

In Judaea, if not in the Diaspora, there was a growing conviction that the time had come, that the age-old struggle between power and piety was about to be resolved in favour of the latter. Little wonder, then, that candidates for the title of Messiah abounded in those days. The Christian Bible mentions two who failed: a certain Theudas and one Judas of Galilee (Acts 5.36-37). There were surely many more. None was finally recognized as the true Messiah because none managed to free Judaea from Roman rule. This was deemed to be the first step in the liberation of all humanity. But the expectations of the people, especially the poor and the downtrodden, were not dashed. The Judaean masses still clung to the belief that a liberator would soon arise, freeing them and establishing God's kingdom on earth. Messianic expectations were most fervent in Galilee, a mountainous region which enjoyed a measure of autonomy from Roman rule and where Jewish nationalism had long been especially militant. It was here that a carpenter's son from Nazareth named Joshua exercised his ministry as a popular preacher and faith healer for some twenty years.

There have been many attempts, by Christians and Jews alike, to portray the so-called 'historical' Jesus. All have failed, but not for want of information. His life and times are well documented in the Gospels—far better than nearly all other major figures of antiquity. Rather, the failure to present modern readers with a convincing portrait of Jesus stems from a misunderstanding as to what the object of history really is. Total reconstruction of the past is beyond anyone's ability. Even if it were possible to collect all existing documentation on a particular subject, the historian would still have to decide which facts are most important. And that choice depends on what the historian is looking for—that is, on his working hypothesis. The study of history must begin with a particular set of questions. Its validity depends on how convincingly these questions are answered.

When dealing with Jesus in a Jewish context—the context in which he actually lived—we are faced with two major questions. The first, and by far the easier to answer, is how to account for the Nazarene's widespread popularity among his compatriots. Then, given this popularity, why did his own people eventually reject him as the Messiah? The answer to the second question depends on a clear understanding of the first. Only by attracting a large following among his fellow Judaeans could Jesus make a convincing claim to be their liberator. Their eventual rejection of this claim is all the more dramatic because they had placed such high hopes in him. Both questions are highlighted in the last week of Jesus's life. On a Sunday, he entered Jerusalem in triumph, with the crowd laying palm branches on the road so that his feet would not touch the ground. Five days later he was dead. To understand what had happened in the interval, we must ask what the Jews of Judaea expected of Jesus and what he was able to offer them.

Any investigation into Jesus's relations with his compatriots must first strip away the centuries-old layers of ecclesiastical tradition which have effectively transformed him into a Christian. In *The Merchant of Venice*, Shakespeare echoes a popular misconception when he has Shylock refer to 'your prophet the Nazarite', who commanded his followers to eat pork. Actually, of course, Jesus did nothing of the kind. He lived and died an observant Jew. Yet even to this day, most Jews prefer to ignore Jesus. Perhaps they are so tired of being called Christ-killers that they do not want to hear any more about him. But Jesus belongs to Jewish history. To exclude the Nazarene from his own people is to acquiesce tacitly in Christianity's appropriation of him.

Among the Jews who have evinced the greatest interest in Jesus are the Zionists who settled in early twentieth-century Palestine and their successors, the present-day Israelis. From Joseph Klausner to André Chouraqui, these authors have, in effect, reclaimed Jesus for the Jews. For a Zionist, there is much to like in him, since he was a Jewish—more properly a Judaean—nationalist. Of the twelve apostles—representing the twelve tribes of Israel—at least one, Simon Peter, regularly carried a sword (Matt. 26.51-52; John 18.10). If Jesus were alive today, he would naturally be an

Israeli and most likely a militant of the religious Right. He would have no more sympathy for the Palestinians than the Jesus of two thousand years ago had for the Canaanites. When a Canaanite woman asked Jesus to cure her daughter, he replied contemptuously that it was not fitting to take the bread of children and cast it to the dogs (Matt. 15.26). Previously, he had advised his disciples not to give that which is holy to dogs or to throw pearls at swine (Matt. 7.6). In a Jewish context, this metaphor has a simple and direct meaning: do not preach to the Gentiles. He forbade them to visit with Gentiles or enter any city of the Samaritans (Matt. 10.5). Nor, he advised, should they pray like Gentiles, who 'repeat empty phrases' in the hope that 'they will be heard because of their many words' (Matt. 6.7). Even those Gentiles who were ready to adopt Judaism did not interest Jesus. He ridiculed the Pharisees because they 'cover land and sea to make a single proselyte' (Matt. 23.15).

Despite his differences with the Pharisees on this point, Jesus was, as Baron has noted, essentially a Pharisaic Jew. What else could he have been? Fully ninety percent of the Jews of Judaea, and nearly all those of the Diaspora, were of the Pharisaic persuasion. These included the Zealots and the Essenes, who were basically Pharisaic in their religious outlook, but differed from the rabbis on politics. In Judaea, the Saducees constituted the dominant minority. They clung to the sacrificial cult of the Temple in Jerusalem and cooperated fully with the Roman governor, by whose authority that cult was able to continue. Unlike the Pharisees, the Saducees had no use for a Messiah, since he would have necessarily undermined their position.

Jesus was no Saducee. He had been educated in the synagogue and clearly longed for the coming of the Messianic age. This may explain why he had no desire to convert Gentiles to Judaism. If the end of history was indeed imminent, proselytism had to be set aside in order to prepare the Jews for the coming of the Messiah. At some point in his ministry he became convinced that he was himself the Messiah. Just how this idea came upon him is not explained in the Gospels. The evangelists Mark (1.18-25) and Luke (1.26-38) both refer to his being born of a virgin as proof that he was indeed the Messiah promised in the Hebrew Bible. Jesus never breathed a word of this to anyone. Perhaps he was ignorant of the particular circumstances leading to his birth (although, if he was truly the Messiah, he ought to have known); or else he knew, but did not want to embarrass his parents. In retrospect, it might have been simpler for all concerned had he come out with it at the very beginning, saying something like this: 'See here. My mother was a virgin when I was born. Therefore, I am the Messiah. Now just follow me and ask no further questions.'

Actually, of course, Jesus was wise not to mention his virgin birth, since this would not have made much of an impression on his compatriots. The Biblical prophesy referred to by Matthew comes from Isaiah 7.14 and is too well known to be cited here. In the original Hebrew, the pregnant woman is rendered by the word *alma*, which means, simply, any woman of child-bearing age, whether a virgin or not. The Hebrew word for virgin is *betula*. Moreover, the original Hebrew text uses the definitive article, indicating that a child will be born to **the** young woman, and not to **a** virgin. The evangelist seems to have used the Greek version of the Bible, which incorrectly translates *alma* by *parthenos* (virgin). All of this would be mere academic hair-splitting were it not for the fact that this particular prophesy has nothing whatsoever to do with the coming of the Messiah and has never been interpreted as such by Jews. The entire story about the child Emmanuel and his eventual ability to distinguish right from wrong is meant to be a sign that the King of Judah will be able to defend Jerusalem against his enemies. Of all the Jews who, at one time or another, aspired to be the Messiah, not a single one ever claimed to have been born of a virgin. And this includes Jesus.

More convincing to his Jewish audience was the fact that Jesus was descended from King David through Mary's husband, Joseph. In Jewish tradition, the Messiah was supposed to be of Davidic ancestry. Not everyone descended from David was necessarily the Messiah, but having him in one's family tree was certainly an advantage. Now we all know that Joseph was not Jesus's real father, but his contemporaries were blissfully unaware of this complication. There are several references in the Gospels to

Jesus as a son of David. (For example, Matt. 9.27.) Those who used this expression obviously considered him to be the Messiah. Jesus's claim to be the liberator so anxiously awaited by his compatriots was based primarily on his remarkable abilities as a faith healer. Jews have long believed that a person whose daily life is guided by moderation and self-discipline will normally enjoy good health. Conversely, they assume that illness is often caused by excess or self-indulgence. It is but a short step from such reasonable principles to the belief that a sick person is somehow possessed of an evil spirit. And since all healing is miraculous in one way or another, the healer can be seen as a miracle-worker, with the ability to expel such demons. Even today, some highly revered Hasidic rabbis are considered to possess healing powers. For them, exorcism is no laughing matter, but a serious obligation to be performed only in the presence of the faithful. When Jesus began to cast out demons from the bodies of sick people in Galilee, he was continuing a well-established tradition, one that persists to this very day. His fame as a faith healer spread throughout Judaea and even to neighbouring Syria (Matt. 4.23-25). Such miraculous cures made the people receptive to his message that the kingdom of heaven was at hand, and that they should prepare for it.

This was the good news that so many Galileans were waiting for. The more miracles Jesus performed, the more they were inclined to see in him the agent of fundamental change. At one point, Jesus asked his closest disciples who the people thought he was. John the Baptist, said one; Elijah, replied another; a resurrected prophet of Biblical times, ventured a third. 'But who do you say that I am?' he queried. It was Peter who answered: 'You are the Messiah!' That they did not reply in unison raises a crucial question: did they know who Jesus was before following him on his mission? To judge by their answers, it would seem that they did not. Their initial loyalty to him stemmed not from any certainty that he was the Messiah, but from a common desire to see Judaea freed from Roman rule. While in Galilee, Jesus and his disciples resembled nothing so much as a resistance cell in Vichy France during the Second World War. Like most members of the French underground, they did not plan military action against a far superior force, but sought to prepare their compatriots for the eventual liberation of their country. Jesus had them all promise to keep silent on his identity (Luke 9.18-21). He had already been called the Messiah by people whom he had cured, and had imposed silence on them as well (Luke 4.41). To be known as the Messiah in Roman-dominated Judaea would invite repression by the imperial authorities. Any so-called 'king of the Jews' (Jesus was of Davidic lineage) was considered dangerous. So he limited his ministry to Galilee, wisely avoiding direct confrontation with Rome.

Jesus Presents His Case

Still, Jesus could hardly go unnoticed. His popularity among the Galilean masses brought him to the attention of the Pharisees. Unlike the ruling Saducees, the Pharisees believed—indeed hoped—that the Messiah would come some day. So they were naturally interested in learning more about this latest aspirant. In Christian tradition, the Pharisees are portrayed as the enemies of Jesus, narrow-minded and hypocritical. Nothing could be further from the truth. Had the Pharisees not taken Jesus's Messianic candidacy seriously, they would have simply rejected him out of hand and warned the people against following an impostor. Instead, they gave him the benefit of the doubt right up to his last few days in Jerusalem. It was their very liberal attitude that led to the many altercations with Jesus that are recounted in the Gospels. For the Pharisees, any Messianic claimant had to be judged on his own merits. The stakes were high. If he was indeed the Messiah, Judaea and all of humanity would be permanently freed from oppression. But if he was not, and the people still believed in him, neither he nor anyone else could save Judaea from the wrath of the Romans.

In an effort to determine whether Jesus was the real Messiah, the Pharisees kept a close eye on him and listened intently to his preaching. The people of Galilee were for the most part poor farmers, who had little time to improve their religious learning. They were impressed with his miracle cures and clung to his every word, even when they did not understand what he was saying. The

Pharisees, on the other hand, did understand Jesus, since most of his preaching was derived from the Hebrew Bible and their own interpretation of it. The Gospels carry extensive excerpts from Jesus's sermons, but seldom explain the Pharisees' reaction to them. Whenever they do question Jesus, he always has the last word. In the end, the Pharisees gave up on Jesus and decided, somewhat reluctantly, that he was not the Messiah after all. To understand why they—and the people at large—finally rejected his Messianic claims, the historian has to imagine what their reaction to his words and deeds must have been. To begin with, Jesus's sayings as reported in the Gospels should be placed alongside the original Biblical texts from which they were derived. By comparing the two, one can only conlude that although Jesus had certainly learned basic Judaism, his understanding of Jewish morality was so flawed as to make him a most unlikely Messiah.

The problems first appear with his particular doctrine about love. Christian tradition has always claimed that Jesus was revolutionary in his emphasis on love, as if the Jews had never heard of it before. But just how did his pronouncements on the subject sound to the Jews of his own day? 'You have heard it said,' he begins, "You shall love your neighbour and hate your enemy." But I say unto you: Love your enemies, bless them that curse you...' etc. (Matt. 5. 43-44). Right from the start, any Jew who had read the Bible would have good reason to be sceptical about Jesus. As we have seen, the commandment to love one's neighbour (actually, one's fellow human being) comes from the book of Leviticus, chapter 19, verse 18. So there is nothing new here. But the part about hating one's enemy appears nowhere in the Hebrew Bible or in Jewish tradition. On the contrary, the Bible is replete with commandments to come to the aid of one's enemy whenever he is in difficulty. 'When you encounter your enemy's ox or ass wandering, you must take it back to him' (Ex. 23.4). 'If your enemy is hungry, give him bread to eat;/If he is thirsty, give him water to drink' (Prov. 25.21).

So where does this nonsense about hating one's enemy come from? To all appearances, Jesus seems to have made it up, perhaps to add rhetorical effect to his preaching. But in doing so, he gave his own religion—and his own people—a bad name. For centuries, Christians have been led to believe that Judaism teaches hatred, even though this has no basis in fact. If Jesus could see the terrible effects of such calumny over the ages, he would have cause to regret it.

Even less enlightening, from a moral standpoint, is Jesus's conclusion. His commandment to love one's enemies may be condoned in view of his haste to see the kingdom of heaven arrive quickly, but it is hardly a guide for living. To love someone is to take sides with that person on all important questions. To love one's enemy is to hate oneself. Such an attitude is, purely and simply, suicidal. Some modern Jews have been accused of self-hatred; it is hardly an admirable quality. Besides, Jesus did not practise what he preached. Anyone who dared to disagree with him was subject to stinging verbal abuse, as in the all too familiar, 'Woe unto you, scribes and Pharisees, hypocrites!' (In particular, Matt. 23.13-15, 23, 25, 27, 28; also Luke 11.44). In this regard, as in many others, Jesus resembles the leaders of some modern-day Hasidic sects, who regularly hurl anathemas at other rabbis, whom they consider less devout, calling them hypocrites (usually enhanced by the adjective, 'godless'). The scribes and Pharisees were not the enemies of Jesus, but merely his critics; and they were not necessarily hypocritical simply because he called them so. The epithets, 'hypocrites', or worse: 'serpents, generation of vipers' (Matt. 23.33), can hardly be considered expressions of love.

Similar difficulties occur when Jesus recalls, 'You have heard it said, "An eye for an eye and a tooth for a tooth." But I say unto you: Do not resist evil. If someone strikes you on the right cheek, offer him the other one as well' (Matt. 5.38-39). The first part comes from Exodus 21.24, but it has nothing to do with vengeance or reprisal. The expression, an eye for an eye and a tooth for a tooth, is in fact a prescription for civil damages following an accident, the compensation varying according to the seriousness of the injury. The loss of an eye would obviously command a higher price than that of a tooth. Judaism has always interpreted this text to mean compensation for accidental injury, not reprisal for wrongdoing. In its penal formulation, an eye for an eye and a tooth for a tooth simply means that the punishment shall fit the crime (Lev. 24.17-22). The Hebrew Bible specifically forbids vengeance (Lev. 19.18). If people took the law into their own hands they would make a mockery of both the laws of man and the law of God. So Jesus's interpretation of Holy Writ is not only incorrect, but slanderous to Judaism as well. It has been used by the enemies of the Jews, including one Adolf Hitler,[1] to justify all kinds of savagery against them.

As for the commandment to turn the other cheek, it may sound sublime at first hearing, but creates problems the more one reflects upon it. Let us say that someone comes over to me and, instead of slapping me on the cheek, tries to hit me on the head with a club. If I do nothing to defend myself, if I do not even parry the thrust, what happens? I can die, leaving a widow and two orphans. Or worse: I can survive as a human vegetable, a burden to my family and to society. This is why the Bible and rabbinical Judaism have always placed a high priority on self-defence. In order to perform *mitzvoth* (literally: commandments, but freely translated as acts of loving kindness), one first has to exist. Any Pharisee within earshot of Jesus must have wondered how he could possibly take such liberties with both the letter and the spirit of Scripture, and still get away with it.

Jesus's twisting of Jewish doctrine to suit his own particular purposes may explain his remarkable antipathy toward the scribes. After all, who were the scribes, but the keepers of Holy Writ? They had to make sure that every word in the written text was properly rendered, so that no one could misinterpret it. On one of the rare occasions when Jesus quotes Scripture correctly, a scribe nearby praises him (Mark 12.29-32). But he shows no sympathy for the scribes in general, often lumping them together with the Pharisees as hypocrites. Could it be that they had upbraided him for misquoting the Bible? They certainly had sufficient cause to do so.

Both the scribes and the Pharisees had serious reservations about Jesus's insistence on performing miraculous cures on the

---

[1]See below, pp. 176 and 261.

Sabbath. The Gospels give the impression that Judaism forbids any kind of healing on the day of rest. Actually, the Pharisees and their rabbinical successors were quite liberal on this point. Their position was based on the maxim that, to save a life, one may violate any commandment, except those forbidding idolatry, adultery and murder. Healing on the Sabbath is therefore permitted when the patient's life is in danger. This criterion, too, was interpreted liberally. A pain, fever or loss of blood were considered sufficient grounds for receiving medical attention on the Sabbath. But in the case of some chronic ailment which did not immediately threaten the patient's life, any attempt at healing would have to wait until the following day.

There were two main reasons for this prohibition. The first, and more obvious, was to allow the healer (the physician, or whomever) his day of rest. Anyone who has ever tried to get in touch with his general practitioner on a weekend well knows how much present-day doctors value their leisure time. There is also a more profound reason for prohibiting all but emergency medical care on the Sabbath. Healing is in itself miraculous, and the Sabbath is no time for miracles. It is a time for reflection, for meditation on one's own conduct and on what the rabbis like to call life's holy purpose. A miracle distracts people from their duty to review their existence on a weekly basis. Judaism has long maintained that miracles are no basis for moral teaching. An old Talmudic tale describes a dispute involving three rabbis, one of whom possesses extraordinary powers. To prove his point on some moral question, he performs such remarkable feats as making a stream run backwards and stopping the bricks of a falling wall in mid-air. Yet his moral argument remains invalid; the miracles in themselves prove nothing.

Every miracle cure effected by Jesus in the Gospels was for some chronic ailment and could easily have waited until the following day. Nearly all took place in synagogues, in front of the congregation and the rabbi. In one instance, he cured a man whose hand was withered (Matt. 12.10-12); in another, the patient suffered from dropsy (Luke 14.2-5). When queried about the need to perform such cures on the Sabbath, Jesus answered, as Jews often do, with another question: if an animal fell into a pit on the Sabbath, would you not be morally obligated to save it? As usual, the evangelists give Jesus the last word; his critics are reduced to silence. Yet, on closer examination, his comparison is not valid. An animal that falls into a pit could die if not rescued promptly; someone with a withered hand can wait until the following day to be cured.

So why did Jesus insist on healing the chronically ill on the Sabbath? Here, one is reduced to conjecture, since the Gospels give no hint as to his motives. What is clear, in any case, is that Jesus believed himself to be the Messiah and wanted to be accepted as such by his fellow Jews. He apparently hoped that his gifts as a faith healer would win the ordinary people over to his candidacy. But there was hardly any point in performing miracles on weekdays when nearly everyone was out working in the fields and could not witness them. Jesus needed an audience, and the best place to find one was the synagogue, which was filled to capacity on the Sabbath. Here was obviously the quickest way to win a popular following.

What is remarkable in all this is not that the Pharisees questioned Jesus on his use of the Sabbath to advertise his Messianic candidacy, but that they tolerated it at all. Why were they so liberal? For one thing, Jesus was a practising Jew and could not be denied access to the synagogue. A pagan faith healer would have promptly been shown the door, but not a Jewish one. Besides, there was always the possibility that Jesus might, after all, be the Messiah. No one knew for certain what life on earth would be like when the Messiah arrived. A general consensus had developed, however, to suggest that once oppression and violence had disappeared, most, if not all, the statutes and ordinances handed down at Sinai would become superfluous. Jesus himself echoed this belief when he said that 'not one jot or tittle' of divine law would pass away until the kingdom of heaven was established on earth (Matt. 5.18). Perhaps it was all right to bend a rule or two so that the Messiah could make himself known.

Was Jesus in fact the Messiah? This question seems to have arisen constantly throughout his ministry and failed to elicit a unanimous response from his fellow Jews. Even his own brothers did not believe in him (John 7.5). 'Do not think that I have come to send peace on earth,' he warned. 'I have come not to send peace, but a sword. I have come to set a man against his father, and the daughter against her mother, and the daughter-in-law against her mother-in-law' (Matt. 10.34-35). The sword metaphor may, as many scholars have suggested, indicate how nationalistic Jesus was. For the rest, however, this declaration hardly befits a Messiah, since Hebrew prophesy stresses that the Messianic age will be one of general reconciliation, in particular among members of the same family (Malachi 3.24). But it probably describes what actually happened during Jesus's own lifetime: whole families (including his own) seem to have been divided as to who he was.

The carpenter's son from Nazareth had little use for family life. He was extremely rude to his own mother, snubbing her with the words, 'Woman, what have I to do with you?' (John 2.4). And he expected the same attitude from his followers. 'If any man comes to me and does not hate his father, mother, wife, children, brothers and sisters—yea, even his own life, he cannot be my disciple' (Luke 14.26). Coming from someone who had already commanded them to love even their enemies, this was a harsh—not to say, contradictory—doctrine indeed. When one of his disciples asked for leave to bury his father, Jesus rebuked him curtly, saying: 'Let the dead bury the dead' (Matt. 8. 22).

Jesus's disciples had some difficulty following his particular moral philosophy. When a woman broke an alabaster box containing a rare ointment and poured it on his head, they objected to such waste. The box and its precious contents might have been sold and the proceeds distributed to the poor, they noted. Jesus replied, somewhat coldly: 'You will always have the poor, and you may do them good whenever you like; but you will not always have me' (Mark 14.7). The part of always having the poor seems to come from the Hebrew Bible: 'For there will never cease to be needy ones in your land, which is why I command you: open your hand to the poor and needy kinsman in your land' (Deut. 15.11). The Biblical commandment enjoins the Israelites to practise charity without delay. Jesus, on the other hand, believed that there was no particular urgency in helping the poor. He saw himself as being more important.

At no point is Jesus more self-centred than when, being hungry, he curses a fig tree because it had no figs for him to eat. Yet the tree was not to blame, for the evangelist makes it clear that this was not the season for figs (Mark 11.12-14). He adds that the disciples heard their master pronounce the curse, but he does not describe their reaction. They were probably just as confused as the countless Christian theologians who have tried to interpret this bizarre act. In another account, the tree promptly withered away (Matt. 21.19). No doubt this is intended to confirm Jesus's remarkable ability to perform miracles. But why should anyone kill a poor, defenceless fig tree simply because it does not bear fruit out of season? The Torah specifically forbids cutting down fruit trees at any time, even those found on enemy territory in time of war (Deut. 20.19-20).

The Test

As long as Jesus limited his ministry to Galilee, he remained relatively safe from arbitrary arrest. The region was not under Roman military occupation; and if the local police tried to apprehend him, there were many Jewish nationalists who would gladly offer him shelter and concealment. By the same token, his fame as a faith healer, although it had spread far and wide, was not enough to win him acceptance as the Messiah from the entire nation. If he truly wanted to be recognized as 'king of the Jews', a title that had both a religious and a political connotation, he would have to go to Jerusalem. As he made his way south from Galilee, he was met by a group of Pharisees who pleaded with him to renounce his mission.'Get away from here, for Herod wants to kill you,' they warned (Luke 13.31). This was a reference to Herod Antipas, the titular ruler of Galilee and son of Herod the Great, whose dynasty had been established with Roman support. So the younger Herod owed his authority, such as it was, to Rome. If he put a price on Jesus's head, it is because he knew that any Messianic claimant was considered seditious by the occupying power in Judaea. Jesus had long known that he was a marked man. Yet he chose to fulfill what he considered to be a providential calling by pushing on to his chosen destination.

The brief passage from Luke recounting Jesus's encounter with a delegation of Pharisees just three days before his fateful arrival in Jerusalem is highly instructive on three crucial points: the Nazarene's relations with the Pharisees, his attitude toward political authority, and his own sense of mission. It shows beyond doubt that the Pharisees were not Jesus's enemies and that they were sincerely concerned with his welfare. Had they been convinced that he was truly the Messiah, they would have guarded him with their lives. The very fact that they implored him to flee indicates that they had serious doubts and hoped to dissuade him from what they viewed as a suicidal venture. But Jesus would not be moved. He had amassed a considerable following as a faith healer and sought to win the support of as many Jews as possible in preparation for the great test to come. To give up now would mean abandoning the apostles and all the other simple folk who had placed their hopes in him. So he answered the Pharisees in these terms: 'Tell that fox [Herod] for me, "I am going to cast out demons and perform cures today and tomorrow, and on the third day I shall have finished my work"' (Luke 13.32). With the bulk of the populace behind him, he was confidently prepared to confront Herod and the Romans. If the kingdom of heaven was indeed imminent, divine providence would surely intervene and stay the hand of force.

Jesus chose to arrive in Jerusalem on the Jewish feast of Passover, which commemorates the Exodus from Egypt. Passover had a special meaning for the Jews of Judaea: by recalling their ancestors' emancipation from slavery in Egypt, it encouraged them to believe that the yoke of Roman oppression would soon be broken. This helps explain the initial outpouring of sympathy for Jesus as he approached the holy city. The crowds lining the streets to welcome him cried out, 'Hosanna to the son of David!' (Matt. 21.9). They clearly expected a king-Messiah who would inaugurate a new and lasting era of freedom. Jesus was forty-nine years old when he made his fateful journey (John 8.57). Forty-nine is seven times seven—a jubilee year for him. If Jesus was ever going to be recognized as the Messiah, and Judaea freed from Roman rule, now was the time.

No sooner did Jesus enter the holy city, however, than he began to dissipate the popularity that had preceded him. His violent physical attack on the merchants and money changers in front of the Temple has long been hailed by Christianity as a telling blow for religious purity. It probably did not seem so glorious to the Jews present. The merchants were selling pigeons (Matt. 21.12), which ordinary people bought to offer as sacrifices. An ox or a calf was too expensive for all but the very wealthy; pigeons were all that the average Jew could afford. The money changers enabled pilgrims from outside Judaea to change their foreign coin into local currency before buying the pigeons. All those who had made the long and arduous trip to Jerusalem in the hope of offering sacrifices at the Temple must have been dismayed at seeing Jesus upsetting the stalls of the pigeon vendors and chasing them from the Temple square. How could the pilgrims offer sacrifices now?

For Jesus, although he attacked the merchants and money changers, did not oppose the sacrificial cult itself. Nowhere in the Gospels does he express a desire to do away with it. The Pharisees, who preferred prayer to animal sacrifice, were careful not to denigrate the Temple because they knew that it embodied the centality of Jerusalem for Jews everywhere. Their attitude toward the Temple and all the ceremonies attached to it may be compared to that of the British Labour Party toward the monarchy, which is generally accepted as a symbol of national unity. The Temple of Jesus's time was no longer that of Solomon. It had been rebuilt by Herod the Great, the flunky of Rome, who hoped thereby to win acceptance for the protectorate by the citizens of Judaea. In this attempt he failed; but the Temple, despite its less than legitimate character, remained a rallying point for most Jews. Jesus's assault on the merchants and money changers, whose stalls reappeared shortly afterward, did not usher in any reforms in Jewish worship. It merely antagonized the pilgrims who had come to the holy city for the purpose of offering sacrifices there.

Disappointment with Jesus following the Temple incident quickly changed to disillusionment once it became known that he recommended paying taxes to Rome. On several occasions, various Pharisees had asked him for a sign that the kingdom of heaven was at hand (Matt. 16.1; Luke 17.20). Jesus not only refused to give such a sign but rebuked them for not accepting his claims on faith alone. This was asking too much. The Pharisees could not assume that all injustice and oppression were about to end simply because Jesus said so. It is precisely because they longed for a liberator that they had to be absolutely sure that they had the right man. The Saducees, of course, did not examine the veracity of his claims, because they were not interested in the Messiah. Only the Pharisees were committed to this quest; they alone would have to determine who Jesus really was. Since he had refused to give them any tangible indication that a new age of peace and brotherhood was imminent, they decided to put him to the test.

The test consisted of a simple question: should the inhabitants of Judaea continue to pay tribute (i.e.: taxes) to Caesar? His answer was equally simple: render unto Caesar that which is Caesar's and unto God that which is God's (Mark 12.17). This was a proper Pharisaic response, but it was not a Messianic one. If the kingdom of heaven was indeed at hand, there would be no need to pay any further taxes to Caesar, since Roman power would quickly vanish with the Messiah's coming. By recommending that taxes continue to be paid, Jesus implied that he did not know when, if ever, the kingdom of heaven would be established on earth. This being the case, there could be more than reasonable doubt concerning his own claims to be the Messiah.

Once word got around that Jesus had favoured paying taxes to Rome, his popular following largely evaporated. Even many of his disciples left him (John 6.66). Jesus was deeply affected by this loss, and his discourse became increasingly incoherent. Speaking to a group of Jews who had formerly believed in him, but who were beginning to express some doubt, he exclaimed: 'You are the sons of your father the devil!' (John 8.44). This was the same man who had earlier commanded his disciples to love even their enemies. He must have been terribly distraught to use such insulting language, though hardly more so than the generations of Jews at whom the same accusation has been leveled by countless Christians ever since. In any case, this outburst made it clear that Jesus was not the Messiah. No one whose mission it was to bring peace and brotherhood to the world would utter such slander.

The chief priests and Pharisees held council to decide what should be done with Jesus. 'This man performs many miracles,' they noted. 'If we leave him alone, everyone will believe in him, and the Romans will come and destroy our land and our nation' (John 11.47-48). They need not have worried about Jesus's popularity, which was falling by the minute. But they were certainly right on the second point. If the religious authorities failed to dissociate themselves from Jesus, the Romans would conclude that they and the entire nation were in revolt. From the Roman point of view, anyone claiming to be the Messiah was, ipso facto, seditious. Once the Pharisees were convinced that Jesus was not the promised liberator of Israel, they had no choice but to let the Romans arrest him.

At this point, the Gospels introduce the character of Judas Iscariot, who, it is said, betrayed Jesus with a kiss. Scholars have long expressed doubt that any such person ever existed: the name Judas may simply have been a code word for the Jews in general. There was certainly no need to betray Jesus, who was extremely visible in Jerusalem at that time. He had to be, if he wanted to make himself known to the Jewish populace. The Romans, whose military patrols covered the entire city, knew who Jesus was and where he could be found. He was quickly arrested by Roman soldiers and brought before Pontius Pilate, the Roman governor of Judaea.

Pilate knew that nationalistic feeling among the Jews was at a fever pitch during Passover week. He deftly defused a potentially explosive situation by offering to release Barrabas, who was then being held in a Roman prison. The Barrabas of the Gospels appears to be none other than Simon Bar-Rabba, a leading Jewish rebel of the time, who had killed someone (probably a Roman soldier) in an attempted insurrection (Mark 15.7; Luke 23.19). For the Jewish masses Barrabas was a real hero, and they were delighted to see him released. They were bitterly disappointed with the faith healer from Nazareth, however, because he had just recommended paying taxes to Rome. In the tense atmosphere of that time, there could be nothing worse than a false Messiah, since he could invite wholesale repression by the occupying power.

Throughout Jewish history, there have been scores of Messianic claimants, one of the most notable being the Turkish Jew, Sabbatai Zevi, in the mid-seventeenth century. Few of these were actually executed. (Zevi himself was sent to prison, where he converted to Islam.) But because Jesus appeared in Judaea at a time when it was under Roman rule, his own claim to be the Messiah was, in itself, seditious. And he paid the price. Crucifixion was a Roman penalty reserved especially for sedition. When Judaea did rise in revolt against Rome in the first and second centuries of the Christian era, many thousands of Jewish insurgents were crucified. Had Jesus been accused of blasphemy and found guilty by a religious court, he would normally have been stoned to death by other Jews. Even under the Roman protectorate, Jewish authorities still had jurisdiction in purely religious matters. The fact that he was crucified indicates the political nature of his Messianic claims.

To what extent, then, were the Jews responsible for Jesus's death? The French historian, Jules Isaac, has answered simply: no more so than the French people can be considered responsible for having executed Joan of Arc, who was condemned to death by a French ecclesiastical tribunal. Until Jesus entered Jerusalem, virtually the only Jewish opposition to his Messianic claims came from the townspeople of Nazareth (Mark 6.1-6) and some members of his own family. The Pharisees naturally wanted to know by what authority Jesus taught, but they gave him the benefit of the doubt throughout his ministry in Galilee. Only when he advised paying taxes to Rome did his own people turn massively against him. So much passion has been expended on this question that it may be worth recalling that Jesus himself did not hold his fellow Jews responsible for his being crucified. His last words, 'My God, my God, why have you abandoned me?' (Mark 15.34) indicate that he counted on divine intervention, even as the end was approaching. Jesus clearly did not expect to die on the cross. But by claiming to be the Messiah in Jerusalem, during Passover, with the Roman authorities on hair-trigger alert, he was putting his life at risk. Yet he pursued this course, hoping for a miracle that never came.

Jesus was taken down from the cross before the sun set on Friday and received a Jewish burial. He died as he had lived—an observant Jew.

A Son of God?

Jesus, then, was a Jewish nationalist who was crucified by the Romans for sedition. Most Jews of Judaea (the only ones who knew Jesus) rejected his Messianic claims, but not the whole of his moral doctrine, which was largely derived from Judaism. The only way to understand the historical Jesus is to read the Gospels as a series of encounters among Jews in a Jewish state, which was then under pagan domination. Modern-day historians and Biblical scholars have increasingly taken this approach, always mindful of the fact that neither Jesus nor his audience spoke Greek, the language of the New Testament. In the broader context of Jewish history, the faith healer from Nazareth appears simply as one of the more illustrious claimants to the title of Messiah, whose hopes to see the kingdom of heaven established in their own lifetimes eventually came to nought.

For pious Christians, however, Jesus is—and indeed has to be—something more: the son of God. By ascribing divinity to him, Christianity inescapably transfers the responsibility for his death from the Romans to the Jews. According to traditional theology, which still prevails in the Catholic, Orthodox and many Protestant churches, Jesus was put to death by the Jews for the crime of blasphemy. Claiming to be the son of God was contrary to Jewish law, say Christian theologians; therefore, he had to die. At the Second Vatican Council, which was called by Pope John XXIII to bring the Catholic church into the modern world, it was decided, after much debate, that present-day Jews could not be held responsible for the death of Jesus nearly two thousand years ago. But the accusation against Judaism still stands, as vivid and implacable as ever. It needs to be re-examined.

Under Roman rule, as has been noted earlier, the Jewish authorities had jurisdiction over purely religious matters. Anyone found guilty of a crime against Judaism was stoned to death, as was the apostle Stephen. Had Jesus committed a crime against Jewish law, he would have suffered a similar fate. Yet nowhere in the synoptic Gospels does he claim to be literally the son of God, just as he never alludes to his virgin birth. He does refer to himself as the son of man. This is a common Jewish term for human being (in Hebrew: *Ben-Adam*), although some scholars believe that, in this particular context, it could mean the Messiah. To the Jews of Judaea, he appeared as a direct descendant of King David—through his father Joseph. The evangelist Matthew (1.1-16) goes to some length to establish the Davidic lineage of Jesus, and with good reason. Otherwise, Jesus would have had great difficulty convincing his fellow Jews that he was the Messiah. The crowds lining the road to Jerusalem to greet Jesus on that fateful Sunday before Passover demonstrated their Messianic fervour by calling him a son of David. Jesus did nothing to dissuade them, for he wanted more than anything else to be accepted as the redeemer of his people.

In Jesus's day, and for some time thereafter, 'son of God' was a popular Jewish expression designating any man who was deemed to be holy. No doubt some of the Nazarene's more enthusiastic followers described him in this way, as did the admirers of other religious leaders. When Jews referred to a man considered to be especially pious as 'a true son of God', they did not mean it literally, any more than the term 'God's children', as found in certain Negro spirituals, alludes to the immaculate conception of all human beings. The fact that 'son of God' was common Jewish usage indicates that it was in no way blasphemous.

Christian theology remains largely unaffected by such historical arguments. It prefers to ignore the Jewish qualities of Jesus, which are precisely those that endeared him to his own people and which help explain his popularity among the Judaean masses. If Jesus had openly attacked Judaism, he would have had few, if any, followers during his lifetime. But Christianity wants—indeed needs—a Christian Jesus, even if no such person ever existed. A

Jewish nationalist who wanted to free his people from Roman oppression would hardly be worthy of veneration. Instead, Christians hold to the belief that God sent His only son to redeem all of humanity with his blood. The death of Jesus, presumably at the hands of the Jews, was therefore willed by God. Now this raises some delicate questions, which Jewish rabbis, not being theologians, prefer to avoid. Let us examine them anyway. To begin with, if God had really wanted to sacrifice His only son, He would have been acting out of character. Had He not earlier prevented Abraham from sacrificing his son, Isaac?

More fundamentally, Jewish law is under attack here, since it is supposed to have dictated the conviction of Jesus by a religious court (John 19.7). If pressed, Christian theologians would admit that Jewish law was ordained by God. It had to be. Without the revelation at Sinai, Hebrew prophesy has no validity; and without that, there can be no Messiah. Unless one accepts the entire Hebrew Bible as being divinely inspired, Christianity loses its theological foundations. Now the question arises: why would a just and compassionate God issue a law forbidding anyone to claim divine lineage and then send His own son to confound those who seek to apply this very same law? If the Torah was valid from the time of Moses on, why should it suddenly lose its validity? Is God consistent or is He not? Is He the 'Rock of Israel,' as Jews like to call Him, or just some capricious deity who can create a religion one day and destroy it the next?

Here we come to the main bone of contention between Judaism and Christianity. It is not about whether Jesus was the Messiah or not, however important that question may be. Rather, it centers on the terms 'Old Testament' and 'New Testament', which do not refer to those documents drawn up by lawyers for people who wish to leave their worldly goods to their heirs. What they signify is: old covenant and new covenant. Christianity maintains that God first established His covenant with the Jews and then, finding them wanting, entered into a new covenant with the church. For centuries, Christian apologists have sought to justify this change by claiming that Judaism was decadent at the time of Jesus and that a new religion was somehow necessary. The fig tree, which Jesus caused to die with a withering glance, has long been a standard Christian symbol for Judaism. In recent years, Biblical scholars of various denominations have come to see it as a fig tree, and nothing more. The presumed decadence of Judaism has been disputed by historians for over a century. Any religion that attracts converts as Judaism did can hardly be considered decadent. Indeed the Judaism of Jesus's day was probably more vital, more dynamic, than it ever has been, before or since.

Yet the term 'New Testament' endures, being fundamental to Christian belief. Christian missionaries have often expressed a sense of frustration at the refusal of Jews to accept Jesus as their saviour. They tend to attribute this stubborn attitude to some imagined perversity or ethnic pride on the Jews' part. Even the most culturally assimilated Jews evince little interest in Christianity. They are generally indifferent to religious arguments of any kind. But to the extent that they accept the existence of God, they assume that He is immutable. If God is indeed eternal and steadfast, He would hardly want to change His religion. If He is not, then history makes no sense at all. God could be Jewish one day (in His sight a day may span thousands of years), Christian the next, and who knows what the day after. By postulating a new covenant, Christianity inevitably destabilized the very notion of divinity. This may explain why Christians are exhorted to **believe** in God, while Jews traditionally accept His existence as an axiomatic truth.

Of all the world's religions, Christianity is the only one that claims to replace another. The church calls itself the new Israel; Christians are supposed to be the heirs to the title of chosen people. With Christianity, the notion of God's election undergoes a fundamental change. Whereas the Jews were chosen to observe divine commandment, and through that observance, to enlighten all of humanity, Christians are chosen for individual salvation. Assuming the heritage of Israel inevitably makes Christianity anti-Jewish. One inherits from the dead, not the living. Therefore, Judaism has to be dead. Its stubborn refusal to die has been a constant thorn in the side of the daughter religion. Judaism has long sought to vanquish idolatry in all its forms. Islam considers itself superior to all other religions. But Christianity alone singles out another faith as being obsolete, namely Judaism. This explains why the Gospels often hold the Pharisees up to ridicule and why later Christian writers portray the Judaism of Jesus's time as decadent. But the key Christian argument against Judaism is that it supposedly caused the death of the saviour. In a stroke the Torah is discredited, since it is said to have dictated that Jesus be crucified for having called himself the son of God. At the same time, the Jews themselves are presumed to be guilty of the crime of deicide.

Deicide! Can there be an accusation as monstrous as this one? For observant Jews, it is inconceivable that God can die. So the notion that they killed Him is simply absurd. But Christians have to believe in the death of God (at least as personified by Jesus); for without it, humanity cannot be saved. Having invented the crime of deicide, Christianity has used it to discredit not only the Torah but the Jews as well. In the process, it endowed them with supernatural powers for evil. As Creator of heaven and earth, God is assumed to be omnipotent. To kill Him, one has to be even more powerful. From this poisonous seed was eventually to sprout the myth of Jewish domination and the Jewish conspiracy to destroy civilization. One wonders what Jesus would have thought of all this. To be sure, he was deeply hurt at not being recognized as the Messiah by most of his compatriots; and in a fit of anger he did call some of them sons of the devil. But would he have approved the vicious campaigns of slander against his own people, and the resulting persecutions committed in his name? Not Jesus, the Jew.

Chapter III

CHRISTIANITY (ALMOST) TRIUMPHANT

THE CRUCIFIXION FILLED Jesus's small band of followers with horror. For two days, they wondered what had become of their master (Luke 24.21). Israel had not been redeemed, and there were certainly no outward signs that the kingdom of heaven was about to be established. What sustained their faith was the belief that Jesus rose from his tomb on the third day after his death and was spirited away to heaven. This vision first came to Mary Magdelene, from whom Jesus had exorcised no less than seven devils (Mark 16.9)—meaning that she was quite mad. It was soon shared by his mother and the remaining disciples. Resurrection was a Pharisaic notion, born of the Maccabean wars. Ordinary Jews, anguished at seeing their finest young men cut down by pagan warriors, asked the age-old question: why does a just and merciful God permit evil-doers to slay the righteous? The Pharisees' reply was necessarily speculative. In the end of days, they reassured the people, the righteous will be resurrected for eternal life on earth. Jesus's followers simply applied this supposition to him. It made no difference to them that resurrection, in the Pharisaic sense, was supposed to take place on earth and not in heaven.

Within Judaea, the small minority of Jews who still believed in Jesus were usually treated with amiable tolerance. The Nazarites (in Hebrew, *Ha-Notsrim*), as they were called, continued to live as Jews—practising circumcision, eating kosher food, praying at the synagogue and resting on the Sabbath. There was no reason to exclude them from the Jewish community simply because they believed that the Messiah had already come. The group led by the apostle James remained committed both to Judaism and to the Messianic promise of freedom. For at least a generation after Golgotha, they continued to yearn for the liberation of Judaea from Roman rule. That the occupying power did not actively persecute them can be explained by the fact that they were as yet few in number. With Jesus safely dead, having been rejected by most Jews as their king, there was little danger that his remaining partisans might lead a popular revolt. Jewish tolerance and Roman indifference allowed the apostles to pursue their missionary campaign in Judaea, as they tried to convince the people that their redeemer had already come and that the kingdom of heaven would soon be established. Curiously, the Acts of the Apostles refers to 'the twelve' (Acts 6.2), even though one of their number, Judas Iscariot, was already dead: he had committed suicide out of remorse for having betrayed Jesus (Matt. 27.5). No successor is mentioned in the Christian Scriptures. The chief spokesmen for 'the twelve' were Peter and James, who lost no time in accusing the Jews present of having killed their master. They had hanged him on a tree, claimed Peter (Acts 5.30). Accusing people of lynching is not the best way to win their confidence, but the Jewish authorities displayed remarkable calm in dealing with this slander. The high priest rejected the charge and accused Peter and James of stirring up trouble (Acts 5.28). In almost any other society, they would have been run out of town. A blood libel is not, after all, something to be taken lightly.

Then Gamaliel intervened. The Acts refers to him as, simply, 'a Pharisee'. This is like calling the Pope a Catholic. Gamaliel was in fact the leader of the Pharisees, a disciple of the great Hillel. He cautioned his colleagues against persecuting Peter and James. 'Do not harm these men, and leave them alone,' he advised. 'For if this plan or undertaking is merely the work of men, it will come to nought. But if it is the work of God, you cannot defeat it' (Acts 5.38-39). In the annals of organized religion, one rarely encounters such broad-mindedness. Imagine what would have happened to Luther, Zwingli or Calvin had they dared preach their new credo in Saint Peter's Square in Rome. They would have swiftly been arrested by the Swiss guards and forced to recant—at the very least. Yet Peter and James were allowed to go on their way, protected by the essential tolerance of Pharisaic Judaism.

Not all the apostles had things so easy. The patience of the religious authorities was exhausted when Stephen accused them of being murderers. He was promptly stoned to death (Acts 7.52-58). But even this did not cause a permanent rift between the Nazarites and the Jewish community at large. The followers of Jesus had no interest in leaving Judaism, which was officially protected within the Roman empire. It was the only minority religion to enjoy such privileged status. Had the Nazarites seceded from it, they would have left themselves open to persecution by Rome. Besides, they had not founded a new religion, but merely a Messianic sect within the very broad and flexible Jewish community.

The basis of the new religion was to be laid by Paul, a Jew from Asia Minor, who had not known Jesus and who was initially hostile to his followers. Once he became convinced that Jesus was in fact the Messiah, he fashioned a belief that was radically different from Judaism: namely that faith in the dead Jesus would save all of humanity from eternal damnation. The classic Jewish view of sin is that every human being has the capacity to do evil as well as to do good. The original sin of Adam and Eve is simply the first act of disobedience to God, which sets all of human history in motion. It is not a fundamental handicap bearing down on people throughout their earthly existence. As a result, Judaism does not speak of salvation in the sense of saving every individual from original sin. Rather, it looks ahead to redemption, to a time when all men learn to live as brothers. God's will to see the establishment of a more perfect universe would somehow be accomplished in the course of history, as human beings, enlightened by His wisdom, lead more purposeful lives.

Paul saw things differently. His theory of sin was largely influenced by his own jaundiced views on sex. Paul was a bachelor, a rarity among observant Jews, and he gloried in his own chastity. 'It is good for a man not to touch a woman,' he declared. 'Nevertheless, to avoid fornication, let every man have his own wife and every woman have her own husband' (I Cor. 7.1-2). Gone is the Jewish doctrine that marriage is a positive, constructive state. For Paul, it is at best a necessary evil. 'I say therefore to the unmarried and the widows: it is good for them to remain single even as I do. But if they cannot contain themselves, let them marry; for it is better to marry than to burn [with lust]' (I Cor. 7.8-9). From the belief that sex is essentially sinful to the dogma that all human beings are conceived in sin, it is but one step.

Paul's sense of insecurity as a Diaspora Jew was another element in his quest for a new religion. He was, from all accounts, thoroughly Hellenized, and Greek was his first language. Just as he sought to justify his own sexual problems by giving them an aura of religious piety, so too did he attempt to drown his uncomfortable religious status in the sea of a new, universal faith. Until Paul arrived on the scene, the Nazarites were simply a minority sect within Judaism. It was he who originated the idea of preaching the Gospel to Gentiles without insisting that they formally join the Jewish community. Thus, the new assembly of the faithful (in other words, the church), would make no distinction between Jew or Greek. So anxious was Paul to eliminate circumcision as a requirement for joining the church that he pronounced it—and all of Jewish law—null and void. He justified this momentous change with the axiom, 'The just shall live by faith [in Jesus as their saviour]' (Gal. 3.11). His reference ostensibly comes from the prophet Habbakuk, 2.4. But the original statement is quite different from Paul's use of it. Habbakuk seeks to encourage those who are disheartened by the apparent triumph of evil over good. He reminds them that the righteous can overcome life's difficulties by remaining faithful to God's law and the morality derived from it. There is nothing in the prophetic text to suggest that faith in a dead Messiah would replace that law. Paul simply lifted this portion from the Greek version of the Bible and applied it to his new doctrine.

Converting the Gentiles was, in itself, nothing new. The Pharisees had been doing it for generations. Jesus, as we have seen earlier, opposed such proselytism and limited his ministry to the Jews of Judaea. When the apostles began to preach to the Jews of the Diaspora, however, they attracted many Gentiles (Acts 11. 19-20). The presence of uncircumcised pagans in the early church provided Paul with a convenient pretext to abolish the whole of Jewish law and custom. The precondition that all male converts to Judaism be circumcised had not, in fact, been universally applied. Some rabbis, albeit a small minority, held that, in certain cases, a ritual bath (i.e.: baptism) would suffice. But all rabbis drew the line when it came to preserving the Torah, which in its most complete sense means Judaism: none was so blind, so obtuse, as to declare all of Jewish beliefs and practices obsolete.

The summary abolition of the Torah and its replacement by a cult based on miracles illustrate Paul's impatience with history. Whereas Hebrew prophesy counseled the righteous to remain faithful to divine law and work patiently for a better world, Paul sought to bypass this long and arduous process. History was too frustrating for him. By converting uncircumcised Gentiles to the new faith, he hoped to bring about a radical transformation of the human condition. Once all of humanity accepted his theology, he reasoned, the kingdom of heaven would arrive in short order.

In his zeal, the new apostle did not hesitate to flatter political authority in the hope of winning its support. If the civilized world were to achieve salvation in the shortest possible time, then the laborious method of making conversions on an individual basis, as the Pharisees were doing, had to be abandoned. Christianity would have to aim at the highest echelon of pagan society and enlist secular power in its cause. Paul's well-known letter to the nascent Christian community in Rome contains this pregnant passage: 'Let every person be subject to the higher powers. For there is no power but of God; the powers that be are ordained by God' (Rom. 13.1). If expounded today, such principles would probably disturb many Christians. Were Hitler, Stalin, Saddam Hussein, 'Papa Doc' Duvalier and scores of other tyrants all ordained by God? Paul had the relatively enlightened rulers of the Roman empire in mind, but such a sweeping statement encompasses all rulers, even dictators. It represents a radical departure from Judaism, which, from Biblical times onward, has always cautioned against putting one's trust in princes (Ps. 146.3).

Post-Biblical Judaism's approach to secular power is aptly summarized in the *Pirkei Avoth*, or 'Sayings of the Fathers'. To this day, it remains the most widely known (and least legalistic) of all the sixty-three tractates of the Mishna, a compendium of Jewish law and ethics that was drafted at much the same time as Paul and his followers established the bases of Christianity. In the *Pirkei Avoth* (1.10) the first political maxim is that of Rabbis Shemayah and

Avtalyon: 'Love work; refuse domination over others; and seek no intimacy with the ruling power.' Rabbi Gamaliel (the same who defended the apostles Peter and John) was even more emphatic. 'Be guarded in your relations with the ruling power, for those who exercise it draw no man near to them except in their own interest. Although they appear as friends when it is to their own advantage, they do not stand by a man in his hour of need' (*Avoth* 2.3). A somewhat different note is sounded by Rabbi Chanina, who advised: 'Pray for the welfare of the government; for without fear of it, men would eat each other alive' (*Avoth* 3.2). Chanina was assistant to the High Priest and therefore in close contact with the Roman authorities. But even if the rabbis accepted secular power as being necessary to avoid anarchy, they would never think of venerating it.

When Paul declared divine law to be obsolete and, at the same time, insisted that secular power was ordained of God, he laid the moral foundations for the worst possible kind of tyranny. Pagan rulers regularly erected temples to one god or another and often claimed to be gods themselves. But their moral authority was limited by the very fact that there were so many competing deities. Judaism postulates the existence of one, all-powerful God, whose law supercedes that of any government. Pauline Christianity, on the other hand, combines the belief in an all-powerful God (albeit in the form of a trinity) with the theory that all secular power is derived from Him. Since divine law was deemed no longer to exist, the laws and decrees of secular rulers, no matter how arbitrary, were theoretically immune to any criticism and could not be opposed.

Once the church became established with its own administrative order, it sought to temper this oppressive system. It created Canon Law, which was every bit as meticulous as that of the rabbis, and insisted that secular power be constrained within specific limits. But until Christianity became the official religion of the Roman empire, the early church had neither an administrative arm nor laws of its own. Its approach to secular power was that of Paul, whose desire to court the Roman political establishment had led him to glorify it. This aspect of Pauline Christianity explains both the eventual political triumph of the Church and the moral dilemma which even the most compassionate Christians have never been able to resolve. Put simply, that dilemma is as follows: should political power, which rests ultimately on military force, be used to bring people closer to God? All attempts to do so have ended in failure.

The Jewish Revolt

In a few short years Paul had created a wholly new thought system, which, in its approach to history and political power, represented a radical departure from classical Judaism. Yet even his new credo did not cause an immediate rupture between the Jewish community (or, more accurately, communities) and the fledgling church. That rupture, when it came, was the result of military victories by Roman armies over a rebellious Judaea. Following the first uprising in the years 66-70, the Romans laid waste to most of Jerusalem, including the Temple. Shortly thereafter, the so-called 'synoptic' Gospels—those of Matthew, Mark and Luke—were written. They indicate a growing separation between the Nazarites and mainstream Judaism. To the evangelists and other Judaeo-Christians, the destruction of the Temple appeared as divine punishment meted out to the Jews for having rejected Jesus as the Messiah. This view cast the pagan Romans as servants of God, carrying out His will. It implied that God is always on the side of the biggest batallions and that military victories are in themselves proof of divine favour. In extolling the powers that be as ordained by God, Paul had proved to be remarkably prescient. With the destruction of the Temple, Christian adoration of power—not only political, but military as well—reached new heights.

Despite the increasing contempt shown by the Nazarites toward Judaism, they remained, at least nominally, within the fold. They still had no interest in leaving it, since by retaining the Jewish label, they continued to enjoy official tolerance from Rome. For the rabbis, the first Christian missionaries were a bother, but hardly more so than some earlier Jewish sects. Obviously, the Jews in general did not share the Christian belief that the destruction of the Temple was an act of divine retribution. They grieved over its loss, mainly because it symbolized the military defeat of Judaea. The Pharisees in particular took heart, since they were now the unchallenged arbiters of Jewish thought and practice. With the Temple in ruins, the Saducees were effectively eliminated from positions of religious authority. The sacrificial cult vanished altogether and was replaced by the synagogue service. Wisely, the Pharisees reserved a place in that service for the *Kohanim*, or priestly caste, and the Levites. This demonstrated not only their tolerance, but also their sense of continuity. The synagogue, heir to the Temple, was now the primary focal point of Jewish worship. Saddened by the military defeat of Judaea, the Pharisees in the Diaspora redoubled their efforts to bring converts into Judaism. Their missionary activity flourished as never before, now that Pharisaism had become the norm for all Jews.

What finally caused a permanent schism between Judaism and Christianity was the second Judaean revolt against Rome, which occurred in 132-135. The Jewish forces were led by Simon Bar-Kochba, who was recognized as the Messiah by both the rabbis and the overwhelming majority of ordinary Jews within that country. For the Nazarites, however, Bar-Kochba could not possibly be the Messiah since **their** Messiah, Jesus, had already come. Bar-Kochba, they reasoned, was therefore a false Messiah and had to be defeated. The Nazarites informed on their Jewish brethren, revealing Jewish troop movements and other military secrets to the Romans. When the rabbis learned of this treason, they lost no time in expelling the Nazarites from the Jewish community. So it was for political, and not religious, reasons that the early Chistians were finally obliged to fend for themselves.

Judaism and Christianity were now openly competing for converts throughout the Roman empire. The defeat of Judaea initially favoured Christianity, as all Jews—even in the Diaspora—were suspected of disloyalty to Rome. Christian missionaries tried to endear themselves to the imperial authorities by claiming that the Jews were habitual rebels and therefore not to be tolerated. Following the reign of Hadrian (117-138), however, Roman persecution of the Jews declined sharply. Hadrian's son and successor, Antoninius Pius (138-161), did issue an edict forbidding circumcision to anyone who was not born a Jew. As an attempt to discourage pagans from converting to Judaism, it failed. Female converts, who had traditionally been more numerous than male, were not affected; and even some pagan men were allowed to enter the Jewish community after only a ritual bath. Finally, the edict was very difficult to enforce, since other Semitic peoples within the Roman empire practised circumcision.

While conversions to Judaism continued apace, the Jews recognized that armed revolt was futile and lost much of their earlier Messianic fervour. Their attitude was expressed in rather picturesque terms by the Judaean sage, Yohanan Ben-Zakkai, who founded a rabbinical academy at Yabneh in northern Judaea shortly after the defeat of Bar-Kochba's forces. 'If you are about to plant a sapling, and someone announces the arrival of the Messiah,' he advised, 'first plant your sapling and then greet the Messiah.' A *modus vivendi* with the ruling power was the order of the day.

The Christian missionaries, on the other hand, were not content with a *modus vivendi*: they sought to make Christianity the official religion of the Roman empire by converting the emperor and the entire political class. Recognizing the threat that such activity posed to the traditional system, imperial authorities initiated an official policy of repression, which reached its climax in the second half of the third century. Christians were actively persecuted—some being thrown to the lions as public entertainment. Meanwhile, the Jewish Diaspora thrived, both economically and spiritually. New synagogues were built throughout the Mediterranean basin, attracting pagans and Christians alike.

The very vigour of Judaism helps explain early (and even later) Christianity's hostility to it. Had Judaism withered and died after the destruction of the Temple, as Christian theologians have long claimed, it would hardly have been a rival to the developing church. And a rival it certainly was, far more serious than any pagan cult. Jewish missionaries were more learned in the Bible than their Christian counterparts. They could rely on an established religious tradition and did not have to improvise. The Christians had to reinterpret the Hebrew Bible so as to convince pagans that it did not mean what the Jews said it did. An entirely new religious calendar had to be devised, with Christmas replacing (often coexisting with) the ancient Roman feast of Saturnalia, while Easter was given a different date from Passover so that newly converted pagans would not confuse the two. In fact, many converts to Christianity not only were attracted to the Passover celebrations, but often preferred synagogue services to those of the church. The Christian Sabbath was moved to Sunday in an attempt to deter this practice. Still, Judaism continued to win converts at the expense of Christianity.

Paul's Winning Strategy

The triumph of the daughter religion came in 313, when a Germanic chieftain named Constantine, who had been consecrated Roman emperor in Byzantium a year before, formally converted to Christianity. Overnight, the Roman empire—or what was left of it—became officially Christian. Actually, paganism survived in Europe until about the year 1000. There can be little doubt, however, that state support greatly facilitated the expansion of Christianity. Through mass baptisms, which were actively encouraged by the civil authorities, thousands of pagans became at least nominally Christian every year.

Just what prompted Constantine to choose the new faith is not entirely clear. He apparently entertained the idea of converting to Judaism, but was dissuaded by his wife, who feared for his virility if he underwent circumcision. It is obvious, in any case, that he was dissatisfied with paganism because it could no longer buttress the existing political system. Reason of state, not morality, was uppermost in his mind. Inasmuch as the apostle Paul had already prescribed absolute submission to the powers that be, Constantine had every reason to choose Christianity, which offered the hope of reinforcing his authority. Thus did Christianity gain an empire, even though that empire was already in an advanced state of decomposition. Constantine's conversion did nothing to stop the rot. Augustine of Hippo wrote *The City of God* to answer educated pagans who argued, with some justification, that the church had actually helped accelerate the empire's decline.

In Western tradition, Christianity's political conquest of the eastern Mediterranean is presented as a victory over Judaism. This, in turn, is supposed to prove the superiority of Christian morality over Jewish and, in particular, that Jesus had revolutionized the world with his doctrine. Even present-day liberals who have long ceased attending church services assume that, since Christianity did eventually become the dominant religion of the West, there must be some moral reason for its success. Perhaps there is, but the teachings of Jesus do not seem to have anything to do with it. The writings of the early church fathers show little interest in what Jesus had to say. They are far more concerned with constructing a new theology than with studying, for example, the Sermon on the Mount. What holds for the theologians applies even more to the first Christian emperor. Since Constantine was motivated primarily, if not exclusively, by political considerations, the teachings of Jesus do not seem to have played any role in his decision to accept baptism.

Yet there is a moral dimension to Christianity's gains, which were made possible by the decline of paganism. As we have seen earlier, paganism received its initial challenge in the fifth pre-Christian century, as the Greek philosophers began to speculate on the meaning of life. The improving standard of living created by the Roman empire cast doubt on the age-old assumption that humanity was subject to forces of nature that could be appeased only through sacrifice. In its decline, the empire further accelerated the disrepute into which paganism had fallen, as the official religion suffered along with the political authority it was supposed to uphold. Indeed all of ancient civilization was in disarray because the economic and social institution on which it was based was no longer viable. That institution was slavery. Without it, the monuments to Roman rule—its roads, aquaducts, baths and other marvels of engineering—would not have been possible. Slavery, in turn, was the result of military conquest, as thousands of captives were consigned to forced labour by the victors. But as the Roman empire reached its geographical limits in the second Christian century and military conquests became rare, the supply of captives fell off drastically. The resulting decline in construction created a general economic depression, in which employers could no longer afford to keep all the slaves they had purchased. These unemployed masses—foreigners whose Latin was imperfect and who were excluded from proper Roman society—found no solace in the official religion. They were quite receptive, however, to the promise of salvation in the afterlife that was offered by Christian missionaries.

Christianity benefited from the moral crisis that eventually undermined ancient civilization. But it was Judaism that had first encouraged pagans to question the accepted morality of the day. And although many pagans were attracted to mystery cults as an alternative to the official religion, Judaism offered them something that the mystery cults could not: an insight into the meaning of life. The influence and prestige of Judaism in the late pagan Roman empire was brought to light in 1962 by excavations in Sardis, in Asia Minor. There, on the town's main street, was unearthed a magnificent synagogue, nearly 120 metres in length, adorned with marble and elaborate mosaics. The local church was far smaller and located in a less desirable neighbourhood. That Christianity eventually became the official religion of the Roman empire should not obscure the moral foundations of its triumph, which had been prepared by the intense missionary activity of the Jews.

It is fruitless to speculate as to what would have happened if Constantine had chosen Judaism, rather than the daughter religion. The Bible and rabbinical sources make it clear that Judaism retained a critical approach to political authority. Jewish missionaries rarely sought to win converts through force and eschewed mass conversions, which in any case were rendered impossible by the requirement of circumcision. Judaism, they believed, will prevail in the fullness of time, when the whole of humanity is enlightened by divine wisdom. It should not be imposed on an ignorant populace by the police, the army and the state bureaucracy. There have been, to be sure, isolated instances of kings and princes who have converted to Judaism; but it was not Jewish policy to seek them out in particular. Constantine, a warrior chieftain who presided over what was still the mightiest empire on earth, would have been an embarrassment to Jewish missionaries, who preferred principle to power.

This choice cost them dearly, as the newly-baptized emperor lost no time in cutting Christianity's influential rival down to size. Imperial edicts forbade conversions to Judaism, imposing the death penalty on both the missionary and his proselytes. Marriages between Jews and Gentiles were likewise outlawed. The construction of new synagogues was expressly forbidden, and those that were destroyed by fire or other causes could not be rebuilt. Harsh as it was, such legislation did not abolish Jewish missionary activity altogether. An empire in decline lacked the power to apply the anti-Jewish decrees in all cases. Nonetheless the first Christian emperor succeeded in his primary aim, which was to curtail the expansion of Judaism. It resumed briefly during the reign of Julian the Apostate (361-363), who restored paganism as the official state religion. Julian looked with favour on the Jews and even thought of rebuilding the Temple in Jerusalem. His successors, however, continued the anti-Jewish policies of Constantine.

Despite official opposition, Judaism remained a moral force in the Mediterranean basin. This is evidenced by the vitriolic diatribes against the Jews by John Chrysostom, who was bishop of Constantinople in the late fourth century. Here can be found some of the vilest calumnies ever uttered by a Christian churchman, as the 'golden mouthed' orator did not hesitate to compare the synagogue to a brothel. He adopted a method used by most of the early church fathers and which became a permanent feature of Christianity: quoting passages from Hebrew Bible out of context and using them to attack the Jews. To support his slander against the synagogue, Chrysostom cited Jeremiah 3.3: 'You have the forehead of a whore.' Further on, he referred to Deuteronomy 32.18: 'You forgot the God who gave you birth' (which was directed at those Israelites who relapsed into idolatry) to prove that all Jews were naturally sinful. From the Christian New Testament came the now familiar accusation that the Jews—all of them—were Christ-killers and that the conquest of Judaea by Rome was divine punishment for the crucifixion.

Chrysostom's polemics did not indicate popular hostility toward the Jews in the region. On the contrary, they were designed to combat widespread Judaizing among Christians. He noted with regret that many Christians were drawn to the synagogue to observe Jewish holidays and fasts. Especially galling, from his point of view, was the widespread practice among Christians of consulting a rabbi to settle their disputes. It was cheaper and more expeditious than going to court, hiring a lawyer and waiting for the Byzantine bureaucracy to inscribe one's case on the docket. The Christians of Chrysostom's day considered rabbis to be wise men and respected their judgement. There were many other occasions on which they visited the synagogue, where the liturgy was more structured and the commentary more forceful than in the early church. The enduring vigour of Judaism was emphasized in 1947 by a Protestant scholar, Marcel Simon, in his exhaustive study entitled *Verus Israel* ('The True Israel').[1] He explained that the early spokesmen for Christianity felt compelled to attack the synagogue, because it continued to attract Christians long after the Temple in Jerusalem had been destroyed. The term 'true Israel' referred, of course, to the church, which denigrated Judaism in order to usurp its place in the divine order of things. Simon, a professor of theology at the University of Strasbourg, effectively laid to rest the venerable myth that the advent of Christianity had somehow consigned Judaism to oblivion.

Given the continued influence of Judaism, it is not surprising that some Christians were tempted to stamp it out once and for all. Wholesale persecution of the Jews was, in fact, official policy in Visigothic Spain during most of the sixth century, and it very nearly succeeded in eradicating Judaism from that country. Yet throughout most of the Middle Ages, Jews survived and prospered. Jewish survival in the Christian era has puzzled Jews and Christians alike. Some consider it simply miraculous. Others, seeking a more rational explanation, ascribe it to Augustine's doctrine, which was eventually adopted by the church after much debate. Augustine held that the Jews should not be forced to choose between baptism and death, as some of his colleagues had proposed. Rather, they should be allowed to survive in an inferior political and social status, as witnesses to the truth of Christianity. Every Jew who freely converted to Christianity would then serve as a reminder to all that the new faith was indeed superior to the old.

As an explanation for Jewish survival, Augustine's doctrine is clearly insufficient because it fails to take into account the realities of power, especially in regard to a religion such as Christianity,

---

[1] 2nd ed.; Paris: de Boccard, 1964.

which venerates the powers that be. Power in mediaeval Christendom varied greatly from one region to another and from one age to another. The Visigothic rulers of Spain were free to persecute the Jews without any hindrance from the church; Augustine's doctrine did not sway them at all. In the eastern Mediterranean, Caesaropapism was the rule. There, so-called 'Orthodox' Christianity was based not on the alliance of throne and altar but on the fusion of the two. This allowed the emperors in Constantinople to interpret Church doctrine, in so far as it affected politics, very much as they pleased. Had they wished to offer the Jews a choice between baptism and death, there would have been little to stop them. Yet, save for a few instances, the Jews in the eastern Empire were allowed to retain their religion, as long as they refrained from proselytism. To understand why, we must recall that the Jews were a sizeable minority in Constantine's realm—twenty percent of the population of Asia Minor and over ten percent elsewhere. Any attempt to impose Christianity on them by force would have led most of them to flee, taking with them their money and their skills. Wisely, the eastern emperors decided to tolerate the Jews, within certain well-defined limits, rather than risk a disruption of the general economy.

In Western Europe, Charlemagne (768-814) and his successors welcomed Jews as merchants, tradesmen, and even farmers. That a significant proportion chose agriculture is evident by the rabbinical *responsa* of the time, many of which were devoted to questions of land tenure and use. The great Rashi (an acronym for Rabbi Solomon Itzhaki) of Troyes, in northeastern France, made a comfortable living by growing grapes. Jews were considered an economic asset by rulers who were badly in need of new tax revenues. Church authorities objected to the influx of Jews in the newly-Christianized West. Agobard, bishop of Lyons and primate of Gaul, complained that ordinary people, as they passed by the synagogue on a Saturday morning, were attracted to the service by the singing, which they could hear through the open windows. He urged Louis the Pious (814-840), the son of Charlemagne, to segregate Jews from Christian society. The emperor refused, since such a measure would hamper the economic activities of his Jewish subjects. His hospitality toward them continued even after his personal confessor, the deacon Bodo, formally converted to Judaism.

Jewish proselytism remained active long after Europe became officially Christian. The French historian Bernhard Blumenkranz devotes an entire chapter to the Jewish mission in his detailed study published in 1960, *Juifs et chrétiens dans le monde occidental, 430-1096* ('Jews and Christians in the Western World').[2] It was hardly surprising, he notes, that the Jews should seek out converts. 'The Judaism of the early Middle Ages, like any other healthy organism, was not content to...survive; it wanted to gain in strength, to increase, to enrich itself with new contributions.' Its most attractive quality was the Sabbath, which allowed for complete rest one day a week. Christian employees of Jews, who enjoyed the Sabbath as a matter of course, thus became drawn to a religion which gave them the same basic rights as their masters. Rabbis tended to regard the newly-baptized peoples of Europe as prime candidates for conversion; in their view, Christianity was merely a half-way house on the road from paganism to Judaism. The converts, for their part, remained loyal to their adopted faith. During the first Crusade in 1096, many accepted martyrdom rather than return to Christianity.

In spite of their missionary activities, the Jews of Christendom enjoyed the protection of most secular rulers. No matter where religious authority lay—with the emperor as in the East or with the Pope as in the West—the welfare of the Jews was ultimately a political question. If the ruler deemed that his Jewish subjects contributed to the overall wealth of his kingdom, he protected them and granted them privileges, such as the right to travel on business, which were denied to ordinary subjects. But should the Jews be perceived as useless or even harmful to the kingdom, they could be despoiled and/or expelled at the ruler's pleasure. The Jews therefore resolved to make themselves as useful as possible to their royal protectors, not only by accepting a greater tax burden than other subjects, but also by making sure that none of their number became

[2] Paris: Mouton, 1960.

a public liability. It was in their interest to maintain strong communal organizations which helped keep vagrancy and crime to a minimum.

Also contributing to Jewish survival was the fact that many Jews lived outside the Christian world. Those of Babylonia enjoyed a large measure of political autonomy and freedom from religious persecution. That the rabbis of that country found the time to record the proceedings of their seminars in the voluminous collection known as the Babylonian Talmud testifies to the remarkable degree of religious freedom there. The rise of Islam in the seventh century had a beneficial impact on Jews and Judaism. Unlike Christianity, Islam does not accuse the Jews of deicide; it does not declare the Torah to be null and void, nor does it claim to be the spiritual heir to Judaism. As Muslim armies conquered much of the Christian world, many rabbis exulted. They had been hard put to explain why the God of history seemed to favour Christianity by allowing it to dominate the entire Meditarranean basin. Now that Christianity was losing ground, they could take heart—and not only for theoretical reasons. The Jewish communities of North Africa received far better treatment from their new Muslim rulers than they had known under the Christians. Those of Spain were saved from almost certain extinction. For them, the Islamic conquest was nothing less than a deliverance.

Holy War

The key to Jewish survival and prosperity, then, was being useful to the ruling classes. In the Muslim world, where deserving Jews were appointed court physicians and treasurers, their success in this regard was remarkable. The rulers of Western Europe rarely admitted Jews into their inner circle, but valued them for their overall economic utility. As European settlement expanded northward, Jews helped provide the economic infrastructure for the new towns and cities. In return, they were protected by the local ruler. This arrangement worked satisfactorily as long as the Jews continued to be useful, and as long as the ruler was able to protect them. Doubtless, mediaeval Jewry had not forgotten the Biblical injunction against putting one's trust in princes or the rabbinical warning against seeking too close a relationship with the ruling power. But there was no choice in the matter: the Jews needed protection, and only the ruling power could provide it.

In Western Europe, the widespread tolerance enjoyed by the Jews ended suddenly with the advent of the first Crusade in 1096. For Christians, the word Crusade still has a positive connotation, signifying any war or campaign for a just cause. For Jews, however, it carries a more sinister meaning. Although they were initially intended to free the Holy Land from Muslim domination, the Crusades' most lasting accomplishment was to unleash popular violence in Europe against the Jews. To understand why anti-Jewish feeling took so long to develop, we must recall that until roughly the year 1000, Europe was not totally Christianized. Not only were there still many pagans about, but the majority of Europeans who were nominally Christian knew very little about their own religion. They had no opportunity to learn, since they could not attend Mass regularly. A continual shortage of clergy meant that the few available priests had to ride on a donkey from one village to another, performing baptisms, marriages and funerals as the need arose (and often after it arose) before traveling on. They had no time to stay and preach.

All this changed with the development, in the tenth and eleventh centuries, of the parish system. Henceforth, priests were assigned to specific churches, where they could attend regularly to the needs of their parishioners and hold Mass every Sunday. This brought the European populace, which in those days was composed mainly of poor, illiterate peasants, into contact with Christian beliefs for the first time. Through weekly sermons, and especially during the Easter season, they were now exposed to the full anti-Jewish content of the Christian scriptures. It does not take much imagination to guess what impression regular quotations from the Gospel, and in particular the Passion narrative, made on such humble folk. A little knowledge is often more dangerous than total ignorance—especially when that little knowledge is based on falsehood. All that most Christians ever learned about the Jews was that they were suppos-edly responsible for the death of the saviour. Thus did anti-Jewish doctrine leave the cloistered realm of theology and become a mass movement.

Popular animosity toward the Jews had been building up for several years before the Crusades, especially in the Rhineland. To ensure their own safety, the Jews sought, and obtained, letters of protection from the German emperor and the leading bishops of the region. The latter were more than mere church prelates; they were prince-bishops, holding political as well as religious authority over the cities they ruled. As such, they commanded armies of their own. In return for protection, the Jews were subject to special taxes **as Jews**, in addition to what they had to pay as merchants or tradesmen. This was a most lucrative arrangement for the bishops, who welcomed Jews into their cities throughout most of the eleventh century.

For the Jews, it turned out to be a bad bargain. The Crusaders took three years to reach Jerusalem. On their way, they attacked Jewish communities in northern France and the Rhineland, usually with the active support of the local Gentile population. The victims were occasionally offered the choice of baptism or death, and some accepted Christianity as an alternative to martyrdom. Most were simply slain on the spot. A Jewish chronicler of the period wrote that the Crusaders were determined to rid Europe of Jesus's enemies (*sic*) before seizing the Holy Land from the Saracens. The protection offered by local rulers was woefully inadequate. In Mainz, for example, the Jews were given refuge in the cathedral, while the bishop's own troops tried vainly to keep the Crusaders at bay. After a brief skirmish, the Jews were slaughtered, and the bishop himself had to flee. When the Crusaders finally conquered Jerusalem in 1099, they killed every Jew they could find.

The impact of the Crusades on Judaeo-Christian relations was far-reaching. Once the genie of popular anger was let out of the bottle, it could not be put back in. On Easter Saturday, 1144, the dead body of William, a tanner's apprentice, was found in Norwich, England. Although the cause of death was never ascertained, rumour had it that young William had been killed by the Jews as part of their Passover ritual. Anti-Jewish riots and lynchings ensued. With William of Norwich began a long series of blood libels, in which the

Jews were accused of killing Christian children for their blood, which was said to be an essential ingredient of unleavened bread for Passover. Just how the Jews had managed to make unleavened bread before the advent of Christianity was never explained. The blood libel is not part of official Christian doctrine, but is clearly derived from it. In the Gospel according to Matthew (27.25), the blood of Jesus is said to fall upon the Jews and upon their children. Popular imagination embroidered on this theme until the blod libel won nearly universal acceptance. It survived well into the twentieth century, notably in Tsarist Russia and Nazi Germany.

Just as the Jews of Europe were faced with popular hatred, their usefulness to the ruling classes began to decrease. The feudal system, which took centuries to be established, gradually pushed the Jews out of agriculture. Feudalism was, in theory at least, a pyramid of allegiances, in which the humblest peasant swore fealty to a minor noble, who in turn became the vassal of a greater lord—and so on right up to the king. Each degree of vassalage was based on an oath, which, as is only normal in a Christian society, was sworn on the Gospels. Since the Jews could not take such an oath, they had tc give up farming. By the end of the eleventh century, there were hardly any Jews in Western Europe who still worked the land. Excluded from the feudal system, the Jews took up residence in the towns. But here too, they met with restrictions from the guilds, which came to dominate trade and commerce. A creation of the new Christian bourgeoisie, the guilds refused to admit Jews. By the twelfth century, the Jews of Northern Europe were reduced largely to peddling and money lending, although they continued to engage in handicrafts in the South. Throughout this period of nascent capitalism, money lending was an exceedingly risky profession in which frequent losses were offset only by usurious rates of interest. This made the Jews hated even more.

With their economic activities thus restricted, the Jews were less attractive to secular rulers as a source of tax revenue. The latter were able to levy new taxes on income derived from the general increase in trade and commerce. As more money flowed into the royal treasuries, kings and princes found the means to engage a permanent civil service, which in turn made tax collection more efficient. The first country to undergo such administrative centralization was England. It was also the first to expel its Jewish subjects, in 1290, but only after they had been thoroughly impoverished by a series of royal exactions. In thirteenth-century France, the crown repeatedly extorted huge sums of money from the Jews until there was none left. They were then officially expelled from the country in 1306, only to be reinvited back less than a decade later, since the royal treasury was once again empty, and the king hoped to gouge them further. Another expulsion followed in 1322, but a financial crisis in 1359 led the king to readmit Jews into France. They were barred from the kingdom definitively in 1394.

Excluded from England and France, the Jews of Europe were still able to settle in less-centralized areas. These included the French-speaking regions that had not yet been incorporated into the kingdom of France, as well as such politically fragmented nations as Italy and Germany. The latter, which was known officially as the Holy Roman Empire, was a hotch-potch of more than three hundred kingdoms, principalities, duchies and free cities, all of which enjoyed very broad autonomy. If Jews were persecuted in one jurisdiction, they could often move to another, not far away. This was far from an ideal solution, but it did allow the Jews to survive and prosper, even in the late Middle Ages. Indeed their survival depended on their prosperity. Not only did a little extra money enable the Jews to get out of a difficult situation when it arose, but their very status as a protected minority implied that they enjoy a higher standard of living than the average. The king or prince expected **his** Jews to increase the general prosperity of the realm. This was possible only if they had money to invest and the skills to make it grow. So on balance, and despite persecutions, Jews lived better than Christians (most of whom were condemned to perpetual serfdom) even as Christianity was dominant in Europe.

Chapter IV

MEDIAEVAL GRANDEUR AND DECLINE

THE ULTIMATE REFUGE for the Jews of Northern Europe was Poland, a vast country, much of it wilderness, with ample room for new inhabitants. Following the Tartar invasions of 1241-42, the King of Poland invited merchants and tradesmen from Germany to settle in his kingdom, hoping thereby to help rebuild its devastated economy. His invitation was widely accepted, particularly by the Jews, whose memories of the Crusades were still fresh. Like their Gentile counterparts, the Jews who moved to Poland from Germany kept mainly to themselves and mingled little with the local population. Such isolation can be explained partly by the very size of the country, since many Jewish villages were far removed from other population centres. A more important factor was the nature of Polish society and the role in it that was assigned to the Jews. As small businessmen, they were rebuffed by the aristocracy and had no interest in joining the peasantry. So they continued to speak German among themselves, but without regular contact with the Gentile settlers from Germany. In time, the Jews of Poland developed a language of their own, Yiddish, which is essentially a mediaeval Rhenish dialect of German, with simplified grammar and sentence structure, containing many Slavic and Hebrew expressions.

Encouraged by the king, the Jewish communities of Poland grew rapidly in numbers and economic status. Their industry, religious observance and social consciousness led to the creation of a dynamic, albeit self-contained, culture. Today's largely secularized Jews look back on that culture with nostalgia and console themselves over their apparent loss of identity by reading books about the joys of Yiddish and about their grandmothers' cooking. Vibrant though it was, however, Polish Judaism suffered in one important respect: lack of regular social and intellectual contact with Gentile society. Throughout the Middle Ages, the Jews of Europe had adopted the language of the country they lived in, not only to communicate with its Gentile inhabitants, but also to converse among themselves. They naturally wrote it using the Hebrew, rather than the Roman, alphabet. This was because few Christians knew how to write, and those that did were typically clerics who used Gothic script to copy religious texts that were of little interest to Jews. By adopting the local vernacular, European Jews were able to maintain contact with Gentile society and often to influence it. In Poland, however, the Jews had no such opportunity. Their social, cultural and religious life developed largely in isolation from that of the surrounding population.

The Polish experience thus marked a radical change from Jewish custom. Judaism, and enlightened self-interest, encouraged the Jews to participate fully in the affairs of the host society, not to live apart from it. Ever since Jeremiah exhorted his people to work for the good of the very Babylon which had taken them captive, a high degree of social integration, consistent with the maintenance of Jewish beliefs and practices, was considered both normal and beneficial. Avoiding contact with Gentiles would have meant forsaking the Jews' historic mission to be a light unto the nations. And despite the efforts of Constantine to prevent Jewish proselytism, it is evident that the Jews did not abandon this mission, even as Christianity strengthened its hold on Europe. The *Manual of the Inquisitor*, written in the late thirteenth century by the Dominican priest, Bernard Gui, contains a whole chapter on how to deal with the Jews, who, the author claims, never miss an opportunity to convert Christians to their religion. Certainly, they were always ready to present the Jewish point of view on moral questions.

Just as Gui was writing his famous manual, rabbis in southern France could be found arguing publicly with Dominicans in religious 'disputations' on the relative merits of Judaism and Christianity. The rabbis were not in the least deterred by the fact that these debates, designed to fortify the faith of Christians and to convert Jews to Christianity, were procedurally rigged in favour of their opponents. Not to participate would leave the field open to the other side.

Jewish converts to Christianity were invited to Jewish homes on the Sabbath and urged to return to Judaism. Christians who had been baptized in infancy were also welcome on these occasions. In Poland, on the other hand, close encounters of this kind were almost non-existent. There, the Jews maintained their religious traditions in virtual isolation from the rest of society. No mission to the Gentiles was feasible.

The Spanish Drama

A more telling blow to Jewish cultural and religious development was the expulsion in 1492 of the Jews from Spain, where they had flourished for over seven centuries in an atmosphere of general tolerance. When the Arabs invaded the Iberian peninsula in 711, the Jews welcomed them as liberators, some actually taking arms against the hated Visigoths. Throughout most of the Middle Ages, the Arabs surpassed Christian Europe in mathematics, science and philosophy; they also enjoyed a higher standard of living. By the eleventh century, many cities in Muslim Spain had street lighting, while London and Paris were still in the dark. The Jews of Spain thrived in the prosperity and intellectual brilliance of Arab civilization. The total output of their religious commentaries exceeded that of all other European Jewish communities put together. Most of these texts were written in Arabic, which was more familiar to Mediterranean Jews than Hebrew. Their authors were seeking a wide audience and did not write merely for other rabbis. Arabic had another advantage over Hebrew in that its larger vocabulary facilitated the exposition of philosophical principles. Through Arab scholars, Spanish rabbis were introduced to Aristotelian philosophy and used it to reconcile faith with reason.

That Judaism can be enriched through contact with Gentile thought is evident in the writings of Moses Ben Maimon, the greatest mediaeval Jewish philosopher, known to all Jews as Maimonides. Born in Cordoba in 1135, he was trained first as a rabbi and later as a physician. His most noteworthy innovation was to apply Aristotle's methods to Jewish religious practice, rationalizing it in philosophical terms. Thus he justified the dietary laws not only on hygienic grounds but also to promote self-discipline. But he did not stop there. The faithful were admonished to limit their consumption of meat—in apparent contradiction to the Biblical permission (Deut. 12.20), 'You may eat meat according to your desires.' Maimonides interpreted the text to mean that one should abstain from eating meat except when overcome by an irresistible craving. In this regard, as in so many others, he was remarkably prescient. Only recently has medical science established that excessive meat consumption can lead to cancer and heart disease. Long before physical fitness became the rage, he prescribed regular exercise as an aid to digestion. Moderation and decorum are the essential characteristics of his philosophy. A truly wise person, he maintained, will dress correctly but without ostentation; clothing is to be neither elaborate nor shabby. Above all, dress should not set one apart from the rest of society—an admonition that the Hasidic Jews of our own day have apparently overlooked.

To most Jews, Maimonides is known primarily for his eight steps or degrees of charity, whose timeless beauty graced the pavilion of Judaism at the Montreal World's Fair in 1967. The lowest is to give with reluctance or regret; the highest is to anticipate charity by teaching one's reduced fellow human being a trade or by setting him up in business. Both the Bible and the Talmud extol charity, which in Hebrew is synonymous with justice. Only Maimonides gave a clear and reasoned prescription for charity that any Jew could follow. He approached social justice in much the same way as he approached medicine: rather than curing disease, the physician's main task should be to keep the patient healthy. By the same token, preventing poverty is more effective than trying to alleviate it through handouts.

The family of Maimonides was forced to flee Cordoba by an army of Islamic militants who invaded Spain from Morocco in 1148. He eventually settled in Cairo, where, after completing his medical studies, he was retained as court physician. In Spain, meanwhile, the Moroccan invasion resulted in a gradual disintegration of

Muslim political authority, which split up into regional caliphates. Taking advantage of this weakness, Christian forces in the north began their reconquest of the peninsula. By the thirteenth century, Spain was a country of three religions. The Jews, having learned Spanish as well Arabic, often acted as business intermediaries between Christians and Muslims. Their high standard of living left them with sufficient leisure time to enjoy the relaxed sexual mores that shocked their coreligionists of northern Europe. Nachmanides (1194-1270), the leading rabbi of Christian Spain, ruled that an unmarried woman may have sexual relations, as long as she takes only one lover. To today's young adults, of course, this is rather tame stuff. But it is remarkably liberal in comparison to earlier Jewish doctrine—to say nothing of Christianity or Islam.

Even as the Jews of Spain continued to live in comparative luxury, their religious writings took on a more emotional tone, far removed from the serene rationalism of the earlier Muslim period. Maimonides, who personally had little use for Christianity, nonetheless defended it in historical terms. It represented an improvement over paganism, he wrote, and would have to suffice until Christians were ready to accept the pure monotheism of the Jews. As Christianity advanced from the north, however, rabbis were summoned to debate with Christian clerics in disputations which were designed to prove the superiority of the daughter religion. Nachmanides participated in many of these encounters, defending Judaism with a verve that impressed many of his Christian listeners. Jewish spokesmen often drew their inspiration from *The Kuzari*, an impassioned defence of Judaism written around 1130-1140 by the great Toledo-born Hebrew poet Judah Halevi. It was a fictionalized account of how the king of the Khazars, a people of the southern Volga region, converted to Judaism in the eighth century after hearing arguments from Jewish, Christian and Muslim authorities. As they came under increasing pressure from Christianity to defend their faith, the Jews of Spain grew less tolerant of dissent within their own community. In 1305, Salomon ben Adret, who had succeeded Nachmanides as chief rabbi, ruled that no Jew under thirty be allowed to study science and philosophy. An exception was made for medical students, but the spirit of free inquiry which had characterized Spanish Judaism for centuries was coming to an end.

The end of Spanish Judaism itself came with the expulsion of the Moors from Granada, their last bastion on the peninsula, in 1492. Spain was now politically Christian, as the kingdoms of Aragon and Castile were formally united by the marriage of Ferdinand and Isabella. Both realms remained separate, however, in virtually every respect: each had its own parliament, legal system, army and civil service. The only institution common to both was the church, and in particular, the Spanish Inquisition. The new Spanish monarchy relied heavily on the Inquisition to impose some measure of centralization on a country where regional loyalties were (and often still are) dominant. Spain was the last of the great European kingdoms to achieve political unity. It was also the last to expel its Jewish population.

Integrated both culturally and economically, many Spanish Jews preferred baptism to exile. The church had long been aware that most Jews who converted to Christianity did so for social and economic reasons and not out of any sincere belief in the moral superiority of the daughter religion. The Inquisition took a dim view of the Jewish *conversos* and readily accepted in evidence any testimony that they were secretly practising Judaism. Any 'new Christian' who washed his hands before meals or who fried food in oil rather than lard or whose chimney did not expel smoke on Saturday was suspect. He was tried before the Inquisition as a heretic and, if found guilty, turned over to the civil authorities for execution. But not even denunciations by jealous neighbours could stop the social ascent of the Marranos, as they were derisively called. Freed by baptism from the restrictions that had formerly hindered them as Jews, they lost little time in gaining access to the liberal professions, the civil service, and even the church. The reaction to their success took a new and particularly vicious form: guilds, universities, and church orders passed statutes—some as early as the fifteenth century—requiring *limpieza de sangre* (purity of blood) for all members. No one with Jewish parents or grandparents could join. For centuries thereafter any Spaniard with 'Jewish blood' was considered an outcast. The last public example of this slander took place in 1904, when opposition politicians in the Spanish parliament accused the prime minister of having Jews somewhere in his family tree.

In our time, Jewish scholars have been quick to point out that such racialism is contrary to official Christian doctrine, which has always recognized the Jewish origin of the apostles and offers salvation to anyone who accepts baptism, regardless of the convert's former religion. Yet the fact remains that all those who helped enact the 'purity of blood' statutes were themselves Christians and, in many cases, sincerely pious. Faced with this apparent contradiction, one must conclude that Christianity, in its historical manifestations, is more than mere doctrine: it is what Christians, throughout the centuries, have made of it. In Spain, Christianity assumed racialist overtones largely because Judaism was so hard to eradicate. So indeed was Islam. The racial statutes were directed at the Moriscos, those Muslims who had converted to Christianity rather than face exile, no less than at the Marranos. But the former Jews remained the main target of Spanish racialism. Not only was their social and economic progress greater than that of the Moriscos, but Spanish Christians showed a greater fear of Judaism than of Islam.

Evidence of this fear can be found in the 1492 decree of expulsion. It refers to 'bad Christians who Judaized' and left the true faith. To counter this practice, the decree recalls, the Jews had been confined in 1480 to specific neighbourhoods in cities and towns. But inasmuch as they continued 'to subvert our holy Catholic faith and to make faithful Christians withdraw and separate themselves therefrom...instructing them in the ceremonies and observances of their religion', expulsion was the only answer. Such religious arguments can easily be dismissed as a mere smokescreen for economic and political ambition, but they do contain a kernel of truth. Although it is difficult to gauge the actual extent of Jewish missionary activity in mediaeval Spain, one thing is certain: no Christian who entered a synagogue in order to receive instruction in the Hebrew Bible or other aspects of Judaism was ever turned away. For the Christian monarchs of Spain who wished to impose both religious and political unity on their very disparate country, the problem was not so much that Jews were busily seeking converts wherever they could find them, but that Christians had become increasingly curious about religion and, in particular, about the source of divine revelation. This led them inevitably to the Bible, including the Hebrew Bible.

The Ghetto

The Jewish presence in Europe became a source of concern for the church as heresies began to develop among the population at large. Heresies are as old as Christianity itself, but they were initially limited to theological disputes. Not until the late Middle Ages did they begin to affect the laity. As we have seen earlier, ordinary Christians knew very little about their own religion until the advent of the parish system in the tenth and eleventh centuries. But educating Christians in the basic elements of their faith was a two-edged sword. The better informed they became, the more likely they were to question church dogma. With the revival of trade and commerce in the twelfth and thirteenth centuries, a few laymen in the towns had enough leisure time to learn to read. Often they read the Bible, translations of which into the vernacular existed long before those of Wycliffe and Luther. Whenever they had difficulty interpreting a particular text, they could ask a priest. But the Catholic clergy were not, as a rule, particularly well versed in the Hebrew Scriptures. Christians seeking guidance on this subject would usually be better off consulting a rabbi. Although rabbis did not actively promote Christian heresy, they might encourage it indirectly through interpretations of Holy Writ that were at variance with those of the church.

In order to curtail Jewish influence on Christians, the Papacy took the lead in isolating Jews from the rest of society. The Lateran Council of 1179 revived anti-Jewish legislation that had long lain dormant, forbidding Christians to work for Jews as domestic servants or to rent rooms in a Jewish home. Another Lateran Council, held in 1215, excluded Jews from public office and obliged them to wear a distinctive yellow badge, usually in the shape of a wheel, on their outer garments. The yellow star, imposed on European Jews by the Nazis, was therefore nothing new. Attacks on Judaism were especially prevalent in France, the centre of heretical activity, during the thirteenth century. The Talmud was declared blasphemous, and in 1240, a general confiscation of books in Hebrew took place throughout the country. In some instances, the church tried to stem the flow of Jewish influence by attracting Jews to Christianity. A Papal decree of 1278 ordered Jews to open the doors of their synagogues to Christian missionaries. No great influx of Jewish converts to Christianity resulted from this measure. So isolating the Jews from their Christian neighbours was considered to be more effective.

The ultimate segregationist measure was the creation of the ghetto of Rome, by Papal decree, in 1555. Jewish quarters in European cities had existed for centuries; the first ghetto had been established in Venice in 1516, largely in response to a wave of Jewish immigrants from the Levant. Despite the restrictions imposed on its inhabitants, the Venetian ghetto was quite prosperous. The ghetto of Rome was something else altogether: a poor neighbourhood of run-down houses and narrow streets enclosed by a wall, whose gates were locked every day at sunset. It was not a Jewish, but a Christian creation, designed less to protect the Jews than to protect Christians from Jewish influence. The Papal bull confining the Jews of Rome to the new ghetto also forbade them to practise medicine among Christians or to have Christians in their employ. They were excluded from the liberal professions and were not allowed to own real estate. The ghetto of Rome served as a model for other ghettos throughout Italy and much of Europe.

Throughout the Middle Ages, Judaism had continued to evolve, to develop and, when the opportunity arose, to take in converts. Despite legal restrictions and increasing persecution, Jewish thinkers had responded vigorously to the many challenges of the outside world. The Jews of Italy, whose ranks were augmented by the arrival of refugees from Spain and Portugal, had been especially innovative. They made ample use of that new invention, the printing press, to expound their arguments on a whole range of moral and philosophical questions. This remarkable intellectual ferment was neutralized after 1555. With the advent of the ghetto, contact with the rest of society was virtually cut off. As a result, Judaism lost its essential dynamic, which depended on continuous interaction between Jews and Gentiles. Jewish missionary activity ceased altogether, for lack of contact with any potential converts. Judaism itself became frozen in time, with mysticism the only remaining outlet for Jewish imagination. Freed from the necessity of having to explain Jewish thought and practice to Gentiles, rabbis stopped explaining them to Jews. Anyone born in the ghetto was a Jew whether he liked it or not. Religious conformity was taken for granted and rigorously enforced. In the cramped, unhealthy conditions of the ghetto, physical and economic survival was uppermost in everyone's mind. Young boys were drilled in the basic elements of Judaism by underpaid and harassed teachers, whose only pedagogical tool was constant repetition. Scholarly inquiry had no place in such a hothouse atmosphere.

The rut into which Judaism had fallen—or rather, been pushed—can best be illustrated by the extraordinary popularity of a book published in 1567 under the title, *Shulchan Aruch* ('The Prepared Table'). Its author was a rabbi, Joseph Caro, whose family had resettled in the Ottoman Empire after having been expelled from Spain. He expressed disquiet at seeing his people tossed up on foreign shores without any centre of Jewish learning to guide and sustain them. So he wrote a four-volume compendium of Jewish law and custom, whose title reflected his approach to the problem: the table was already prepared; all the guests had to do was sit down and partake of the feast. The *Shulchan Aruch* proved to be exactly what the hard-pressed Jewish communities in Europe and the Mediterranean needed: a quick reference guide to daily observance. An unauthorized one-volume abridgement, which allowed even the untutored to follow basic Jewish practice, became even more popular than the original. Judaism thereby survived, but at a terrible cost: Jews were no longer required to reason together. When confronted with one of the many moral dilemmas that occur in everyday life, rabbis formerly poured over the Bible and the Talmud, usually consulting with colleagues over the finer points of interpretation. Now, however, a quick glance at Caro's code provided them with a ready-made answer.

As Judaism adopted a defensive position, emphasizing survival rather than development, so did Christianity. The year 1555, which saw the creation of the Roman ghetto, also marked the religious peace of Augsburg, by which the lines of demarcation between the Catholic and Protestant regions of Central Europe were officially laid down. With minor modifications, they remained in force until the twentieth century. Protestantism was the ultimate heresy, the one which the Catholic church could not eradicate. Its rapid rise in the first half of the sixteenth century can be traced first of all not to ecclesiastical corruption, as has often been claimed, but to the very strength of the Catholicism from which it originated.

Luther, like Wycliffe and John Huss before him, was a member of the Catholic clergy. He taught at a university, which, like all others in Europe, was Catholic; and it was there that he first came into public prominence by challenging, in the traditional academic manner, the widespread practice (now obsolete) of selling indulgences. The chapel door, on which Luther posted his 95 theses, was the university bulletin board. Whenever a professor wished to engage in a serious discussion on some question within his academic field, this is how he would make his propositions known. On theological matters, the Papacy naturally had the last word. But within the framework established by the church hierarchy, a wide range of subjects could be discussed. The entire educational system of mediaeval Europe was meant to serve the church by supplying it with a fresh crop of priests and theologians every year. Their enthusiasm and sense of commitment were the best insurance against ecclesiastical stagnation or corruption.

Without Catholic universities, the revolt sparked by Luther would have been unthinkable.

Spawned in academia, Lutheranism was eventually rescued and sustained by state power. When Luther was summoned to defend his views before the Diet of Worms in 1521, he was given a safe-conduct pledge. In itself, this was nothing new: John Huss, the brilliant and impassioned Bohemian cleric, had received a similar promise when he appeared before the Council of Constance in 1414. But Huss was burned at the stake as a heretic, whereas Luther received the protection of the Elector of Saxony. Huss had wanted to reform everything: the church and civil society alike. At the core of his doctrine was the premise that all human beings, including the ruling classes, are subject to divine law. An avid student of the Bible, Huss had elaborated such teachings without recognizing that they were fundamentally Jewish in nature; he cited Jesus of Nazareth as his sole authority. Nor did he seem to realize that their application would endanger the entire power structure of mediaeval Europe. Luther, on the other hand, followed the traditions of Pauline Christianity. He concentrated on spiritual matters and was content to leave secular rulers to their own devices. Within a few years, nearly half the German princes rallied to Luther's new religious formulation, thus freeing themselves from Papal authority.

The emancipation of the state from ecclesiastical control allowed Protestantism to gain a footing in Catholic Europe. Here too, the Protestants were heirs to Catholic tradition, which looked to the state as its closest ally. Early Christian missionaries, inspired by Paul's epistle to the Romans, spread the Gospel by first converting kings and princes, whose subjects were then baptized as a matter of course. In the late Middle Ages, the state again proved its usefulness by executing those whom ecclesiastical tribunals had found guilty of heresy. To ensure that the state did not get out of hand, mediaeval Popes played off one ruler against another. In particular, they regularly supported the King of France against the Holy Roman Emperor in Germany. This traditional policy backfired in 1302, when the French king, Philip the Fair, had

Pope Boniface VIII kidnapped in reaction to the bull, *Unam Sanctam*, which asserted Papal supremacy over the entire world. Boniface soon died, broken both in body and in spirit. His successors were French nominees, who presided over a court in Avignon, under French domination. This disgrace was compounded in 1378 by the election of two Popes, one in Avignon and the other in Rome. By 1414, there were three, each excommunicating the other two. Thus did the alliance of throne and altar work to the detriment of the latter.

The logical outcome of this trend was the creation, in 1534, of the Church of England. Its founder was that notorious glutton, adulterer and murderer, Henry VIII, who had not wanted to reform anything at all. He was at odds with the Pope over the latter's refusal to annul his marriage to Catherine of Aragon and decided to become head of the Catholic church in his own country. While Henry was still bickering with Rome, Calvin and other Protestant leaders attracted a following in continental Europe and Scotland. Their arguments were largely theological and moral. But the English king was not concerned with either theology or morality. The church he established was Protestantism in its essential form: a state religion—no more, no less, committed to supporting the nation's power structure. Contemporary Anglicanism seems innocuous enough, but for centuries it provided a moral alibi for the worst excesses of its country's class system and imperial conquests.

Within two generations of their inception, the Protestant churches virtually ceased to proselytize and settled into a comfortable existence as pillars of local society. In reaction, Catholicism largely reformed itself, eliminating the more egregious cases of corruption and vesting even greater authority with the Pope in Rome. An uneasy truce prevailed, with neither side able to increase at the expense of the other. The Wars of Religion, which were actually political conflicts played out under the guise of doctrinal disputes, showed that religious passion could still inflame the masses into hating the other side. By then, however, both Lutheranism and Calvinism were established churches, every bit as much as Catholicism; and the leaders of all three had lost most of their missionary zeal. Christianity as a whole ceased to expand; and the Jews, caught between the opposing Christian factions, were content to survive.

For the ghetto, while it restricted the Jews' freedom, did offer them some protection against an increasingly hostile society. The popular passions which manifested themselves in the wars between Catholics and Protestants, were also directed against the Jews. Just how strongly Judaeophobia held sway among the unlettered European masses in the late Middle Ages can be seen in a remarkable book published in 1943 by an English rabbi, Joshua Trachtenberg. Under the title, *The Devil and the Jews*,[1] it shows how Jesus's invective in John 8.44 had developed into an ideology which demonized the entire Jewish people. Some zealous clerics reasoned that since the real Messiah had already arrived, the one awaited by the Jews was none other than the Antichrist. Popular imagination took over from there, accusing the Jews of being in league with the devil. By the fourteenth and fifteenth centuries, mass violence against the Jews was commonplace. Behind ghetto walls, they enjoyed some protection—for the time being at least.

The System Breaks Down

One country where ghettos were hardly needed was Poland; and with the exception of the ecclesiastical seat of Cracow, none was created. The Jews of Poland, who were for the most part isolated in their villages and who continued to speak Yiddish among themselves, had little contact with the population at large. Their intellectual and spiritual influence on Christian Poles was therefore slight. And although the church continued to portray the Jews as Christ-killers, secular power made no attempt to segregate them, as in Italy, or expel them, as in Spain. The Polish monarchy's

---

[1] 2nd ed., Cleveland: Meridian Books, 1961.

official policy of toleration was dictated by enlightened self-interest: it needed the Jews.

More than in any other European country, the Jews of Poland had mastered the art of survival by making themselves useful to the ruling classes. Not only did they pay special taxes to the king in return for his protection, but they also entered into a close working relationship with the greater nobles. Polish aristocrats, whose social standing was closely tied to their careers as army officers, usually left the running of their estates to Jewish managers. These vast holdings were devoted mainly to grain production, which, in itself, was not especially profitable. When distilled into alcoholic beverages, however, the grain harvest yielded handsome benefits. In time, many Polish Jews became involved, willy-nilly, in the production and distribution of hard liquor. The estate managers sold this produce to other Jews, who are usually referred to in Jewish history books as 'innkeepers'. To accept this definition one must recall what an inn actually was in those days before tourism existed. It was not a hotel; the few, modest rooms available were used only occasionally by bona-fide travellers. In most instances, they were rented out to prostitutes. The entire ground floor of a typical inn was given over to the sale and consumption of hard drink. In other words, the typical Polish country inn of the late Middle Ages was a tavern and a brothel.

It is unlikely that Jewish inkeepers enjoyed the social role that had evolved to them in Poland, but they had to make a living somehow. What is certain is that, as accessories to drunkenness and sexual licence, they contributed to tensions between Jews and the Polish population in general. The church did not help matters. When priests inveighed against the evils of drink, they could not fail to note that the purveyors of liquor were of the same stock as those whom Jesus had called sons of the devil. So the Jews, it seemed, were still doing Satan's work! For mediaeval Christians, many of whom spent more time in the tavern than in church, the devil was terribly real—far more so than God Himself. Inasmuch as the innkeeper was typically the only Jew with whom the average Polish peasant had regular contact, the tendency to equate Jews with the devil was very strong indeed.

The wealthier Jews' privileged contacts with the Polish elite created ill feeling not only among Polish peasants, but even more so among the Ukrainians. When Poland annexed large areas of the Ukraine in 1569, thousands of Jews were brought in to manage the estates that had been taken over by Polish nobles. An entire network of Jewish administrators was thus created, with Jews in charge of practically everything that yielded a profit: agriculture, forestry and mining. Village government was subservient to Jewish overseers, and Jews dominated the trade in alcoholic drink no less than in Poland. Especially humiliating to the local population was the Polish practice of using Jews as tax farmers throughout most of the Ukraine. Tax farming was an old custom, usually involving local notables, so that poor folk were at least being exploited by their own kind. But the Jews in the Ukraine were clearly foreign, and popular animosity toward them grew year by year.

Among the Jews themselves, the growth of a wealthy elite serving the Polish nobility was likewise a source of considerable resentment. A Jewish oligarchy maintained its hold on society by marrying its sons and daughters to the children of rabbis. Religious sanction allowed it to stifle dissent within the community. Private correspondence of the fifteenth and sixteenth centuries, which was published in Israel by Haim Ben-Sasson in 1959, reveals the bitterness felt by the poorer elements of Polish Jewry. The rich alone are honoured in the synagogue, they complain. Rabbis busy themselves with purely ritualistic matters, leaving urgent social problems unattended. Sealed off from the outside world, the poor Jews of Poland had no one to turn to for solace. They grudgingly accepted the system because it offered them physical protection, if little else.

By the mid-seventeenth century, even this meagre advantage was swept away. A revolt by Ukrainian Cossacks against their Polish landlords in 1648 quickly degenerated into a wholesale massacre of the Jews. The Polish monarchy and nobility proved incapable of protecting their Jewish subjects. In fact, they could hardly protect themselves. In 1654, The Tsar of Russia allied him-self with the Ukrainian rebels and annexed large areas of White Russia and Lithuania, which had been under Polish rule. Once the turmoil subsided, more than one hundred thousand Jews had perished, often in circumstances whose horror rivals that of the Nazi genocide. In a stroke, the symbiotic relationship between Jews and Polish secular power was destroyed. Since the expulsion of Jews from Spain, Poland was the one country in Europe where they could be assured of survival. Now this assurance was gone. In their shock and confusion, the Jews of Europe groped about for a miracle.

The answer to their prayers came from a somewhat unlikely corner—the city of Smyrna in Asia Minor, where in 1665, Sabbatai Zevi, the handsome son of a Jewish merchant, proclaimed himself the Messiah. He lost no time in asserting dominion over Palestine and in abrogating certain Jewish fasts as a sign that the kingdom of heaven was nigh. His call for deliverance was heeded by hordes of European Jews, who sold their businesses and personal effects in a headlong rush to emigrate to the Holy Land. Even the arch-sceptic Spinoza (who remained in his native Amsterdam) saw no reason why the Jewish commonwealth should not be restored. But Zevi's territorial claims vexed the Turkish authorities, who had him imprisoned. Forced to choose between conversion to Islam and death, the would-be Messiah readily abandoned Judaism. He died, a Muslim, in 1676.

In a more rational epoch, Zevi's betrayal would surely have cooled the ardour of his followers; indeed, his claim to be the Messiah would not have been taken seriously in the first place. But such was the temper of the times that the general longing for a redeemer did not abate. Some distraught Jews waited patiently for Zevi's resurrection. The rest were attracted to other Messianic claimants, who were not lacking in those days. One of the most notable was a Polish adventurer named Jacob Frank, who in 1755 announced that he was the reincarnation of Sabbatai Zevi and joyfully proclaimed that the traditional Jewish prohibitions on certain forms of sexual activity were no longer valid. For many dejected

Jews of Poland, this proved to be a powerful drawing-card, and the Frankist sect attracted a large following. Condemned by the Polish rabbinate, Frank converted to Catholicism in 1759, along with most of his flock. Frankism, which was associated in the popular imagination with sexual orgies, was now thoroughly discredited. But poor Jews everywhere, especially in Poland, continued to seek redemption.

The Messianic sects of the seventeenth and eighteenth centuries all failed because their leaders could not make good on their promises. To comfort the downtrodden Jewish masses, a message of hope was needed, but one which did not identify any one person as the Messiah. In that way, the message could be renewed from one generation to another. Its author was a Jewish lime digger from Galicia, Israel Ben Eliezer (1700-1760), who withdrew to the forest as a hermit and studied various plants for their healing powers. On returning to society, he became so famous for his herbal remedies that Jews and Gentiles alike came to him to be cured. Dubbed *Baal Shem Tov* ('Master of the Good Name') by his disciples, he taught that devotion was more important than scholarship. Classical Judaism, as exemplified by Hillel, had always stressed the importance of education. In Hillel's view, an ignorant person could never be truly pious (*Avoth* 2.6). This concept was now turned upside-down: the simple soul who sought communion with God was held to be holier than the most learned rabbi.

Baal Shem Tov's followers called themselves *Hasidim* or 'pious ones', in conscious imitation of a Messianic sect that had flourished in Judaea during the Maccabean period. The movement gained many adherents and eventually survived an edict of excommunication published by the chief rabbi of Vilna in 1772. By then, the Hasidim had tempered somewhat their initial opposition to scholarship and maintained an uneasy coexistence with traditional Judaism. But they never were, and never became, 'ultra-orthodox'—a catchword of contemporary journalism that would have been utterly incomprehensible in the late eighteenth century. Hasidic Judaism remains fundamentally anarchistic, as its followers continue to turn their backs on society and seek communion with God—either directly or through a *Tsadik* ('righteous one'), a mystic considered to possess extraordinary spiritual powers. Such single-minded pursuit of personal holiness will, they believe, be rewarded some day by the coming of the Messiah. The meteoric rise of Hasidism, with its rejection of established society, both Jewish and Gentile, is evidence that the mediaeval framework which was supposed to ensure the viability of Jewish communities in Europe had outlived its usefulness.

The Hasidim recognized implicitly that the old system had failed, but they were not interested in creating a new one. They wanted out, period. Their movement assumes that history has no purpose: the only option for the pious is to do God's bidding and await the Messiah. Not all Jews took this fatalistic approach, however. As printed books became increasingly available, individual Jews everywhere were exposed to the secular belief in human progress that was then sweeping Europe. It was based on the indisputable fact that the scientific discoveries of the seventeenth and eighteenth centuries had helped bring about a general, though unevenly distributed, improvement in the standard of living. The most immediate benefits were in agriculture, where more efficient methods of cultivation and new crops, such as the potato and the turnip, resulted in a healthier diet for most people. Material progress led some advanced thinkers to postulate a general improvement in society, with legal disabilities abolished or at least attenuated, so that each individual might contribute the full measure of his capabilities. For the Jews, who for centuries had to endure a multitude of obstacles to their advancement, this was welcome news indeed. Those who could read and understand the latest treatises on social philosophy eagerly took up the secular belief in human progress. In a self-conscious imitation of the French *siècle des lumières* and the German *Aufklärung*, they called their movement the *Haskala*, or Jewish enlightenment.

Chapter V

A NEW DAWN?

THAT AN INTELLECTUAL REAWAKENING was underway among European Jews in the mid-eighteenth century can be seen by the case of Moses Mendelssohn. The son of a poor Biblical scribe from Dessau, Mendelssohn gained prominence as a secular philosopher with the publication of his first work, *Philosophical Conversations*, in 1755. He was soon invited to the court of Frederick the Great, who marvelled that a Jew could speak proper High German. Nearly all German Jews of the time spoke a heavily-accented *Judendeutsch*, similar to the Yiddish of their Polish brethren. Mendelssohn was fluent in several languages and eventually translated the Pentateuch into German. He was not, strictly speaking, the first secular Jewish intellectual in history; that distinction belongs to Spinoza, who lived a century earlier. But whereas Spinoza rejected religion except on grounds of social and political utility, Mendelssohn remained a committed and observant Jew. To Gentiles he appealed for tolerance, treating religion as a private matter. If Christians allowed him to practise Judaism in the home or synagogue, he would not call their beliefs into question. This meant abandoning the Jewish mission, but by the 1750's, it seemed a dead letter anyway. Oppressed by the ghetto system and reeling from the persecutions suffered a century earlier, the Jews of Europe were hardly in a position to seek out converts.

The political, social and economic status of most European Jews at the time was, quite simply, wretched. The Polish monarchy, which had provided them with sanctuary for some five centuries, was itself in the process of advanced disintegration and would soon be partitioned among its more powerful neighbours. Elsewhere, Jews were tolerated by local authorities on an *ad hoc* basis. The Hungarian town of Buda allowed a small Jewish community to exist within its limits; but across the Danube in Pest, any Jew caught spending the night was subject to a heavy fine. Vienna expelled its Jews in 1670; Prague followed suit in 1744. The French monarchy did not apply the edict of expulsion to Jews who lived in areas annexed to France since 1394, but instead allowed local governments to decide whether, and on what conditions, they could remain. Their situation in Alsace, which had become a French province in 1648, was particularly dismal. Denied access to handicraft trades and the liberal professions, most Alsatian Jews eked out a living as pedlars and dealers in second-hand goods as they struggled to pay the special taxes imposed on them for the privilege of residence.

A way out of their predicament was suggested by the emergence, in the early eighteenth century, of the court Jew (*Hofjude*) in Germany. With the Holy Roman Empire reduced to a legal fiction by the Treaties of Westphalia in 1648, the more than 300 German petty states and principalities gained virtually complete sovereignty. Their rulers employed Jews as bankers and suppliers to the army for much the same reasons that had prompted Muslim caliphs in the Middle Ages to appoint Jews as court treasurers: being outsiders, Jews could not form, or even become a party to, an opposing faction within the court. They could therefore be trusted with the state finances. In Alsace, where Germanic traditions persisted long after the province became nominally French, the official supplier to the French army in the second half of the eighteenth century was a Jew from Strasbourg named Cerf Berr. In an effort to improve the economic condition of his coreligionists, he invested his substantial profits in three factories, which employed Jews almost exclusively. This was a step in the right direction, but it did little to alleviate the community's general misery.

In 1780, the Jews of Alsace decided to appeal to the French Council of State for a relaxation of the restrictions under which they had to live and work. Their leaders, who were none too confident in their own powers of literary expression, asked Moses Mendelssohn to draft a suitable petition. Mendelssohn, in turn, approached a cultivated Prussian nobleman, Christian Wilhelm Von Dohm, in the belief that such a plea would have greater effect if written by a

Christian. Dohm produced a two-volume work, entitled, *Concerning the Civil Improvement of the Jews.* His argument was simple: Jews may be more corrupt, more inclined to sharp business practices and fraud than other people; they are indeed clannish and often antisocial, but that is because society rejects them. Admit them fully into society; allow them to enter agriculture, the liberal professions, the guilds and even the army; and their social behaviour will greatly improve. Only by being granted full civil rights can Jews become useful to the state, he concluded.

The theme of making the Jews useful was soon taken up in other European countries. In 1782, the Austrian emperor, Joseph II, issued an edict of toleration in which he announced 'Our goal to make the Jewish nation useful and serviceable to the State'. To this end, they would henceforth be allowed to enter the trades and professions, to own real property wherever they liked, and to frequent places of public amusement. Such measures were designed to release the Jews of Austria from the bonds of poverty into which a tangle of legal restrictions had placed them. The more prosperous they became, the more taxes they would pay to the crown. Joseph was the first European head of state to make such sweeping reforms.

But it was in France, and not central Europe, that the civil status of the Jews became a subject for public debate. Alone among European countries, France had within its borders two very distinct Jewish communities: the larger of the two, comprising mainly the Jews of Alsace and Lorraine, was excluded from society and lived in general poverty; the Jews of southern France, on the other hand, enjoyed a greater degree of social acceptance and were far more prosperous. Most remarkable of all was the small but dynamic Jewish community of Bordeaux, which was descended from Marranos who had fled Spain in the early seventeenth century and who were given permission to settle in France by the pragmatic King Henry IV. In a revealing study entitled *The Sephardic Jews of Bordeaux*,[1] Frances Malino explains that the original

---

[1]University of Alabama Press, 1978.

Marrano settlers had only a fragmentary notion of Judaism when they arrived in France. They had to rediscover their Jewish heritage, build synagogues and observe the Jewish Sabbath in order to be accepted as upright bourgeois by the local gentry. Then, clean-shaven and dressed in conservative business suits, they were able to participate in the growing overseas trade of that bustling seaport. For those enlightened Frenchmen who sought to make all elements of the population more productive, Bordeaux was a shining example of what Jews could do if given the chance.

Mindful of these possibilities, the Royal Society of Metz, in northeastern Lorraine, announced a literary competition in 1785 on the subject: 'Are there ways to make the Jews happier and more useful in France?' Metz was on the very border between Western and Central Europe. Its French-speaking elite was well-versed in the latest philosophical writings of Montesquieu, Voltaire and Rousseau; but within its *juiverie*, or Jewish quarter, were crowded several thousand poor souls who still spoke a Jewish dialect of German and whose very mode of existence was foreign to the other townspeople. In addition, some Polish Jews had settled in Metz when Lorraine was ruled by the former Polish king, Stanislas Lesczinsky, before being ceded to France in 1766. Once the literary competition was announced, notices were posted in the synagogues of Metz, urging the faithful to make themselves more useful to society. But this was easier said than done: like their brethren in Alsace, the Jews of Lorraine were severely restricted as to how they could earn a living.

Their hardships were well known to a local priest, Henri Grégoire, whose entry, *An Essay on the Physical, Moral, and Political Regeneration of the Jews*, was tied with two others for first prize in the competition. Unlike his fellow laureates, Grégoire approached the Jewish problem from a social, rather than a purely philosophical, point of view. A frequent visitor to the *juiverie,* he noted that Jewish population growth had already outstripped the community's meagre economic resources. If Jews were not allowed to become more productive by engaging in the same trades and professions as the rest of society, they would become a burden on the state. Grégoire saw the Jews' propensity to marry young as a prime cause of the problem. Whereas Christians tend to put off marriage until they can support a family, even the poorest Jews rush headlong into wedlock, seeking in a happy home life some consolation for their misery. 'Of all peoples, the Jews are the most eager to procreate, and the hope of seeing the Messiah emerge from their race makes them even more diligent in fulfilling the precept ["Be fruitful and multiply"] that they believe the Book of Genesis has imposed on them.'

Grégoire's analysis was correct—as far as it went. The Jewish rate of natural increase was in fact greater than that of Christians. Early marriage was a factor, to be sure, but there were others. Because Jews traditionally took a bath once a week (on Friday afternoon, just before the Sabbath) and washed their hands before eating, they enjoyed better hygiene than Gentiles. This may explain why relatively fewer Jews than Christians perished in the bubonic plague, or Black Death, of the fourteenth century. Because Jews were seldom drunk, their sexual potency and fecundity remained undiminished. For the same reason, wife-beatings were extremely rare in Jewish homes. And of course Jews did not give any of their children to the church, to remain celibate. Only expulsions and persecutions had prevented the Jews of Europe from making serious demographic inroads on Christian society.

By the eighteenth century, outright persecution of the Jews had largely ceased, while expulsions were rare and confined to a few localities. Even more important, the agricultural revolution of the period stimulated population growth in general and that of the Jews especially. As new methods of cultivation produced greater harvests, new crops, such as the turnip and the potato, provided the lower classes with more nutrients than they had consumed previously. As a result, fewer poor people died young of malnutrition, and the social pyramid widened at its base. With an increased life expectancy, the poorer elements of society grew faster than the middle classes or the rich. Poor Jews—a visible minority if there ever was one—were especially noticeable as the century drew to a close. Something had to be done about them.

The winning essays of the Metz literary competition were published in 1788. All three laureates agreed that the Jews should be granted the same rights as other people in order to become happier and more useful to society. In the past, the Jews had survived by making themselves useful to the sovereign power—that is, the king or prince who ruled over them. Now, on the eve of the French Revolution, as sovereignty was about to be assumed by the people, the Jews had to become useful to the nation as a whole.

A Jewish Revolution

Born of an attempt by King Louis XVI to reduce the national debt by taxing his country's privileged classes, the French Revolution soon concentrated on re-establishing all of society on a new constitutional basis. Central to this reform was the social contract, an idea previously put forward by Jean-Jacques Rousseau. Instead of a sovereign ruler, acting through such intermediaries as the nobility and the church to protect his passive subjects, society was to be based on a contract between the government and the governed. In return for paying taxes, serving in the army and obeying the laws of the land, the people were to live in freedom, their fundamental rights guaranteed by delegated authority. The new nation would no longer be composed of privileged and unprivileged orders, but of citizens—each enjoying the same rights and subject to the same obligations as the rest. A citizen was defined as being anyone who lived in France and who obeyed its laws, regardless of his social class, ethnic origin or religion. Inevitably, this definition would have to include the Jews.

Admitting Jews as full-fledged members of French society was not a foregone conclusion, however. For most delegates to the Constituent Assembly, the Jews seemed to be a nation unto themselves, with their own laws and customs. These objections were overcome, however, by a flood of petitions drafted in excellent French by Jews from all over the country, who insisted on being granted equal rights with other citizens. 'It is true that we practise a religion different from that of the majority,' read one such appeal. 'But that only serves to ensure the fidelity of our oath.' Even the Jews of Paris, who numbered but one thousand and who had no legal right to live in the capital, sent a petition of their own. In 1790, after much debate, the Assembly voted to grant citizenship to the Jews of southern France. Those of the north were accepted as Frenchmen a year later. Abbé Grégoire, who was a member of the Constituent Assembly, was one of those most instrumental in having the Jews of France admitted into civil society. But the real impetus toward equal status came from the Jews themselves. They were tired of being parias and longed for the dignity and well-being that citizenship offered.

Those who voted for emancipation were not all friends of the Jews, still less of Judaism. Even Abbé Grégoire expressed the hope that once the Jews regained a measure of human dignity, they would see the light and convert to Christianity. The Gentile proponents of civil rights for the Jews sought to make society function more efficiently by making everyone equal under the law. The welfare of the Jews was, in their view, subordinate to that of the nation. One who best exemplified this approach was Napoleon Bonaparte, who reformed the French legal system by issuing the civil code which bears his name. When Bonaparte turned his attention specifically to the Jews—which was not very often—he assumed that it would be in the best interests of France for them simply to assimilate. He himself was a culturally assimilated Corsican, whose vision of society was influenced by his military experience. Soldiers may have different duties to perform on the battlefield, but they all must wear the same uniform and march in step on the parade ground.

Napoleon was enough of a realist, however, to recognize that the Jews of France were not about to assimilate in his own lifetime. Since he could not eliminate Judaism, he decided to make it an instrument of state policy. A similar approach had characterized his relations with the Catholic church. In a concordat negotiated with—or rather, dictated to—the Pope in 1802, Bonaparte turned official Catholicism, which had opposed the French Revolution, into a political ally. In particular, a new catechism instructed Catholic schoolchildren to be loyal to the regime. Enlisting the support of Judaism was more difficult, since there was no established Jewish religious organization to deal with. So Napoleon decided in 1807 to convene an assembly of Jewish notables—rabbis, businessmen, and members of the liberal professions—to which he gave the overblown title of 'Grand Sanhedrin'. To these worthies he put a certain number of questions, all of which centred on one theme: given the fact that the Jews have laws of their own, could they be counted on to observe those of France and remain loyal to the French state? The 'Sanhedrin' gave its answer directly, citing Rabbi Samuel of Babylon, who in the third century had laid down the principle that 'The law of the kingdom is the law'. Thus reassured, Napoleon accepted Judaism as one of France's official religions, alongside Catholicism and Protestantism. Rabbis were henceforth to be paid from state funds, and a central Jewish administrative council, or *Consistoire*, was established to oversee religious practices and to act as intermediary between individual Jews and the state. To commemorate this achievement, Napoleon had a medal struck in 1808. It depicted Moses, on bended knee, receiving the Ten Commandments from the French emperor!

Judaism thus became an official religion in France and was subject to the same degree of centralization that characterized the entire Napoleonic system. In many respects it resembled French Catholicism—a dignified, respectable cult which honoured tradition and showed proper respect for political authority. French rabbis of the nineteenth century were men of considerable erudition, but showed hardly more innovative qualities than could be found among the Catholic clergy. In other countries as well, Judaism tended to resemble the dominant religion. Where there was an established church, as in England, Judaism took on an official character, with a centralized rabbinical authority. In Germany and the United States, where various Protestant sects coexisted somewhat uneasily with Catholicism, synagogues were more independent of one another. German Jews welcomed Napoleon's armies with joy, for with the French conquest came the promise of release from centuries of discrimination.

The majority of the Jews in Germany responded to their new-found freedom by adopting a series of ceremonial changes to the synagogue service. Henceforth, men and women could sit together, in imitation of the family pew common to Christian churches. Organ music was introduced, and many of the prayers were recited in the vernacular. The service itself was shortened, and everyone was expected to arrive on time. In religious teaching, emphasis shifted from legal prescriptions to the prophetic values of Judaism. The Reform movement swept throughout most of Germany in the first half of the nineteenth century, encountering little opposition until some German Jews protested that the reformers had gone too far. They objected mainly to the pick-and-choose approach of the modernists; one had to accept the whole Torah without reservation, they said. In opposition to Reform, the minority called itself Orthodox, so that, in historical terms, 'Orthodox' Judaism is actually the more recent version. That some Jews wished to retain the traditional ceremonies and practices is perfectly understandable, but 'Orthodox' was a poor choice of words. It is derived from the Greek and means, literally, right-thinking. Yet Judaism was never particularly concerned with what its adherents thought; it laid far more emphasis on what they did. 'Orthoprax' would have been a more appropriate term.

Many of the criticisms levelled against the reformers in the nineteenth century are still being voiced today, and they have not been ignored. In recent years, the use of Hebrew in Reform synagogues has increased, as has Torah study among their members. The principal virtue of Reform, in any case, is in its approach to history: alone among the various currents that have run through contemporary Judaism, it recognized that emancipation has obliged Jews to modify their traditional lifestyle. Orthodoxy, while allowing its adherents to dress in normal business attire and practise whatever trade or profession they choose, prefers to ignore the entire question. So does 'Conservative' Judaism, a uniquely American version, which came into existence in the late nineteenth century and seeks a middle ground between Orthodoxy and Reform. Since most American Jews emancipated themselves simply by leaving Europe, they are largely unaware of the historical dilemma posed by the Napoleonic decrees.

Whatever their outward differences, European Jews of the nineteenth century shared a common belief in secular progress. And they had good reason to do so. Following the agricultural revolution of the eighteenth century, the industrial revolution of the nineteenth created an era of prosperity and general well-being not seen since the Roman empire. The Jews, of course, prospered greatly. But more than that, they witnessed an extraordinary improvement in the overall quality of life. Sanitation is a prime example. The steam engine made possible the creation of central pumping stations, which, by the second half of the nineteenth century, brought running water to millions of homes. As a result, many Gentiles took to washing their hands before meals—a custom that had previously been condemned as Judaic. Now, however, this particular aspect of Jewish tradition seemed to be justified by technological progress.

The reverse side of the coin was that, if science and technology alone were sufficient to make the world a better place to live in, there would seem to be no further need for Jewish doctrine. And if Jewish doctrine no longer has a role to play in human experience, then the Jews themselves cease to be the chosen people. They were chosen, we recall, to enlighten the nations and to lead suffering humanity to a new era of peace and understanding. But the technological innovations of the nineteenth century had already alleviated much of human suffering. So perhaps the world would reach its golden age without the benefit of Judaism. Engulfed in a tidal wave of social and material progress, the Jews themselves hardly gave any thought to the role assigned to them in Holy Writ. They were happy to be members of a religion that enjoyed—in principle—official state recognition. Reform Judaism did maintain that the Torah and the prophetic writings carried a unique ethical message for all of mankind. In practice, however, the reformers did little to publicize this message beyond their immediate milieu.

Those who professed Orthodoxy could hardly be expected to renounce the idea of being chosen, but they were content to let the Messiah bring humanity closer to God. Once Jews cease to believe in their own mission, Judaism loses its cutting edge. There is no longer a historical imperative for anyone to remain a Jew.

There was even less incentive for anyone to become a rabbi. During the ancient and mediaeval periods, rabbis had been teachers and judges. Jewish emancipation reduced both functions to a symbolic level. On being admitted into society, Jews rushed to send their children to secular schools, which gave them access to the better-paying careers and professions. Religious education—the only kind that had existed in the ghetto—was now administered outside the regular school curriculum, if at all. The rabbi's role as judge was superceded when Jews became subject to the laws of the land. Jews could still bring cases before a rabbinical court if they felt so inclined, but its decisions were no longer legally binding. Only in the synagogue could the rabbi still make his presence felt, and in fact his role in the service grew at the expense of the cantor's. At the same time, however, synagogue attendance diminished, often for lack of interest. Besides, many Jews who might have attended Sabbath services were prevented from doing so by having to work on Saturday.

Still, there was no turning back. Having petitioned the civil authorities for equal rights, European Jews were in no mood to return to the ghetto. They had gained far too much in material benefits and individual self-esteem to accept the legal disabilities that had burdened their ancestors. The Jews had worked long and hard for their own emancipation; they would now have to adjust to it.

Difficult Assimilation

After the drama of the French Revolution and the Napoleonic period, Europe settled down to business. In spite of occasional rumblings on the left, the old nobility managed to retain power largely by co-opting elements of the new industrial bourgeoisie. The

Jews, whose leaders were drawn mainly from the retail trades and the liberal professions, were overwhelmingly liberal—that is, they supported the middle-class programme of constitutional government with equal rights guaranteed for all citizens. Napoleon's defeat at Waterloo in 1815 had been a major setback for Jewish emancipation. Throughout Central Europe, and even in France, Jews lost many of the rights that had been granted them earlier and were left in a kind of limbo: they had abandoned the ghetto, but were not fully accepted into society.

In Eastern Europe, their situation deteriorated with the final partition of Poland in 1815. Most of that hapless country was absorbed by the Russian empire, with smaller areas going to Prussia and Austria. For the Jews of Poland, who had found their niche in an economy based on private enterprise, the transition to Russian rule was harsh indeed. Russia had no capitalistic tradition similar to that of Poland. All major industries were in the hands of the state, in particular the production of alcoholic drink. On being annexed to Russia, the Jews of Warsaw sent a petition to the Tsar (in French, to show how serious they were), requesting that the confiscated distilleries be returned to them. The petition was refused. Even without this source of income, the Jews of Warsaw were still relatively well off, since the Polish territory annexed in 1815 enjoyed some measure of autonomy until 1830. After that, however, they had to face the full thrust of Tsarist tyranny. The Polish monarchy had long been tolerant of minority religions, such as Jews, Protestants, and Orthodox Christians. The Russian empire, on the other hand, prided itself on its strict Orthodoxy, with the Tsar serving as head of both church and state. Moscow was glorified as the third Rome, the historical and spiritual heir to Rome and Byzantium. Although the Tsars had long wanted to annex Poland, they had no use for its Jewish inhabitants, who were treated simply as outcasts.

In Germany, the Jewish question was dealt with on a piecemeal basis: a few German states granted Jews equal rights, while others imposed restrictions. For some Jews, whose appetite for complete equality had been whetted by the Napoleonic reforms, there was a relatively easy way out of this dilemma: baptism. The descendants of Moses Mendelssohn chose this path, as did many others. By converting to Christianity, well-educated Jews could become *salonfähig*, or socially acceptable. For those in the liberal professions, being admitted into polite society was a prerequisite for material success. One such Jew was a lawyer from Trier named Herschel Marx, who was descended from a long line of rabbis. He converted to Christianity in 1816, taking the name of Heinrich. Trier, on the western edge of Germany close to Luxembourg, was a predominantly Catholic town. Yet Marx chose Protestantism, The Vienna settlement of the previous year had given Trier and the surrounding region to Prussia, whose ruling classes were Protestant. By joining that particular branch of Christianity, Marx hoped no doubt to ingratiate himself with the new power elite. One Sunday in August 1824, he took his seven children to church and had them all baptized. The youngest, a serious little boy named Karl, was then six years old.

It is impossible to determine what made Karl Marx ashamed of his Jewish origins—taunts by schoolmates, neighbours' ridicule, or perhaps even remarks by his own father—but ashamed he certainly was. With the zeal of a convert, he studied philosophy and theology at the University of Berlin. His mentor, the Protestant theologian Bruno Bauer, had recently written that the Jews ought not to be emancipated because they were narrow-minded. Their religion was particularistic, whereas Christianity was universal (a common argument at the time, less so today). Marx answered with a book—his first—entitled, *On the Jewish Question*, in which he stood Bauer's argument on its head. It is not the Jews who should be emancipated, he claimed; rather, society should be emancipated from the Jews, and especially from their commercial ethic. 'The god of the Jews is money,' he concluded.

In his later writings, Marx concentrated on propagating socialism, but he never missed an opportunity to disparage Jews in the process. In *The Class Struggles in France,* an essay on the Paris revolution of 1848, Marx identifies each Jewish capitalist specifically as a Jew. The other capitalists are simply members of that dreaded class, the bourgeoisie. Marx delighted in insulting as Jews those leaders of rival socialist factions, who happened to be of Jewish ancestry like himself, but who had never been baptized. Thus he would call Ferdinand Lasalle, the leader of the German Social-democratic Party, a 'Jewish nigger'.

Marx was not merely ashamed of once having been a Jew. His entire public life was driven by the desire to create a new religion-substitute, in which there would be neither Jew nor Christian. With his comrade-in-arms, Friedrich Engels (another alienated Jew), he proclaimed that religion was 'the opiate of the people'. Just as the apostle Paul had argued that, within the church, there was neither Jew nor Greek, so Marx sought to abolish all religious distinctions in his new philosophy. Whereas Judaism urges the faithful to love work, Marx viewed work as alienating. No doubt it was, for the many industrial workers who had to perform the same repetitive task several hundred times a day. But Marxism found only a minority following among Western proletarians, most of whom preferred immediate improvements in their standard of living to dreams of a world revolution. The most enthusiastic Marxists were the rootless intellectuals, university graduates who could not find work commensurate with their education, and in particular many bright young natives of countries in Africa and Asia that were colonized by Europe. The alienated of the world could now unite under Marxism. Marx was similar to Paul in his veneration of power; only by seizing power, he wrote, could the proletariat ever be free. He was the apostle Paul of the industrial age, a living example of what can go wrong when Jews are made to feel ashamed of their ancestry and religious heritage.

For European Jews in general, the situation was far less dramatic. By 1871, legal emancipation was an established fact throughout the continent, with only a few holdouts, such as Spain and Russia. British Jews acquired legal equality gradually, just as the suffrage in Britain was extended bit by bit over the years. That was the pragmatic British way. The new German Reich and the reformed Habsburg monarchy of Austria-Hungary gave the Jews within their borders equal rights—not out of any sincere concern for their welfare, but because it was the simplest thing to do. Having defeated the liberal insurgents in 1849, the ruling classes of Central Europe belatedly recognized that constitutionalism was in their own interest. A written constitution allowed for centralization, thus reinforcing the authority of the crown. Laws had to be uniform throughout the realm in order to facilitate internal trade and commerce, which were now expanding rapidly thanks to the railways. Under these conditions, there was nothing to do but put the Jews under the same laws as everyone else.

Emancipation did not lead directly to the total assimilation of the Jews, to their disappearance as a distinct group. For one thing, they did not branch out into all the different trades and professions that were now open to them. Very few chose agriculture, as Abbé Grégoire had so ardently wished. Even during the French Revolution, when the sale of so-called 'National Property' (the vast landed estates taken from the church to pay off the national debt) allowed them to buy land, hardly any showed the slightest interest in becoming farmers. That would have entailed moving into a village where everyone else was a Christian and where practically all social life revolved around the local church. Nor did Jews rush to join the army. Some French Jews chose a military career, but nearly all of them became artillery officers, for whom mathematical skills were essential. The infantry attracted only a handful of Jews, the cavalry even fewer. In Germany, the officer corps was virtually closed to Jews, since no one who was not a noble could rise above the rank of lieutenant.

Having rejected careers in agriculture and the army, Jews continued to live in urban areas, thus facilitating social contacts with their own coreligionists. As synagogue attendance declined, newly-built Jewish community centres attracted the non-observant, in particular young people, eager to make friends, and the very old, who sought an escape from boredom. By the late nineteenth century, Jewish conversions to Christianity diminished considerably, especially in Germany. There, the Jews had created a respectable, middle-class society of their own and were *salonfähig* enough to suit themselves. They felt no urgent need to be accepted by the Gentile elite. The history of German Jews during this period is one of unparalleled success. Not only did they excel in the law, medicine and retailing, but they soon availed themselves of their newly acquired rights to develop careers in science, journalism, the arts, and education. Although their scholarship was almost exclusively secular, it did encourage the more pious members of Germany Jewry to apply scientific investigation to religious questions. The resulting *Wissenschaft des Judentums,* or science of Judaism, showed that an ancient faith could flourish in a spirit of free inquiry.

The growth of a Jewish intelligentsia did not please everyone. Jewish scholars and artists rarely referred to Christianity in their works. They were not afraid to break new ground and were less constrained than their Christian counterparts by the weight of tradition. Critics accused them of trying to secularize, or even de-Christianize, art and literature. Actually, the Jews were trying to create a culture that they could feel comfortable with. Similarly, in politics, they rarely favoured right-wing candidates, who nostalgically recalled the good old days when everyone knew his place. For the emancipated Jew, the old days were not good at all; he was compelled by past oppression to look forward to a brighter future.

More generally, the problem was that while Jews had been emancipated, Christians had not. The latter were not freed of their anti-Jewish prejudices. This is where the French Revolution had erred in its treatment of the Jewish question. The assumption that the situation of the Jews could be normalized simply by granting them equal rights was only partly correct. The rest of society had to be educated in understanding the Jews and Judaism. No attempt was made, either in public education or in the press, to do so. So the old animosities remained, partially obscured by a wave of material progress that, by 1900, seemed endless.

Backlash

In the early 1880's, a new word entered the general vocabulary: anti-Semitism. It had been coined in 1864 by a German polemicist,

Wilhelm Marr, to foster hatred of the Jews on racial grounds. The fact that many Jews are not Semites and that most Semites are not Jews did not deter Marr or his followers. They succeeded in convincing many people that the Jews possessed certain, specifically Semitic, racial characteristics, which made them enemies of Western civilization. Judaeophobia was nothing new in the West, but just why anti-Semitism—both the word and the deed—became popular virtually overnight, has never been satisfactorily explained. The usual argument is that, as European society became more secular, hatred of the Jews changed from religious to racial.

In reality, however, the perceived secularism of the late nineteenth century was limited to the political and juridical spheres. There is little evidence that ordinary people suddenly gave up being Christians. On the contrary, the 1880's were a period of intense religious revival. A prime factor in making Christians more conscious of their religious heritage was the rise in literacy. The public elementary school was the child of the industrial revolution. Workers had to know how to read in order to operate their machines properly. But public education was not always secular. In many countries it was entrusted to religious orders, often because the state lacked sufficient funds to train and pay lay teachers. Even in those jurisdictions where the state alone ran the public school system, the local priest or pastor was usually allowed to dispense religious instruction at set times during the week. The education boom in the nineteenth century had much the same effect on the evolution of Christianity as the introduction of the parish system in the eleventh: in both cases, religious belief was more widely spread among the masses. Just as the study of history in the public schools fostered national consciousness among people whose horizons had previously been limited to their native town or village, so did religious instruction contribute to the propagation of Christian doctrine.

This doctrine was, in the late nineteenth century, as anti-Jewish as ever—perhaps even more so. Animosity toward the Jews and Judaism increased as they were perceived to have benefited from the political and social changes set in motion by the

French Revolution. The reforms of 1789 had deprived the Catholic clergy of its status as the first estate, or order, of the realm. Christianity itself was not directly affected; but the church had clearly lost influence, in both political and economic terms. The confiscation of the landed estates belonging to the church, although it did not directly benefit the Jews, was coincidental to their accession to civil society. For superficial minds, it seemed that the Jews had won benefits at the expense of both the church and that other privileged order of the Old Regime, the nobility.

In France, neither the clergy nor the nobles were terribly concerned about their loss of official privilege because they were able to recover most of their real power after the defeat of Napoleon in 1815. Their confidence eroded, however, in 1880, when the republicans took control of the Third Republic. After France's defeat at the hands of Germany in 1871, the French electorate had given royalists a majority in the National Assembly because they were the only candidates willing to accept the conqueror's terms. Once the peace treaty was signed and ratified, there was no further need to keep the royalists in power. A republican majority was elected to the lower house, or Chamber of Deputies, in 1876 and to the Senate in 1879. Shortly thereafter, a republican became President of the Republic. With the levers of political power firmly in their grasp, the victors lost no time in appointing their sympathizers to public office. Royalists were dismissed from the police, the judiciary and the civil service, and replaced by loyal republicans. Only the French army and navy escaped this wholesale purge. Public education was made secular and obligatory for all. No immediate advantage accrued to the Jews, but the country's traditional ruling classes clearly lost ground. In towns and villages throughout France, political battles raged between the local noble, whose chief ally was the parish priest, and the republican challenger, aided by the public schoolteacher.

For the church, the loss of power was especially galling, and it fought back through a vigorous campaign of evangelization. Here, new technology was a big help. The ancient Christian custom of pilgrimages to holy places, which had fallen into disuse in the late

Middle Ages, was revived with the growth of rail passenger service. Railway companies would often offer the local priest free passage for leading his parishioners on a pilgrimage by train. It may be just coincidence—or perhaps providential—that the young Bernadette Soubirous had her famous vision of the Virgin Mary just as a railway line was being built through her native Lourdes. Pilgrimages were not, in and of themselves, anti-Jewish; they served primarily to reinforce the faith of simple folk in miracles. More ominous was the opening of amateur passion plays, such as the one performed every decade since 1634 in the Bavarian village of Oberammergau, to rail tourism. This nasty remnant of Christian folklore, drawn broadly on the Gospels, had always contained many anti-Jewish references. The traditional version nonetheless held the devil primarily responsible for Jesus's death. In 1860, a new text was adopted. It had been written by a local priest and assigned all guilt to the Jews, who were portrayed throughout as the Nazarene's sworn enemies. Confined to the local population, such sorry spectacles were bad enough; shown to visitors from afar, they openly challenged the supposedly liberal values of modern society.

Still more effective in promoting both religious belief and anti-Jewish feeling was the Christian press. Just as religious education in elementary schools instilled Christian beliefs in young children, so did newspapers serve to propagate the faith among adults. Not only did a large readership exist by 1880, but the invention of the rotary press at that time made the mass-circulation daily possible. In France, the leading Catholic newspaper was *La Croix*, which was founded by the Assumptionist order in 1882. It regularly accused the Jews of France of being in the pay of Germany (French Protestants were said to be agents of Great Britain) and assumed that the Rothschilds bought and sold republican politicians at will. At bottom, however, the journal's anti-Jewish polemic was religious. French historian Pierre Sorlin has explained in his doctoral thesis, *La Croix et les Juifs*,[2] that the main accusation against the Jews was that of deicide. As the

---

[2] Paris: Grasset, 1967.

eternal enemies of God (*sic*), they were presumed to be innately evil. This would explain their desire to subvert Catholic France. Deicide was the common thread which held the paper's anti-Jewish diatribes together. *La Croix* is still France's leading Catholic newspaper. Since 1945, it has abandoned the theme of deicide and rarely attacks Jews as such. In the late nineteenth century, however, it regularly spewed anti-Jewish propaganda which was firmly rooted in Christian tradition. Neither the French church nor Pope Leo XIII disavowed this policy.

An intense religious revival, occurring just as the church lost a large measure of political power, helps explain the sudden growth of anti-Semitism in the early 1880's, especially in France. Only about eighty thousand Jews lived in France at the time, as compared to half a million in Germany. Yet it was in France that anti-Semitism first became a popular movement—not because society had suddenly turned secular, but because the state had. The political triumph of the republicans in 1880 convinced many French Catholics that the state was no longer their ally. It was henceforth officially neutral, and not biased toward the church. Any state with a pro-Christian tilt would see to it that the Jews be kept in their proper place. In a neutral jurisdiction, they could rise to wherever their ambitions and talents might take them. Anti-Semitism was rooted in fear, not of the influence that Jews actually had, but of what they might gain in the future.

The racial component of the new Judaeophobia came not from the secularization of Christians, but from that of Jews. The latter were no longer a visible minority. Nearly all had shaved their beards and dressed like everyone else. There was still a tendency for some Jews to gesticulate while talking; but by 1880, their discourse no longer set them apart from the majority. The Jews of Western Europe, and those of France in particular, were now so culturally integrated that they spoke the national language without accent or inflection. This is why the racial definition of the Jew caught on so quickly. The ideal of the emancipation movement—being Jewish at home and French (or German or whatever) outside—had been realized only too well. Identifying the Jew as a member of an alien race would presumably allow his enemies to recognize him.

The anti-Jewish racialism of the late nineteenth century was entirely consistent with a particular strand of Christian history. Even before the 'purity of blood' laws directed at Marranos and Moriscos in Spain, Thomas Aquinas referred to the Jews as a race in his advice to the crusader king of Cyprus. They should be kept far from positions of influence, he warned. Once the Jews were ghettoized and forced to give up missionary activity, they became little more than an ethnic minority. Many of the so-called 'racial' characteristics attributed to the Jews were the result of being cut off from the rest of society. The fact that they did not assimilate completely even after legal emancipation gave further credence to the racial definition now being imposed on them. More fundamentally, their stubbornness in refusing to recognize Jesus as their saviour was considered by many Christians to be a hereditary trait. Such seemingly innate perversity could be attributed to racial characteristics. And even though official church doctrine continued to recognize the Jewish origins of the twelve apostles, most people usually identified only one as a Jew: the 'traitor' Judas.

Chapter VI

JEWS ON TRIAL

IN FRANCE, WHERE ANTI-SEMITISM erupted with such *éclat*, its chief polemicist was a free-lance journalist named Edouard Drumont, who had been an atheist throughout most of his life. One day in 1882, Drumont got religion—or so he claimed—and began to attend Mass regularly. Shortly thereafter, he founded an anti-Semitic weekly called *La Libre Parole* ('free speech'). The start-up funds for this publication appear to have been contributed by royalists, who hoped that popular Judaeophobia would work to discredit the Republic. This was a radical departure from established tradition. During the Middle Ages, the ruling classes were supposed to protect their Jews from popular violence. Since the French Revolution, however, and more obviously since 1880, the Jews were no longer anyone's to protect. They were, in theory at least, citizens, with the same rights as their Gentile compatriots. Certainly they no longer paid special taxes for protection. Popular hatred of the Jews had not abated, however, and some royalists sought to make political capital from it.

As a political issue, anti-Semitism made little headway in the nineteenth century. Its first real test came in the 1886 elections to the Paris city council. Paris, the seedbed of revolution for nearly a century, would never have elected royalists to its municipal government. So a slate of anti-Semitic candidates was presented instead. They all lost, despite a vigorous campaign waged by *La Libre Parole*. As the Nazis were to learn several decades later, elections could not be won on Jew-baiting alone.

The Jewish question has always been more moral than political. As such, it has little to do with the Jews themselves, whatever their faults may be. Rather, it reflects popular apprehensions about the basic values of society and the direction it seems to be taking. Among the social innovations that worried people in the 1880's were urbanization and the gradual blurring of class distinctions. Since the Jews favoured an urban, relatively egalitarian society, they were often held responsible for these changes. *La Libre Parole* had many subscribers in Brittany, where there were hardly any Jews, but which suffered from chronic unemployment and a continuous flight of young people to the larger cities. Anti-Semitism has always thrived in areas whose inhabitants fear a threat to their traditional way of life.

Western France was also a prime market for Drumont's two-volume diatribe against the Jews, entitled *La France juive* ('Jewish France'), which was published in 1886 and went through several editions. His thesis, if such it can be called, was that France was being taken over by the Jews. But he furnished little evidence in its support. Most of his rambling book is a hotch-potch of anti-Jewish legends handed down from the Middle Ages. The old myth about the ritual murder of Christian children to make unleavened bread for Passover is there, along with well-poisonings and other sordid bits of Christian folk-culture. But hateful though it is, Drumont's book can hardly be called racist. It contains none of the pseudo-scientific arguments later used by the Nazis against the Jews. Rather, his entire anti-Jewish polemic is firmly rooted in Christianity—beginning, naturally, with the Jews' presumed responsibility for the death of Jesus.

Drumont was well connected with some high-ranking officers in the French army. It was from this source that he learned in 1894 that a Jewish officer in the general staff was suspected of selling military secrets to Germany. That a Jew could rise to a position in the general staff of a major military power was remarkable in itself; only France then possessed such a distinction. The officer in question, an artillery captain named Alfred Dreyfus, was patriotic to a fault. His parents had left their native Alsace in 1871, in order to remain French. He had no debts, was not given to drinking, gambling or womanizing, and enjoyed a life of tranquil domesticity with his wife, the daughter of a wealthy diamond merchant. Drumont published a report in *La Libre Parole* about the suspected Jewish traitor without investigating its veracity. His articles prompted the army high command to act quickly, lest it be accused of laxity by other anti-Semitic periodicals. On the most fragile of circumstantial evidence (a vague resemblance between the handwriting of Dreyfus and that on an incriminating document), the Jewish captain was accused of high treason. He was found guilty by a court-martial, stripped of his rank and condemned to spend the rest of his days in the French penal colony on Devil's Island.

This harsh sentence drew little criticism at the time. The vast majority of French Jews preferred to keep quiet, for fear that their own patriotism might be called into question. It would have been most improper for them, without producing any new evidence on this matter, to cast doubt upon the decision of a military tribunal. The one leading political figure who did so was the Socialist leader, Jean Jaurès, who publicly expressed regret that Dreyfus had not been shot! Only the accused's brother, Matthieu, and a Jewish journalist from the south of France, Bernard Lazare, tried to re-open the case, at first without success.

But the leakage of military secrets to Germany continued. This prompted another high officer, Colonel Picquart, to do some investigating on his own. He came to the conclusion that Dreyfus was not the culprit and submitted his findings to the general staff. Picquart was posted to Tunisia for his pains. Before leaving, however, he sent a copy of his report to the speaker of the French Senate. Thrust into the rough-and-tumble world of politics, the Dreyfus case now became the Dreyfus Affair. The government still refused to admit that a judicial error had been committed. 'There is no Dreyfus Affair!' exclaimed the harassed premier, Jules Méline, in answer to a question from the opposition in parliament on 4 November 1897. Méline knew that re-opening the case could destroy his fragile governing coalition, which was based on an alliance between conservative republicans and former royalists who had come to accept the new regime. The opposition Radicals, the party of small business and agriculture, knew this too. They intended to use the Dreyfus Affair to bring down the government and assume power themselves.

The army high command played into the Radicals' hands. In an attempt to cover up its initial blunder, it forged new 'evidence' against Dreyfus. The forgery was soon discovered, however; and its author, a certain Colonel Henry, committed suicide in prison. Right-wing groups in Paris reacted to this embarrassment by staging violent demonstrations, often breaking into Jewish shops and assaulting their owners. When one agitator actually struck the President of the Republic at a public function in 1899, some of the moderate republicans in Méline's cabinet resigned, depriving him of a parliamentary majority. They then allied themselves with the Radicals to form a new government. The Radicals soon appropriated for themselves the spoils of victory, filling posts in the civil service with party stalwarts. This was the famous *révolution dreyfusienne,* by which the lower-middle classes in France gained political influence on a national scale.

Smarting at their defeat, the former royalists who had supported Méline blamed a 'Jewish syndicate' for having put the army in such a bad light in order to rehabilitate Dreyfus. There was no Jewish syndicate. Even after the affair became political, most French Jews preferred to keep a low profile and refused to take sides publicly. Dreyfus himself gained little from the Radicals' political triumph. He was re-tried by the War Council, the highest judicial instance in the French army, and sent back to Devil's Island. In 1906, long after the public clamour had subsided, he was pardoned by the President of the Republic and promoted to the rank of colonel. By then, he was a very sick man. The real traitor was never brought to justice.

Whatever its outcome, the Dreyfus Affair—the great national debate which tore families apart for more than a generation—was not about Dreyfus, but about France. The entire country was, at one point, about evenly divided between *dreyfusards* and *anti-dreyfusards.* The former were not, save for a very small minority, friends of the accused, still less of the Jews. They called for a re-trial simply because a breach of justice had been committed. All French citizens, they argued, had equal rights under the law. If the rights of any citizen are violated, then the social contract is broken, and the nation as a whole is weakened. Their definition of nationality was contractual, not historical or cultural. French citizens, in their view, included anyone who was a party to the social contract. The *dreyfusards* did not fight anti-Semitism directly; they were not even concerned with the fact that Dreyfus was a Jew. Instead, they insisted that he was a Frenchman, and therefore entitled to the same consideration as any other.

But was Dreyfus really French? To ask this question is not to impugn his patriotism, which was unshakable, but to attempt to define the historical character of France and, by extension, that of the West in general. For the *anti-dreyfusards*, France was more than a mere community of people bound together by a social contract. It was, and had to remain, a nation with deep roots in the past, a nation in which nearly 98 percent of the population was baptized, a nation of villages and small towns, where the local church was the focal point of society. If the French nation is a living organism nurtured in a common spiritual tradition, a Jew cannot become a true Frenchman because he has not shared in that tradition. Therefore, so ran this argument, it would be folly to weaken the nation by holding one of its most revered institutions, the army, up to ridicule. There is a saying in French: *Toute vérité n'est pas bonne à dire* ('Some truths are best left unsaid'). Not all opponents of a re-trial were professed anti-Semites. Many believed simply that even if Dreyfus was innocent, it was better for the nation as a whole that he continue to rot on Devil's Island. France, in their view, was a Catholic country. To tear it asunder over a Jew would be degrading.

The issue raised by the Dreyfus Affair has never been resolved, either in France or elsewhere. Yet if it may be examined dispassionately, the *anti-dreyfusards* would seem to be closer to the truth. Jews are French citizens in the legal and political sense, but they are not fully part of the French historical community. Their history, through no fault of their own, is indeed different from that of other Frenchmen. No matter how long certain Jewish families have lived in France, they lie outside the mainstream of French religious tradition, which is Catholic. Even French Protestants, who account for little more than two percent of the population, are all of Catholic ancestry. Jews are not. Only by denying the historical importance of Christian tradition can Jews in France and other Western democracies feel totally at home. But they are only deluding themselves if they try.

Self-defence

Confronted with organized slander and violence, the Jews of France did little to defend themselves. Not only were they numerically weak, but the institutional mold into which they had been cast by Napoleon left them without the means to take independent political action. Their most important initiative in Jewish affairs was the founding of the *Alliance Israélite Universelle* in 1860. The *Alliance* helped raise the educational and living standards of poor Sephardic Jews outside France by creating schools not only in French North Africa, but throughout the Muslim world, as far east as Baghdad. Aside from religious instruction and a school cafeteria which served kosher food, there was little to distinguish these Jewish schools from those of France: the curriculum and language of instruction were the same. By gaining access to French and to the vocational training offered at the secondary level, Jewish youth of North Africa and the Middle East attained a certain level of wealth and Western culture—often exciting the envy of their Muslim neighbours. At the same time, the *Alliance* served the interests of France by helping to extend French influence throughout the region. It was not active within France, however, nor did it take a stand on behalf of French Jews during the Dreyfus Affair.

The Jews of Germany, on the other hand, began to organize an effective defence against anti-Semitism shortly after the new Reich came into existence in 1871. In this, they had two advantages over their French coreligionists: far greater numbers, and more freedom of action due to the relatively decentralized political authority in Germany. Those who think of the German-Jewish experience solely in terms of Karl Marx and Adolf Hitler will no doubt be surprised to learn that most Jews in pre-1914 Germany were neither ashamed of their identity nor the willing victims of persecution. Such is the inescapable conclusion of two well-documented monographs published in the 1970's: *Jewish Reactions to German Anti-Semitism, 1870-1914*, by Ismar Schorch,[1] and

---

[1] New York: Columbia University Press, 1972.

Jewish Activism in Imperial Germany, by Marjorie Lamberti.[2] These complementary studies show that the Jews of Germany took three avenues of approach in dealing with their enemies. The first was judicial: individual Jews and sometimes the entire community were encouraged to bring suit under the criminal code against their slanderers. The Jews also took political action, supporting parties that were most likely to defeat anti-Semitic candidates. Finally, there was a concerted effort to enlighten the public about Judaism, as rabbis and other Jewish scholars wrote in defence of the ancient faith against charges by Christian theologians. In all three areas, the Jewish defenders not only scored victories against their detractors; they also reinforced the community's will to live as Jews.

Taking anti-Semites to court was a slow and often frustrating process. It was not always easy to persuade individual Jewish victims of defamation to file a complaint. In early cases, the defendants were usually acquitted or given a suspended sentence. Fines, when levied at all, were light. The founding in 1893 of the *Centralverein deutscher Staatsbürger jüdischen Glaubens* ('Central Association of German Citizens of the Jewish Faith') opened the way to more effective action. Its legal department, which by 1902 was handling more than a hundred cases annually, built up a massive jurisprudence on the question. As the courts imposed heavier fines, and even imprisonment in some cases, the incidence of anti-Jewish libel began to decrease.

Political action was likewise not immediately productive. It was directed against those conservative politicians who expressed fear that the entry of Jews into civil society would undermine its Christian foundations. Their immediate aim was to bar Jews from any form of state employment, especially teaching and the magistrature. Some hoped eventually to rescind Jewish emancipation altogether. Jews could help defeat anti-Semitic candidates only in those urban districts where they were sufficiently numerous to hold the balance of power. The party receiving their vote—usually the Progressives—tended to take Jewish support for granted. Once

---

[2]New Haven: Yale University Press, 1978.

elected, it was slow to propose legislation protecting the rights of Jews. In time, however, Jewish activism did bear fruit. The number of avowed anti-Semites in the Reichstag dwindled over the years until, by 1907, there were none left. Animosity toward the Jews did not cease altogether; many professional and fraternal associations still excluded them. But the Jewish question was no longer a political issue in Germany. It re-surfaced only after the First World War and the advent of Bolshevism gave rise to new fears that traditional social values were being threatened.

Jewish self-defence in politics and before the courts was relatively straight-forward. In the religious sphere, it required immense tact and discretion. To defend Judaism without directly attacking Christianity was fraught with difficulties. Yet the Jews of Germany had to confront this issue because emancipation, in the sense of complete equality, had not been accepted by the Christian majority. Even culturally assimilated Jews eventually understood that attacks on Judaism tended to undermine their status as German citizens. As early as 1871, the Jews of Berlin found themselves involved in a religious dispute. It originated in the conversion of seven Christians to Judaism that year—an unusual occurrence, but one that was perfectly feasible within the new framework of religious freedom. The Supreme Council of the Prussian Evangelical Church not only denounced the conversions; it also ordered that, in future cases, the apostate's name be read from the pulpit and that the congregation be warned against joining a religious community that rejected the son of God and hates him to this very day (*sic*). A protest from the governing board of the Berlin Jewish community forced the Protestant body to recant, at least partially. It had not meant to condemn Judaism, but merely conversions to Judaism.

The Jews had similar preoccupations, though they would never think of expressing them by deprecating the dominant religion. A few years after its creation, the *Centralverein* issued a blistering polemic against conversions to Christianity. Such apostasy destroys Jewish families and robs Jews of their self-respect, it read. As long as some Jews were willing to convert in order to enter the civil service or other positions that would otherwise be barred to them, discrimination would continue. This line of reasoning appealed to the Jews' civic pride, rather than to any spiritual considerations. By 1913, however, the leaders of the *Centralverein* had come to realize that the essential issue was not merely civic equality, but Judaism itself. The Jews would never truly enjoy their legal rights until the spiritual right to be Jewish was fully recognized.

The defence of Judaism in pre-1914 Germany fell to a small group of scholars, nearly all of them Reform rabbis. They were reacting at first to a particular form of religious defamation developed by some German Protestant theologians, which was generally known as the Higher Criticism of the Bible and referred to in Jewish circles as 'the higher anti-Semitism.' With painstakingly structured arguments, the Jewish apologists refuted the most egregious canards, such as the claim that the commandment to love one's neighbour applied only to Jews, and that the Torah was similar in all essential respects to other Semitic codes of the pre-Christian era. More generally, they challenged the notion that Judaism was a mere prelude to Christianity and cast doubt on the Protestants' ability to study Jewish doctrine without any knowledge of Hebrew.

In 1900, the respected Protestant theologian Adolf Harnack gave a series of university lectures, which were published soon thereafter as a book entitled, *Das Wesen des Christentums* ('The Essence of Christianity'). To prove the superiority of the daughter religion, Harnack characterized the Judaism of Jesus's time as rigidly legalistic and lacking in magnanimity. Such calumnies, though hardly new, aroused much resentment in a Jewish community whose educational level was, by the turn of the century, far higher than that of the Christian majority as a whole. A young Reform rabbi, Leo Baeck, answered Harnack with a book entitled *Das Wesen des Judentums* ('The Essence of Judaism'), which was published in 1905. Baeck argued that, far from condemning the Jews to dry legalism, divine commandment is the most effective, if not the only, way to improve the human condition. His book was a milestone in Jewish history. For the first time, a general justification of Judaism was available to the reading public in the vernacular. It was addressed primarily to Jews, culturally integrated Jews who knew little or no Hebrew, and did much to restore their self-respect. Being written in German, it was also available to any German-speaking Christian who wished to learn about Judaism. Few were in fact interested; but the opportunity was there, waiting on library shelves to be seized upon. 'Judaism lies open for all to see,' wrote Baeck in his concluding paragraph.

Gaining recognition for Judaism on its own merits was the theme of Hermann Cohen, professor of philosophy at the University of Marburg, himself a formerly assimilated Jew who had rediscovered the religion of his forebears. In 1907 he took up an idea proposed half a century earlier by the founder of the *Wissenschaft des Judentums*, Leopold Zunz. It was to have the Jewish fraternal organization B'nai B'rith pay the salaries of instructors appointed to teach Judaica in the leading German universities. Cohen argued that, for Judaism to be taken seriously, Jewish studies must achieve equality in scholarship. Toleration does not imply equality, he reasoned; it must eventually be replaced with 'justice and truth.' This meant that not only Jews, but Christians as well would have to learn the truth about Judaism.

Even the most ardent defenders of Judaism in Germany stopped short of recommending active proselytism. The risk of a wholesale religious polemic, with the Jewish camp at a severe numerical disadvantage, was far too great for a missionary campaign to be attempted at the turn of the century. With the Second Reich at the peak of its power and prestige, the self-confidence of ordinary Germans would not have tolerated any calling into question of the dominant religion. German Jews too had grown in self-confidence, as a direct result of being integrated into Gentile society. Their mastery of the German language, their increased social and cultural awareness became powerful tools in the reasoned defence of Judaism. Such reasoned debate was possible, however, only in a civilized society placed under the rule of law. Germany was not forever to remain so.

Return To Zion

The emancipation of the Jews was largely a Jewish undertaking. The French Jews who petitioned the Constituent Assembly greatly facilitated their own accession to citizenship. Those who founded the *Alliance Israélite Universelle* helped raise the living standards of their coreligionists in Muslim countries. The German Jews' largely successful struggle against discrimination in the Second Reich allowed them to make fuller use of their legal rights. But there were some countries where legal rights—either for Jews or for Gentiles—barely existed. The most important of these, in terms of its Jewish population, was Tsarist Russia. For the Jews of Russia, the only certain way to gain protection of the law was to seek it somewhere else—in other words, to emigrate. The steam engine made this possible. By 1880, most areas of Russia were linked by rail to the Baltic, the Black Sea ports, and Western Europe. A few thousand Jewish emigrants left Russia that year; most went to the United States, with others choosing Argentina, Canada, France, Britain and Germany. The tide of Russian Jews fleeing Tsarist tyranny rose from year to year, until by 1914, over two million had left the Russian empire. By emigrating to relative freedom, the Russian Jews were, in effect, emancipating themselves.

To flee oppression by settling in another country under a more tolerant ruler was the traditional solution for the harassed Jews of Europe. But as the Polish experience had already shown, the safe haven could in time become precarious. To put an end to this constant wandering, a few visionaries suggested that the Jews found a state where they could live in freedom under their own laws. Among the earliest was a physician from Odessa, who had previously favoured assimilation as a solution to the Jewish problem. His name was Leon Pinsker; and his pamphlet, provocatively entitled *Auto-Emancipation*, was published (in German, the language of science) in 1882. With the dispassionate calm of a doctor examining his patient, Pinsker diagnosed the Jews as being sick, incapacitated by centuries of oppression and alienated by virtue of their minority status everywhere. Let them regain their faculties by becoming politically sovereign, he reasoned, and they will rejoin healthy, upright humanity.

Pinsker's appeal did not fall on deaf ears. The movement to create a Jewish nation-state was already under way. In 1881, a small band of young Jewish men and women from Russia established an agricultural colony in Palestine, just north of the old port city of Jaffa. They called it *Richon Le-Zion*, or first in Zion. For centuries, pious old Jews had left for Palestine in order to be closer to God when they died. The latest arrivals were not pious; they went to Palestine not to die, but to live. Early life on the colony was harsh; the *halutzim*, or pioneers, knew very little about farming and had to learn it, literally, from the ground up. They won the financial support of Baron Edmond de Rothschild, who even sent them plants from his own vineyards so that they could grow grapes in their new settlement.

The Jews of France and of other Western democracies saw the Zionist experiment as a possible solution for their oppressed brethren in Russia, but hardly expected to require a refuge themselves. Even the Dreyfus Affair did not shake their confidence. But it came as a body blow for Theodor Herzl, who was covering the trial of Dreyfus as a reporter for a Viennese newspaper. Herzl thought of himself as an emancipated Jew—so much so that he did not even bother to have his two sons circumcised. He knew little Hebrew and was thoroughly integrated into the cultural life of the Austrian capital, where he had dabbled in the theatre before becoming a journalist. Like most Jews of Central Europe, Herzl considered France to be the most enlightened country on the continent, the first to grant civil rights to its Jewish minority. His disillusionment was only the more crushing. When Dreyfus was publicly stripped of his rank, the French crowd did not shout, 'Death to the traitor!' as might be expected in such circumstances, but 'Death to the Jew!' So even in civilized France, Jews were not safe from popular hatred. Herzl resolved to put things right in a short book published in 1896. It was entitled *Der Judenstaat*, which does not mean 'The Jewish State', as the English translation reads, but 'The State of Jews'—the state founded by Jews, belonging to Jews. Herzl was not interested in religion; the state he proposed was not to be Jewish in a religious sense. What mattered to him was that Jews be politically sovereign there.

Only by having a state of their own, argued Herzl, could the Jews effectively overcome anti-Semitism, which, he claimed, 'increases day by day and hour by hour among the nations'. What is more, it is bound to increase, because the more the Jews are hated, the more subversive, the more revolutionary they become. Here, Herzl had the Russian Jews in mind; those of Western and Central Europe were fiercely loyal to the countries of which they were citizens. In one of those flashes of genius that come occasionally to visionaries, he noted in passing that the root cause of anti-Semitism was 'our loss of the power of assimilation during the Middle Ages'. But he did not propose trying to recover the power to Judaize. Herzl was a man in a hurry. His book is not a learned treatise on Jewish history, but a political manifesto. He knew that he had to over-simplify in order to win general acceptance for his plan, which he summarized as follows: 'Let sovereignty be granted us over a portion of the globe large enough to satisfy the rightful requirements of a nation; the rest we shall manage for ourselves.' Ever the optimist, Herzl confidently predicted that 'the Jews, once settled in their own State, would probably have no more enemies.' Christian nations would be delighted to rid themselves of these recalcitrant elements, whose departure would leave jobs open for their Gentile rivals.

Once Herzl got around to organizing a Zionist movement, however, he encountered difficulties that he had not anticipated in his cheery prospectus. He had originally assumed that a state for Jews could be created wherever space was available; Argentina (where some Jewish farming settlements already existed) and Uganda were his first choices. But the Jewish masses of Eastern Europe were more attached to the Bible than he was. They would not have Zionism without Zion—that is, anywhere else but in the Biblical land of Israel. So Herzl bowed to their wishes and sought meetings with the Ottoman authorities, who had ruled Palestine for centuries. After long waits in stuffy anterooms, he found no sympathy for his plan, only a vague promise to tolerate the Jewish settlers as long as they did not make trouble. Pope Pius X was even less sympathetic. Since the Jews refused to recognize Jesus of Nazareth as their saviour, he reminded Herzl, the church was not about to recognize the Jews. In 1903, the Zionist leader visited Russia in the hope of getting the government to persuade the Ottoman Turks that a large area of Palestine should be set aside for Jewish colonization. Of the Russian leaders, only Count Serge Witte, the minister of finance, showed any interest in the proposal. Witte assured his visitor that he would do all he could to encourage the Jews to leave Russia—by giving them a kick in the pants! 'I am a friend of the Jews,' he added. 'In that case,' replied Herzl wearily, 'we hardly need enemies.'

When Herzl died in 1904, exhausted by constant rounds of speechmaking and appointments, Zionism had gained a small but growing following among the Jews of Russia. An American Zionist movement was also created; but its aims were largely philanthropic: to help poor Russian Jews get settled in Palestine. The Zionist organizations in Germany had a similar purpose, plus that of instilling pride in German Jews through athletic and cultural encounters. For most Jews, however, Zionism remained a marginal movement until the Second World War. Rabbis usually avoided it. The Orthodox condemned Zionism as heretical; the restoration of a Jewish commonwealth in Palestine, they said, would have to await the coming of the Messiah. Reform rabbis asserted that Jews were loyal citizens of the countries in which they lived and therefore had no need of a Jewish state.

In France and England, Zionism enjoyed little support among individual Jews and even less in political circles. The French government, although anti-clerical at home, pursued France's traditional policy of supporting Latin Christians in the Levant. It therefore took a dim view of Jewish settlement in Palestine. The British already had oil interests in the region and were involved in a joint venture with German firms to build the Baghdad railway. Zionism had no place in their Middle East policy.

British indifference changed to support as a direct result of the First World War, which pitted Britain against the Ottoman Turks for control of the Middle East. Legend has it that David Lloyd George, who became prime minister in 1916, was influenced by Chaim

Weizmann, the Russian-born chemist, whose work in Manchester was vital to British munitions development. While it is certainly true that Weizmann did bring Zionism to the attention of the British government, it is equally true that great powers do not base their policy on sentiment. Britain's eventual sponsorship of Zionism did not result from any sympathy for the Jews, but was a by-product of the complicated wartime relations with its ally, France.

Foreseeing the demise of the Ottoman empire, British and French diplomats met in 1916 to carve out respective spheres of influence in the Middle East for their two countries. A secret agreement gave Syria and Lebanon to France, while Iraq and the Arabian peninsula went to Britain. The fate of Palestine, an area essential to the British if Iraqi oil was to reach the Mediterranean without passing through French-held Lebanon, was left in abeyance. Britain assumed overall jurisdiction, but control of the Holy Places was deemed to be French. In the succeeding months, the French subtly made known to London just what their interpretation of the term 'Holy Places' was. The whole of Palestine was sacred; therefore France should assume control over all of it!

Britain countered by enlisting Zionism in support of its own Middle Eastern ambitions. It brought the Jews into Palestine ('up to a point', as some Foreign Office types would say) in order to keep the French out. On 2 November 1917, Foreign Secretary Balfour published a letter he had written to Lord Rothschild, head of the Board of Deputies of British Jews, stating that 'His Majesty's Government look with favour on the establishment of a Jewish national home in Palestine'. This is not what Weizmann and other Zionists had in mind—namely, the establishment of Palestine **as** the Jewish national home; but it was close enough. Even the proviso that British sponsorship should not be construed so as to diminish the rights of Palestine's non-Jewish population or those of Jews elsewhere did not dampen the Zionists' enthusiasm.

Anglo-Jewry viewed the Balfour Declaration with mixed feelings. Other than Lord Rothschild himself, who saw Palestine as an eventual haven for the persecuted Jews of Eastern Europe, its leaders were massively anti-Zionist. A resolution voted on 18 November by the Board of Deputies of British Jews thanked the government for their 'sympathetic interest in the Jews as manifested by' the Declaration, but stopped short of endorsing its contents. The Council of the Anglo-Jewish Association passed an identical motion a short time later, but its president, Claude Montefiore, voiced his 'grave and serious misgivings' about the new policy. Among English Jews, only the little people—mainly immigrants from Tsarist Russia—were at all Zionist, and they had neither power nor influence. Weizmann made no secret of his aversion to the Anglo-Jewish establishment. He preferred to deal directly with the Gentile political elite; and, for the moment at least, his tactic paid off.

The Balfour Declaration had no immediate effect on the outcome of the war. In particular, it did not rally to the Allied cause those Jews who did not already favour it. In the fall of 1917, there were over two million Jews in uniform. Apart from the Zionist volunteers from Eastern Europe who formed three Jewish brigades in the British army, none fought as Jews. The rest served under different flags and often shot at one another. The Jews of Britain, France, and the United States continued to support the Allied war effort; those of Germany and Austria-Hungary, that of the Central Powers. The masses of Russian Jews were caught up willy-nilly in the October revolution and the ensuing civil war. Only in Palestine itself did Britain's new policy produce any concrete results. The Turkish army, fearing the existence of a Zionist fifth column, swept through the Jewish areas of Jerusalem, killing most of their inhabitants and forcing the rest to flee.

Russian Encounter

At the turn of the twentieth century, it was not in Palestine, but in Russia that the Jews found themselves in the forefront of political and social change. In no other country were Christianity and imperialism so closely linked. The Russian monarchy had embarked on its expansionist course when Vladimir, the ruler of Kiev, embraced Christianity early in the eleventh century. He chose the Orthodox version, being closer to its Byzantine source than to Rome. This made him heir to the Caesaropapist tradition created by the first Christian emperor, Constantine. By choosing to be called Tsar, a title derived from the Latin Caesar, the Russian monarchs laid claim to imperial authority. Orthodoxy was intended to give this authority divine sanction, since the Tsar was also head of the Russian church. Catholic rulers had to yield to the Pope on religious matters. The English monarchy, once it became Protestant, had titular authority over the Anglican church; but its political power was circumscribed by an increasingly assertive Parliament. Not so the Tsar of Russia. He reigned supreme, unencumbered by ecclesiastical or legislative restraints. Being Orthodox, he naturally tended to view other Christians as heretics and had every reason to maintain the religious purity of his realm. His own political authority was at stake.

If other Christians appeared as heretics in the eyes of the Tsar and the Russian Orthodox church, the Jews were simply infidels. They had to be kept out of holy Russia at all costs. In 1550 the King of Poland asked Tsar Ivan IV (known familiarly as 'Ivan the Terrible') to allow Jewish merchants from his kingdom to do business in Russia, pursuant to a commercial treaty between the two countries. Ivan flatly rejected this request on the grounds that the Jews 'import poisonous herbs [medicines] into our realm and lead astray the Russians from Christianity.' As Russia began to absorb Polish territory in the seventeenth century, however, it found itself taking in large numbers of unwanted Jewish subjects. The Jews were perceived as a threat to both the religious homogeneity of Russia and to the power of the Tsar. How to deal with them became a permanent conundrum in Russian ruling circles. The first solution hit upon, and one which was attempted repeatedly for centuries, was forced baptism. It failed because only a small minority of Jews were willing to accept Christianity; and of those who did, many became indifferent (and not very loyal) Christians. Moreover, the number of Jews in Russia continued to grow not only through natural increase, but primarily as a direct result of that country's westward expansion. The more Polish territory the Tsar annexed, the more Jews he had to worry about.

The Jewish question in Russia became still more acute in 1815, when the Vienna settlement gave the Tsar most of the Polish territory that he had not already acquired through previous partitions. The Russian empire now had the largest Jewish population in the world—over two million souls. Unlike Western rulers, the Tsar was not their protector, but their persecutor. In 1827, Nicholas I decided to grind them down through long terms of service in the army. Here too, the contrast with the West could hardly be more striking. Since the French Revolution, military service was deemed to be a civic duty, incumbent on all healthy adult males. The Jews of France were proud to do the usual two- or three-year stint as a sign of their equality with other citizens. In Russia, however, military service was more like a prison sentence. Conscripts were chosen by lot for a period of service that usually lasted twenty-five years. For the Jews, conditions were even worse, since they could be drafted at the age of twelve for a six-year period of preparatory training in addition to their regular tour of duty. In a confidential memorandum, the Tsar wrote that conscripting Jews 'will move them most effectively to change their religion.' Service in the army was also used to eradicate the 'Judaizing heresy', which affected some Russian peasant communities in the early nineteenth century. Without actually converting to Judaism, several thousand simple folk adopted certain Jewish customs, such as resting on Saturday, practising circumcision, and refusing to eat pork. The army became their penitentiary.

Jewish conscripts in the Tsar's army were subject to constant harassment (latrine duty was a favourite) by their superiors until they accepted baptism—and often afterward. Several thousand young men were thus lost to Judaism by the mid-nineteenth century, but their numbers were more than offset by natural increase. Because of their eagerness to raise large families and their assiduous personal hygiene, Jews experienced the fastest population growth of any group in the Russian empire. Yet Nicholas I was so intent on having them baptized that he failed to make good economic use of them, as Western rulers had learned to do. Excluded by imperial decree from many spheres of the economy and the liberal professions, the Jews of Russia were mostly too poor to be productive.

The Crimean War of 1854-1856 drew attention to the more grievous shortcomings of Russian society. When it became known that Russian soldiers were dying in droves for lack of medical attention, Tsar Alexander II decided to have Jews admitted to medical school. An educational revolution followed. From 1.25 percent of Russia's secondary school population in 1853, Jewish males accounted for more than 13 percent of a larger enrollment twenty years later. Alexander II was the closest thing to a liberal that had ever ascended the throne of Russia. He hoped to turn all his subjects, including the Jews, into patriotic Russians. Educated Jews, who soon became fairly drunk with this heady whiff of liberalism, took to speaking Russian with one another. Some even published Russian-language periodicals in which they regularly proclaimed their undying love for the motherland.

This happy state of affairs came to an abrupt end when Alexander II, who had already begun to reverse his liberalizing policies, fell victim to a dynamite bomb on 1 March 1881. The new Tsar, Alexander III, was a religious zealot, who announced shortly after his coronation that the liberal experiments of his predecessor would be abandoned. Once the government-subsidized press published unconfirmed reports that Jews were involved in the assassination (in fact, only one of the conspirators was Jewish), it became clear that anti-Semitism was once again official policy. In mid-April, a series of anti-Jewish riots broke out in several cities of southern Russia. The pogroms, as they came to be known, began with attacks on Jewish shops and homes, but soon degenerated into wholesale lynchings. Although they appeared to be spontaneous, these crimes clearly had official support: the police did not intervene until the government in Saint Petersburg gave the word. In the face of energetic protests from Britain and the United States, it decided to call a temporary halt to the pogroms. Instead, the Jews of Russia were presented with a series of official disabilities. Their access to the liberal professions was severely restricted, as were the areas where they were allowed to reside. In 1891, Moscow was added to the list of Russian cities that were off limits to Jews.

A general pauperization of Russian Jews was the result. Only three percent possessed any investment capital. Many were

Luftmenschen, people who seemingly lived on air, with no visible means of support. Even the handicrafts (such as shoemaking, tailoring and carpentry), which had long sustained the Jewish masses, were made precarious by the advent of mechanized industry. More and more Jews had to seek low-paying factory jobs for want of anything better. Russia was not the only country with a Jewish proletariat. Large numbers of Russian-Jewish immigrants to Western countries had to work in sweatshops. But the immigrants were convinced that even if they could not rise above their station, their children would eventually prosper. No such hope existed for the Jewish factory workers of Russia. They viewed themselves—correctly—as a class condemned to permanent exploitation, excluded from Russian society not only because they were industrial wage-earners, but mainly because they were Jews. In 1897, an assembly of Jewish proletarians met in Vilna to found the Jewish workers' league, or *Bund*. Its socialist programme included a pledge to promote autonomy for each national group, including the Jews, within the Russian empire.

With the formation of the *Bund*, the Jewish masses now joined the disparate elements in Russia that sought a wholesale transformation of the repressive Tsarist regime. The government, which had traditionally considered the Jews subversive, now redoubled its campaign against them. But like almost everything else in the ramshackle Russian empire, anti-Semitism was often bungled. It left the government open to ridicule and further weakened the social fabric. Tsarist Russia displayed a contradictory and confused attitude toward foreigners. On the one hand, it actively sought their capital and their markets; on the other, it tried to protect itself from Western cultural and political influence. A similar ambivalence prevailed in its policy toward the Jews. Those who had money were allowed to stay; those who had not were hounded into exile. In the eyes of the state, all were suspect.

As the twentieth century opened, the Tsarist regime actively used anti-Semitism to deflect popular discontent from its own social tyranny. A monstrous pogrom in the Bessarabian city of Kishinev during Easter week of 1903 received government support. But the most glaring example of official Jew-baiting was the trial in Kiev in

October 1913 of Mendel Beilis, a Jewish factory worker accused of having ritually murdered a Christian boy two years earlier. To buttress its case, the prosecution introduced testimony from a priest, Father Justin Pranaitis, to the effect that the Jews regularly needed Christian blood for their religious practice. If this were so, then ritual murder trials should have been an everyday occurrence, involving thousands of Jews, and not merely the unfortunate Beilis. Yet despite the priest's 'expertise' and other equally damning testimony, a jury of semi-literate peasants and townspeople voted for acquittal on the grounds of insufficient evidence.

With the Beilis trial, the Tsarist system reached its moral nadir. No Russian Jew—indeed no civilized person anywhere—could consciously support it. The outbreak of the First World War in 1914 revealed the extent to which centuries of oppression had enfeebled Russian society, rendering it incapable of meeting the challenge of modern combat. In particular, the tradition of using the army as a correctional facility resulted in a severely demoralized fighting force. Russian soldiers were often sent into battle without boots or rifles. They were told to pick up the necessary equipment from their fallen comrades. For the Jews of Russia, the situation was even more painful. Many had fought bravely for the motherland in the war against Japan in 1904, and a new generation of Russian Jews stood ready to defend their native soil in 1914. Instead, they were constantly hounded by both civil and military authorities, accused of espionage, driven to desert or rebel. When the Tsarist regime was overthrown in March 1917, not a single Jew rose to defend it.

The downfall of Tsarist absolutism marked an end to a centuries-old institution in which the state was the official guardian of the Christian faith. Eastern Orthodoxy persisted in Russia even under the Communists, as it did in Greece and Serbia. But Greece and Serbia were not great powers and therefore could not successfully impose Orthodoxy on large areas of the world. Tsarist Russia continually nourished such ambitions. The narrowly religious nature of the old Russian regime was made plain in 1890, when Tsar Alexander III penned the following note in the margin of a plea from one of his advisors for a more tolerant policy toward the Jews: 'But we must not forget that it was the Jews who crucified our Lord and spilled his precious blood.' Throughout history, there had been Western rulers who, at one time or another, persecuted their Jewish subjects; but none was so blind as to base official policy on the myth of deicide. Even Queen Isabella did not refer to the crucifixion in announcing the expulsion of the Jews from Spain. Only the Tsar of Russia used it to justify his anti-Jewish measures.

Faced with such single-minded enmity, Russian Jews could not give the regime the same wholehearted loyalty as was common among their coreligionists in the West. They contributed to the Tsar's overthrow not only by joining, *en masse*, the various opposition groups that sprouted in Russia before 1914. Their very presence in a regime dedicated to the triumph of Orthodox Christianity was in itself a highly destabilizing influence. Thus they acted as a catalyst for historical change in helping to bring about the end of Caesaropapism. That odious tradition had originated with Constantine, but the Roman empire in decline lacked the power to pursue it fully. Taken to its logical conclusion by the Tsars, it was discredited in 1917. Even the Russian nationalists of today do not talk of reviving it. But, as is the case with all sweeping change, there was a price to pay. And the Jews would pay dearly.

Chapter VII

PRELUDE TO DISASTER

WHEN THE BRUTAL TSARIST regime was swept away in March 1917, the Jews of Russia rejoiced. The provisional government soon lifted the disabilities under which they had suffered so long by declaring them and other minorities to be equal citizens under the law. In return, the vast majority of Rusian Jews supported that government in its attempt to establish a liberal democracy. Even among the masses of Jewish factory workers who favoured socialism, most remained loyal to the *Bund* during the seven-month interval between the two Russian revolutions and were not initially attracted to Bolshevism. Yet when Lenin and his followers seized power in November 1917, Jews quickly rose to positions of authority in the Communist party leadership. Indeed, no other political movement in history, with the obvious exception of Zionism, has had such a high proportion of Jewish activists. The first president of the Central Committee of the Party was Jacob Sverdlov, a Lithuanian Jew. Four other Jews sat on the original Committee, out of a total membership of twenty-one. Grigorii Zinoviev (Apfelbaum) served for many years as president of the Third International. A. A. Yoffe led the Russian delegation to the peace talks at Brest-Litovsk and used his diplomatic immunity to spread Communist propaganda within Germany. A Galician Jew, Karl Radek (Sobelsohn), put the press under Communist control and helped create the Party's world-wide propaganda mill. Maxim Litvinov (Wallach) became foreign minister and enabled the Soviet Union to gain admittance to the League of Nations.

None of these figures was the least bit religious. They all approved the Party's efforts to stamp out Judaism by converting synagogues into workers' clubs and restricting the use of Hebrew. A Yiddish-language press was tolerated as long as it served to indoctrinate its readers in Communist ideology. The Jewish Party leaders were the first to applaud when, in 1919, the revolutionary government officially declared Zionism to be petty-bourgeois and reactionary. They rightly sensed that it was a serious rival to their own particular brand of secular Messianism.

For what was socialism, after all, if not a plan to establish the kingdom of heaven on earth without divine assistance? For centuries, the rabbis had counseled patience: the Messiah would come in his own good time. To many young Jews of Eastern Europe, however, such advice rang increasingly hollow in the nineteenth century. The traditional religion-oriented Jewish society was not even capable of protecting the Jews, they noted. How could it possibly redeem all of humanity? The industrial revolution not only highlighted the inequalities of bourgeois society; it also provided the means of eliminating them by distributing the newly-created wealth among all classes of the population. From their parents and teachers, these impatient young Jews inherited a sense of social justice that is fundamental to Judaism. The Torah, for example, commands employers to pay their workers, whether native-born or foreign, each day before sundown (Deut. 24.14-15). But since religion had obviously not helped the older generation escape misery, political—and, if necessary, revolutionary—action seemed imperative. In an age when Jewish population growth was especially strong, these educated but underemployed young radicals were too numerous to be restrained by their elders.

Of all Jewish radicals in the early twentieth century the most illustrious—and to his enemies the most fearsome—was Trotsky. Born Lev Davidovich Bronstein to a wealthy farmer in the Ukraine, he constantly downplayed his Jewish background. He seems to have received little religious education from his parents. His father was illiterate—a rarity among Jews—and his mother observed only a minimum of Jewish practice. At the age of seven, Trotsky was sent to a Jewish elementary school, which he hated. Learning was by rote: the pupils had to recite each verse of the Pentateuch, first in Hebrew, then in the teacher's Yiddish translation, until they knew it by heart. Trotsky would never admit to knowing Yiddish; his parents spoke a mixture of Russian and Ukrainian at home. Yet he must have picked up more than a smattering of the Jewish vernacular at school. His insistence that he was not a Jew either by religion or by nationality is understandable in view of the role he eventually played as second in command of a movement, which, in its early stages at least, was dedicated to world revolution. While proclaiming himself an internationalist, however, Trotsky was not indifferent to the sufferings of other Jews. From Vienna, to which he had been exiled as a revolutionary, he wrote scathing attacks on the prosecution in the Beilis trial. The pogromist policies of the Tsarist regime, he argued, had condemned it beyond reprieve.

January 1917 found Trotsky in New York, where he was welcomed as a contributor to the *Jewish Daily Forward*. With a circulation of over 200,000, that Yiddish newspaper was the largest socialist organ in the United States. The Jewish masses of New York were, at the time, overwhelmingly pro-German and anti-Russian. To them, Germany appeared as a harbinger of progress, since it had the largest socialist party in the world in 1914. Trotsky's articles condemning the Tsarist regime enjoyed an enthusiastic readership. In March, however, the *Forward* abruptly withdrew its support for Germany, following a report that the German foreign ministry had secretly promised Mexico large portions of the American Southwest in return for participation in an eventual war against the United States. In a front-page editorial, the paper's editor, Abraham Cahan, called upon all Jews to come to the defence of the republic which had taken them in. After a bitter exchange with Cahan, Trotsky left both the newspaper and the American shore.

On his arrival in Russia, Trotsky found the Bolsheviks in despair. The hated Tsarist regime had been overthrown at last, but not by them. The return of Lenin and his close associates helped raise their morale but brought them no closer to power. It was Trotsky who, guided largely by instinct, advised the Bolsheviks first to seize power in the capital, Petrograd, and then to consolidate it throughout the country. The instrument of consolidation was the Red Army, which Trotsky organized and led. He hit upon the idea of appointing political commissars to motivate the troops and to report back to the revolutionary government on the state of their morale. At a time when the *halutzim* of Palestine had just begun to equip themselves with small arms as protection against Arab attacks on their settlements, this bespectacled Jew, a trained mathematician and avid reader of Aristotle, was commanding entire divisions.

Jews joined the Red Army in large numbers—less out of love for Bolshevism than for sheer self-preservation. Whenever the White Russian forces entered a Jewish village, they tried to kill all its inhabitants. In Minsk and some areas of the Ukraine, several Red Army regiments were almost entirely Jewish. Knowing that his Jewish troops had nothing to lose, Trotsky often sent them into battle first, to soften up the enemy while his fighting spirit was still intact. They endured appalling losses; but the Reds eventually won the civil war, thus enabling Bolshevism to triumph in Russia.

Because of his brilliant leadership and courage, Trotsky was the obvious successor to Lenin on the latter's death in 1924. He was forced out of power by Stalin, however, and had to seek exile once again, this time in Mexico. There, he was to write an article in 1937, noting with regret that the Communist regime had not eliminated anti-Semitism in Russia. Three years later, he was assassinated in Mexico City by a thug hired by Stalin. Like Paul of Tarsus and Karl Marx before him, Trotsky believed that humanity could be liberated from oppression if only the right people took power. For Paul, these were the early Christians; for Marx and Trotsky, the industrial proletariat took the place of God's elect. In both cases, real power was assumed by a faceless bureaucracy which soon lost sight of its original mission.

Even with Trotsky exiled to Mexico, the Soviet Communist Party still numbered far more Jews than their population would normally warrant. The reason was simple: when the Bolsheviks seized power, large numbers of educated Russians and foreign capitalists fled the country, never to return. To fill the vacuum, the inexperienced Communists turned to whoever possessed sufficient intelligence and initiative. It did not seem to be terribly important at first that a large proportion of these new people were of Jewish origin. Litvinov was a typical example. His youthful ambition had been to become a librarian. He entered the diplomatic service only because the new regime needed him there. In time, a mainly

Gentile Communist elite was trained to handle—and often to mishandle—the affairs of state and the economy. So Jews were no longer in such demand. Their numbers in the Party and its hierarchy began to decline in 1922. Among the old Bolsheviks purged by Stalin in 1937 were many Jews. They had served their purpose and were now rewarded with a bullet in the brain.

But the memory of Trotsky and other Jewish atheists lingered on, long after they had ceased to contribute to the edification of Soviet or world Communism. Just as Jews had been drawn into the power vacuum left by the demise of the Tsarist regime, so they rode the wave of revolution in the successor states to the German and Austro-Hungarian empires. In Bavaria, a socialist government under former journalist Kurt Eisner briefly held power just after the First World War. Eisner was assassinated in February 1919 by a right-wing nobleman. Rosa Luxemburg, whose Jewish origins were more obvious to her enemies than to herself, led an unsuccessful Communist revolt in Berlin in 1918. She was arrested and killed on her way to prison. Hungary saw the establishment of a Communist regime, which lasted six months under the unsure leadership of a Jewish intellectual named Béla Kun. He was forced to flee when his government was overthrown by elements of the Romanian army. Despite their failure to retain power, these idealistic revolutionaries unwittingly played into the hands of Western anti-Semites, who pointed to the Jews' place in the vanguard of the Left as a dreaded portent of things to come.

The Conspiracy Myth

From beyond the grave, the defunct Tsarist regime wrought vengeance upon its Jewish adversaries. Its weapon was a crude pamphlet, published in Russia in 1905 and entitled, *The Protocols of the Elders of Zion*. Here was laid out, in turgid prose, what purports to be the secret deliberations of a supreme Jewish council, held somewhere, sometime, under the chairmanship of an un-named rabbi, for the purpose of plotting world domination. To undermine Christian civilization, the elders recommend establishing republics everywhere and then assuming power when the inevitable chaos ensues. Financial speculation will enable the Jews to reduce entire countries to misery and then to buy out the national economies with their ill-acquired wealth. By encouraging labour agitation, rich Jews can easily bring modern industrial society to its knees, the better to dominate it. In a stroke, the opposition between Jewish capitalists and Jewish socialists is seen to be feigned; their interests are in fact identical! The rabbi urges the faithful to marry Christian maidens as a first step toward the complete penetration of established society. Given the traditional hostility of rabbis everywhere to intermarriage, an astute reader would immediately conclude that the *Protocols* were nothing but a monstrous hoax. But few readers of this bizarre document were astute; fewer still had any understanding of Judaism.

Demonizing the Jew, endowing him with supernatural powers, is as old as Christianity itself. By accusing the Jews of deicide, the daughter religion made them appear to be more powerful than God Himself. In Christian tradition, the Antichrist, the 'son of sin' first mentioned in Paul's second letter to the Thessalonians (2.3), is widely assumed to be a Jew. What gave the myth of Jewish world-domination widespread credence was the French Revolution and the reaction it engendered. As early as the 1790's, a few Catholic polemicists saw the Revolution as part of a plot concocted among Jews and Freemasons. Further embellishments on this theme throughout the nineteenth century led to the first edition of the *Protocols* in France around 1890. The text was largely a plagiarism of an earlier attack on emperor Napoleon III, who was characterized as harbouring Machiavellian plans for world rule. By substituting the fictitious Jewish council for the real emperor, the author—or rather, forger—of the *Protocols* attributed such plans to the Jews. In 1905, a paranoid Russian named Sergei Nilus, who was personally convinced that the reign of the Antichrist was imminent, translated the French text into Russian, added a few 'protocols' of his own and published the entire forgery. He received the encouragement of the *Okhrana*, the Tsarist secret police, whose director found them useful to justify the pogroms. The first editions sold poorly. Not many Russians were then ready to believe that the Jews, who were subject to incessant humiliations by the

Tsarist regime, were quite as powerful as Nilus made them out to be. The Bolshevik seizure of power and the ensuing civil war in Russia gave the *Protocols* a new lease on life. White Russian prisoners of war were found to be carrying in the pockets of their uniforms mimeographed excerpts from the pamphlet. They had, their captors soon learned, been told by their officers that they were fighting to save Holy Russia from Jewish control. With the victory of the Red Army, White Russian émigrés took copies of the *Protocols* to the West, where they soon appeared in translation. In the United States, the yellow press was quick to publicize the myth of a world-wide Jewish conspiracy. Thus, the *Chicago Tribune* of 19 June 1920 ran an inflammatory article under the headline: 'Trotsky Leads Jew-Radicals to World Rule. Bolshevism Only a Tool for His Scheme.' Many simple-minded Americans, already petrified by the Red scare that was then sweeping the country, accepted such sensationalism as the truth.

Among those Americans who took the Red menace seriously, the most influential was the pioneer auto magnate, Henry Ford. From May to October 1920, Ford's newspaper, *The Dearborn Independent*, ran a series of articles inspired by the *Protocols*. These were published in October of that year in book form under the title, *The International Jew*, with Ford himself listed as the author. In fact, the articles and the book based on them were written by a German who had worked for his native country as a propaganda agent in the United States until 1917. But with Ford's name on the cover, the book sold well—half a million copies in its American edition alone. It held the Jews responsible for virtually every modern innovation—except the motor car, of course—that Ford disapproved of. The sports clothes craze that swept across America after the First World War was taken to be just another example of how Jews seek to entice Gentile youth into lewd behaviour. Following the threat of legal action by the American Jewish Committee, Ford recanted in 1927 and disavowed author-ship of the book. By that time, however, it had been translated into several languages, including German.

Few educated people in the West took Ford's book, or the *Protocols* from which it was derived, at their face value. The august *Times* of London was at first inclined to give Nilus's pamphlet the benefit of the doubt when it first appeared in English in 1920. A few months later, the paper honourably admitted its mistake and pronounced the *Protocols* a total imposture. But the pamphlet, like some evil genie let out of its bottle, could not be suppressed. Hitler was inspired by it and based entire pages of *Mein Kampf* on its crude allegations. The Nazi party was founded in 1920, the same year that the *Protocols* began to circulate in the West. Hitler ordered the party organization to distribute copies of the German translation to members and sympathizers. He also saw to it that the German edition of *The International Jew* was readily available at party offices. Thus did the myth of Jewish world domination feed on itself. Worse, as Norman Cohn has shown in his revealing study, *Warrant for Genocide*,[1] it provided the Nazis with a moral justification for their subsequent anti-Jewish policy.

The anti-Semitic paranoia abated somewhat during the prosperous years of the 1920's, only to flare up again with the coming of the Depression. In the *Protocols*, the 'Elders of Zion' had vowed to create economic chaos; and there it was. Anti-Semites were quick to recall that they had predicted just such a catastrophe. More fundamentally, the Depression seemed to invalidate a tradition that originated with Charlemagne, who had admitted Jews into his kingdom in order to encourage trade and commerce. Throughout the Middle Ages and most of the modern period, it was widely assumed that the social function of the Jews was to bring prosperity to the countries which had received them. This is why they were tolerated in the first place. Jews were very much present in the industrialized world during the 1930's, and yet the global economy contracted drastically. The onset of hard times led many basically decent people, who were not ordinarily anti-Semitic, to conclude that the Jews were not doing their job. In that case, one could infer that they should no longer be tolerated.

---

[1] London: Eyre & Spottiswoode, 1967.

The Depression brought Jews to prominence in another way—as repairmen for a broken-down economy. Low production and high unemployment tended to discredit the traditional elites in democratic countries. (They had already been discredited in the totalitarian states.) So people from the outside were called in to help put the system back together again. Among these outsiders were many Jews. Such was the approach of Franklin D. Roosevelt on assuming the Presidency of the United States in 1933. He surrounded himself with a group of high-powered advisors whom he called his 'Brain Trust'. Their job was not to destroy capitalism but to make it work again. Since several members of the 'Brain Trust' were Jews, American anti-Semites lost no time in calling the New Deal a 'Jew Deal'. Some even insinuated that Roosevelt, an authentic representative of the Protestant gentry, had been born a Jew and had changed his name from Rosenfeld.

The political scene was even more dramatic in France, where Léon Blum, the Jewish leader of the Socialist Party, became premier in June 1936. Blum was not the first French Jew to hold such high office; that honour belongs to Jules Simon, a conservative republican who was head of government for a few weeks in 1876. But Simon had no policy, beyond that of maintaining the republic. Blum, on the other hand, energetically pushed through the legislature a series of social and economic reforms that were long overdue, some having been enacted in Germany fifty years earlier. These included the forty-hour work week, mandatory paid annual vacations for all employees, guaranteed pensions and universal medical insurance. A wheat board protected farmers from exaggerated price fluctuations, while the railways were nationalized and made more efficient. This ambitious programme became law in the amazingly short span of four months.

Blum's approach to power was unique and owed much to his Jewish heritage. The son of a Parisian furrier, he had originally hoped to become a writer, but was discouraged by novelist André Gide, who disparaged his literary efforts as being too Semitic in tone. On entering politics, Blum joined the Socialists but entertained no illusions of being himself a member of the proletariat. Rather than seeking power as Trotsky had done, he saw himself in the role of a manager, exercising political authority as trustee for the working classes. His managerial approach was essentially Jewish; Jews had been managers, both in the West and in the Islamic world, for centuries. It helps explain why Blum did not allow himself to become corrupted by political power. He was, above all, a sincere democrat, who readily relinquished the office of premier once his governing coalition began to weaken.

Regarding Nazi Germany, Blum's policy was tempered by his knowledge that France was ill-prepared militarily and could not count on any tangible help from Britain. When Hitler's territorial claims on Czechoslovakia reached crisis proportions in the fall of 1938, Blum was no longer premier. He used his position as head of the Socialist Party to argue that France must honour her treaty obligations to the Czechs, despite the risk of war with Germany. Blum was no warmonger. As a Socialist, he was deeply committed to the cause of peace and understanding among peoples. But he felt that France's reputation as a great power was at stake. For the anti-Semites, who were both active and vocal in France at the time, this was proof positive that the Jews wanted war with Germany. A new conspiracy theory was hatched: it held that French Jews were pushing for war in the hope that France would be defeated, just as Russia had been in 1917. They would then profit from the ensuing disorder and seize power, in true Bolshevik fashion. This bizarre logic failed to take Hitler's already obvious anti-Jewish policy into account. If France lost a war to Germany, French Jews would surely meet with a fate similar to that of their coreligionists in Germany and Austria.

Yet the myth of a Jewish conspiracy to lead France to military disaster found a hard core of believers in 1938. It was encouraged by the publication of a book in the fall of that year entitled, *La guerre juive* ('The Jewish War'). Its author, Paul Ferdonnet, claimed that everyone in France who opposed a policy of appeasement toward Nazi Germany was either a Jew or (as in the case of Henri de Kérillis, a Breton Catholic) a puppet of the Jews. Realizing the divisive nature of such arguments, the French government enacted a law in the spring of 1939 banning appeals to hatred based on racial or religious grounds. All anti-Semitic propaganda ceased overnight. Ferdonnet was found to be in the pay of the Nazis and fled to Germany, where he took to the airwaves. From the Reich's powerful transmitter in Stuttgart, he broadcast daily in French, warning his listeners that a war between France and Germany would benefit only the English and the Jews. Few Frenchmen were won over by such arguments; most would shrug their shoulders in disbelief, referring to him as 'Ferdonnet the traitor'. After France's humiliating defeat by Germany in 1940, however, they became more receptive to such twisted reasoning.

Hopes and Fears

In one of the more memorable scenes from Noel Coward's play, *Cavalcade*, two newlyweds are planning their future while leaning on the deck rail of an ocean liner. Lost in love, the honeymooners see nothing but happiness ahead: a home of their own, children—the usual. The groom then decides to photograph his lovely bride as she stands with her back to the rail, her wrap gracefully draped over a life preserver. Once the picture is taken, she removes the garment, and we see the name, *S. S. Titanic*, painted on the buoy. Letting the audience in on an impending tragedy, of which the stage participants are blissfully unaware, is a well-known dramatic technique; and many playwrights have used it to good effect. For a historian to pass judgment on his subjects for not having a crystal ball, however, would be crude and dishonest. This caveat should be borne in mind when dealing with the Jews during the period between the two World Wars. They simply did not know what was going to happen to them.

For the different Jewish communities of Europe, the 1920's were a period of considerable promise. The only great power that had elevated anti-Semitism to the level of official policy was the Tsarist regime in Russia, and now it was gone. The advent of Communism meant an end to pogroms (except, occasionally, by anti-Communists) and to the official disabilities under which the Jews had suffered. Even after Stalin revived unofficial discrimination against them, the Jewish masses of Russia were still generally better off than they had been under the Tsars. Nazism was not yet a source of concern. Hitler's failed putsch in 1923 brought discredit upon the movement, which five years later managed to win only 2.6 percent of the popular vote and a mere twelve seats in the German Reichstag.

The independence of Poland, a direct result of the Allied victory in 1918, initially infused Europe's largest Jewish community with optimism. When Trotsky's Red Army invaded Poland, however, all Jews were suspected of collusion with the Communists. Those in the Polish army were interned as possible traitors, while a pogrom was unleashed against Jewish civilians. Under Marshall Pilsudski, who assumed power in 1926, the situation of Polish Jews greatly improved. They enjoyed civic equality until his death in 1935. In the major cities especially, Jews basked in a new-found sense of freedom. As Isaac Bashevis Singer has reminded us, a young Jewish woman in Warsaw during the late 1920's found opportunities for personal expression that her mother and grandmothers had never dreamt about. She could bob her hair. She could smoke cigarettes (then considered positive proof of her emancipation). She could even take a lover—and not necessarily a Jewish one. Some Jews were so caught up in the general euphoria that they began to speak Polish at home, instead of Yiddish. In such happy circumstances, the immigration quotas imposed by the United States in 1924 did not dishearten the Jews of Eastern Europe. Most did not want to leave, and those that did could find other Western democracies willing to take them. These included France, Britain, Canada and Germany.

Under the Weimar Republic, the Jews of Germany prospered and flourished as never before. Their role in education, journalism and the liberal professions was far greater than their numbers—less than one percent of the total population—would seem to warrant. They were also very active in such new ventures as radio, the recording industry and the cinema. Most noteworthy were their achievements in science. Of all Nobel prizes awarded from 1901 to 1936, nine percent went to Jews from Germany and Austria. The lifting of quotas and other discriminatory measures enabled them to give the full measure of their talents. Imbued with a new-found sense of confidence, many German Jews set out to re-Judaize their secularized brethren. Surely the most spectacular manifestation of this trend was the growing Zionist movement, which concentrated on instilling pride in being Jewish. Less apparent but every bit as productive was a privately-organized campaign for adult Jewish education. It was led by the philosopher Franz Rosenzweig, who had nearly converted to Christianity in 1913, but returned to Judaism after having attended a Yom Kippur service at a small synagogue for Eastern European immigrants in Berlin. After the war, he organized the Free House of Study in Frankfurt, where Jews from all walks of life were re-introduced to the basic tenets of their religion and encouraged to apply them to contemporary problems.

Whether they realized it or not, the Jews of Germany did benefit as a group from the decline of the old aristocratic order and the greater social mobility which ensued. Many other Germans, however, expressed nostalgia for the pre-1914 era, when their country enjoyed seemingly unchallenged power and prosperity. Disillusioned war veterans, hard-pressed peasants and the lower middle classes whose savings were wiped out by inflation formed the core of the new Nazi movement, which promised a return to former glory. Not all Nazis were fervent anti-Semites, but their view of society necessarily ran counter to that of the many Jewish writers, artists and scientists. Compounding the problem in Germany, as elsewhere, was the growing belief in a world-wide Jewish conspiracy. On 24 June 1922, Foreign Minister Walter Rathenau was assassinated in Berlin by a group of young right-wing terrorists who had read and believed every word in *The Protocols of the Elders of Zion*. At their trial, they testified that Rathenau, a Jew, though not an observant one, was the official German delegate to some imaginary Jewish world-government. They also claimed under cross-examination that his sister was married to the Bolshevik Radek. (She was, in fact, the wife of a Berlin physician.) Fortunately, Germany was still a country where the rule of law prevailed; and the criminals were brought to justice. The terrorist group to which they belonged was banned, and a new law made it a criminal offence to claim that Rathenau had ever been an 'Elder of Zion'.

The rule of law was threatened, however, by the rise of Nazism. Propelled into prominence by the Depression, the Nazis increased their parliamentary representation from twelve to over a hundred in the general elections of September 1930. The German Jewish leadership was well aware of the danger posed by Hitler and his minions. The official organ of the *Centralverein* urged its readers to leave party affiliations aside if necessary in order to support whatever candidates seemed most likely to defeat the Nazis. Unfortunately, the Jews of Germany were too few in number to deny Hitler his victory. He became Chancellor on 30 January 1933, in accordance with strict constitutional procedure. From then on, there was no legal way for German Jews to oppose him, and armed resistance was out of the question. Their only solution was to emigrate, which they did in ever increasing numbers until, by 1938, most of Germany's Jews had left the country where they and their families had lived for centuries.

In the past, Jews expelled from one country could usually find refuge in another. Those who fled Spain in the late fifteenth century were absorbed primarily by Turkey and the Muslim caliphates of North Africa. Smaller numbers were later admitted to England, Holland and France. The situation in the 1930's was vastly different. Whereas Jewish refugees had been prized by kings and princes for their value in stimulating the economy, now it was widely feared that they would take other people's jobs away. The immediate cause of this fear was the worldwide economic Depression, but earlier economic crises had not deterred rulers from admitting Jews into their kingdoms. What was different this time was not so much the severity of the economic contraction, but the fact that democratic governments of the twentieth century had to take public opinion into account. The fear of increasing unemployment as a result of Jewish immigration was totally unfounded. Those Jewish refugees from Nazi Germany who were admitted to Western democratic countries founded businesses which hired more people than they displaced. But beneath this fear was popular anti-Semitism, fanned by economic hardship and the myth of a Jewish conspiracy. Absolute rulers could ignore, or even oppose, such base phobias. The democratically elected governments of the West took them seriously—all the more so since many legislators were themselves caught up in the collective hysteria.

Under the circumstances, the German Jews fared reasonably well, since most eventually found refuge somewhere. Britain took in some 50,000, including those from Austria, which was annexed to Hitler's Reich in February 1938. Another 40,000 found a haven in France, which was already inundated with exiles from all over: Armenians, White Russians, anti-Fascist Italians and, since 1938, Spanish republicans fleeing the advance of Franco's armies. So the French effort was really quite commendable. Far less so was the performance of Canada, whose government traditionally favoured immigration to fill up that country's vast spaces. Yet even those German Jews who promised to buy vacant land and take up farming were refused entry. When asked how many Jewish refugees should be allowed into Canada, the head of the immigration section at the External Affairs ministry replied callously, 'None is too many.' From 1933 to 1948, Canada took in only 5,000 European Jews, or about a third as many as Bolivia, a poor country with far fewer resources. The United States did little better: with a population nearly eleven times that of Canada, it accepted 57,000 Jewish refugees. The annual immigration quotas for Germany were not even filled in most years from 1933 to 1941, as American consuls refused visa applications from thousands of qualified and solvent German Jews. At one point, Roosevelt toyed with the idea of resettling some of them in Alaska, but dropped it in the face of strong opposition from Congress and the State Department.

By 1938, the world was divided between those countries that wanted to get rid of their Jews and those that refused to accept them. In the summer of that year, an international conference on refugees met at the French resort town of Evian, on the Lake of Geneva. It had been convened by Roosevelt, primarily in the hope that Latin American countries might take in more Jews. Only one made an unequivocal offer of resettlement: the Dominican Republic, whose government seized this opportunity to ingratiate itself with the United States. With great fanfare, it announced that 100,000 Jews would be admitted. A total of 6,000 were actually allowed in. The other Latin American governments were decidedly reticent; they were not eager to receive large numbers of German-speaking merchants, lawyers, physicians and academics, who might compete with their own elites. In the end, little was accomplished. When the government of Poland appealed to the Evian conference for help in resettling the Jews it wanted to get rid of, the delegates threw up their hands in dismay. It was difficult enough trying to find havens for those Jews remaining in Germany and Austria. Resettling the 3.3 million Jews of Poland was beyond contemplation.

As the refugee problem became more acute, attention turned to the American Jewish community, which, with five million members, was now the world's largest. Over 60 percent of American Jews were of so-called 'Russian' origin, their families having fled Tsarist tyranny. They had made great strides since arriving in the United States and repaid their host country with a heartfelt demonstration of patriotism. Although they represented only 3.5 percent of the total American population, Jews accounted for 4.5 percent of their country's voluntary enlistments and battlefield deaths in the First World War (as they would in the Second). With the return of peace, the sons and daughters of Jewish immigrants rose to prominence in various fields—music, radio, sports and the cinema. Some were drawn to a business venture that seems to have had particular appeal for many urban immigrants and their children: organized crime. In 1919, the gambler Arnold Rothstein accomplished the never-to-be-duplicated feat of fixing a World Series simply by bribing eight players of a baseball team. He was later shot to death by his rivals' henchmen while leaving a (non-kosher) restaurant.

When not making newspaper headlines, American Jews could often be found discussing among themselves the purpose of their Jewish identity: whether to be socialists, Zionists, or just plain Americans 'of the Jewish persuasion'. It was a lively time; the Hitlerite tragedy had not yet helped create the 'We-are-one' conformity that has since stifled all original thinking on the subject. The Jews of the United States expressed their Jewishness in various ways: in humour, as exemplified by the Marx brothers; in music, as when Benny Goodman transformed the Yiddish song, 'Bei Mir Bist Du Schoen', into a rousing swing classic, or in religion. With the interwar period came a new generation of American-trained rabbis, such as Robert Gordis, Abba Hillel Silver and Milton Steinberg. All were captivating orators, whose mastery of English was enhanced by their Biblical culture, and all wrote popular books on Judaism in the vernacular. Each sought, in his own way, to add something uniquely Jewish to the American historical experience. After 1933, the community became increasingly preoccupied with developments in Germany. When the Nazis announced a boycott of Jewish shops in Germany on 1 May 1933, Jewish business leaders in the United States replied by organizing a boycott of German products and services. This well-meant gesture backfired. German Jewish businessmen pleaded with the Americans to lift the boycott, since some of the German goods exported to the United States came from, or included components made by, Jewish firms. The German Jews argued, moreover, that the American boycott gave credence to the Nazis' claim that Germany was the victim of a worldwide Jewish conspiracy. Although the boycott remained in effect, it did the German economy little harm, and perhaps even some good. Certain rich Americans travelling to Europe preferred to book passage on German ships, knowing that there would be no Jews on board. The boycott's failure serves to illustrate the essential powerlessness of the American Jewish community, reputedly the most powerful in the world. No matter how hard American Jews tried to influence the course of events, they remained political and economic lightweights.

On the refugee question, American Jews were stymied at every turn. They petitioned, they lobbied—all to no avail. Roosevelt made no attempt to have the State Department admit more Jews from Hitler's Reich. He was too sensitive to the charge that his New Deal was a 'Jew Deal' to give the appearance of being under excessive Jewish influence. When Jewish refugees required a guarantee that they would not become a public charge in the United States, many American Jews came forward individually to sponsor them. In some cases, the sponsors did not even know the people whom they were endorsing. The champion in this regard was Arthur Taubman, a self-made millionaire who owned a chain of auto parts stores. He obtained entry for some 500 refugees by claiming that they were all his relatives. American Jewish service organizations, whose funds had been sorely depleted by the Depression, managed to find housing and employment for any new arrivals who needed help. But they had no influence on government policy. The plight of Jews under Nazism was brought into sharp focus by the saga of the *Saint Louis*, a German liner, which left Hamburg for Cuba in May 1939, with 930 Jewish refugees on board. All had official landing permits, for which they had paid 150 dollars each. But when the ship docked in Havana harbour, the Cuban authorities declared that these permits were no longer valid. The ensuing drama has since given rise to a pernicious myth of American Jewish indifference to European Jewish suffering. In the opening chapter of his book, *Never Again*, the late Rabbi Meir Kahane paints an utterly false picture of American Jews gamboling in the surf and attending dog races in Miami Beach, totally unmindful of their German coreligionists, who were then being tossed about on the high seas. The American Jews ought to have done something, he exclaims petulantly. In fact, they did as much as they could. On learning of Cuba's refusal to honour its own documents, the leaders of the Joint Distribution Committee, a New York-based Jewish organization founded to help resettle refugees, took the first available flight for Havana. There, they offered to post a five-hundred-dollar-bond for each and every passenger of the *Saint Louis*. The Cuban officials were unmoved; and after a week of fruitless pleading, the American Jews had no choice but to fly back to New York, their mission a failure. One wonders what Rabbi Kahane would have done in their place. The ship was forced to leave Cuba and made for Antwerp, where its human cargo was dispersed among those countries that were willing to grant temporary asylum: Belgium, Holland, Britain and France.

The approach of war in Europe made American Jews count their blessings. Life in the United States was not always easy for them. The effects of the Depression were compounded by the discrimination they often faced in jobs and housing. There was widespread Judaeophobia at home to contend with, as Father Coughlin vituperated against the Jews in his weekly radio broadcasts, and Representative John Rankin regularly spewed anti-Semitic venom in his speeches to the Congress. But at least America was protected from Hitler's legions by the broad Atlantic.

The war in Europe had already commenced when the Jewish calendar turned over a new year, and a new century. The first of Tishri 5700 fell on 13 September 1939, as the Wehrmacht was slicing through Poland. In synagogues throughout the United States, Jews gave thanks for being spared the horrors of war. One New York rabbi, in his Rosh Hashana homily, compared the great American republic to Noah's ark atop Mount Ararat, safe from the raging flood. He had no way of foreseeing the extent of the tragedy that would soon befall the Jews of Europe.

Britain's Dilemma

One country had already been designated as a refuge for Jews fleeing persecution: Palestine. Shortly after the First World War, Britain received a formal mandate from the League of Nations to administer Palestine in accordance with the Balfour Declaration. This meant that the mandatory power was to facilitate Jewish immigration with a view to establishing a Jewish national home there. When the terms of the mandate reached the Palestinian Arabs, they rioted in 1919 and again in 1921. Scores of Jews were killled, and their homes and shops destroyed. The late professor Elie Kedourie, a specialist in the modern Middle East and himself a Jew, later remarked that Palestine was quite possibly the worst place to create a Jewish state. It was inhabited by a tightly-knit Arab society, with a Sunni Muslim majority, which would regard an influx of Jews as an invasion of its ancestral homeland. That the Palestinian Arabs bitterly resented Jewish settlement is beyond doubt. But what other people on earth would have accepted the creation of a Jewish state in its midst? In the seventeenth and eighteenth centuries, various European powers had been able to settle the Western hemisphere without the consent of its indigenous population. But the Jews were not a power, with an army and navy at its disposal. The Arabs, for their part, were better organized and far more conscious of their history than the natives of the Americas. The Zionists recognized their own weakness and the Arabs' strength. They realized that British support was essential to the success of their programme, in the initial stages at least.

The British government, meanwhile, had grown cool toward Zionism since the turbulent days of 1917. Having been granted authority over Palestine, it no longer needed the Jews as a rationale to keep France out. British civil and military administrators in the mandated territory were not at all interested in promoting a Jewish national home. On a personal level, they found the Arabs easier to deal with than the Jews. Among senior political figures, only Churchill, who became colonial secretary in 1921, was still personally committed to the Balfour Declaration. His perception of the Jews was friendly, if a bit paternalistic. Only by encouraging Zionism, he believed, could Britain win the great Jewish masses of Eastern Europe away from Bolshevism. He therefore set out to persuade the Palestinian Arabs that Jewish immigration would not cause them any hardship. The Arabs were not convinced. To placate them, Churchill made two significant concessions. The first was to allow Jews into Palestine only to the extent that the country's economy could absorb new immigrants. Cyclical Jewish unemployment in Palestinian cities during the 1920's gave this measure an *ex post facto* justification. The other was to divide Palestine along the Jordan river, the eastern portion being reserved for Arabs. The Emirate of Transjordan, which Britain created in 1922, was strictly off limits to Jews, as its successor, the Kingdom of Jordan, still is. The British governor of the new sheikdom, Sir Alec Kirkbride, recalled in his memoirs that the Colonial Office had intended Transjordan to be a home for Palestinian Arabs displaced by Jewish settlement.

But the Palestinian Arabs did not want to be displaced. Jewish settlers would buy land, usually at greatly inflated prices, from absentee Arab landlords, for the purpose of cultivating it themselves. This meant that Arab tenant farmers, who were forced off the soil that they and their families had tilled for generations, now had to find work elsewhere. Given the highly structured nature of Palestinian Arab society, where everyone was presumed to know his place and to occupy it, this was far from easy. The displaced Arabs tended to gravitate to the cities, where they were joined by job-seekers from Egypt, Lebanon and Syria, who were attracted to the burgeoning economy of Palestine. These uprooted elements became a receptive audience for demagogues who incited them to attack the Jews. A new wave of anti-Jewish riots broke out in Palestine in 1929, following a decade of slow but steady Jewish immigration. The British army was able to quell these disturbances, but its commanders grew uneasy in what they perceived to be their role of protecting Jews.

In the 1930's anti-Semitism became official policy in Germany, while in Poland and Romania, the state tacitly encouraged increasing acts of violence against Jews. As a result, Jewish immigration to Palestine rose dramatically: 30,000 new arrivals in 1933, 42,000 in 1934 and 62,000 in 1935. Coupled with natural increase, this drove up the country's Jewish population from 192,000 to 355,000, a gain of nearly eighty-five percent. In response, the Palestinian Arabs staged an indefinite general strike in April 1936, which soon degenerated into armed rebellion against the mandatory power. Since British troops alone could not quell the revolt, the civil administration allowed a Jewish police force to be created, while tolerating the *Hagana*, a Jewish militia founded in the early 1920's. The general strike was called off in October 1936, following appeals from the rulers of Transjordan, Iraq and Saudi Arabia. Sporadic fighting continued well into 1938, however, with the Jewish militia assisting British troops in the pursuit of Arab rebels.

A royal commission was convened in London in 1936 to examine the problem and, after hearing testimony from both Jews and Arabs, recommended that Palestine be partitioned. The Jews were to get Galilee and the coastal plain, extending just south of Jaffa; everything else would go to the Arabs, save a British enclave stretching from Jerusalem to Jaffa, which would eventually become part of the Arab state. The Zionists were divided over whether to accept the plan. Weizmann first compared it to the judgment of Solomon: cutting the baby in two. He soon changed his mind, however; a rump Jewish state was better than none at all. The Arabs rejected partition outright and insisted that all Jewish immigration be halted immediately. But Jewish population pressure continued to mount, as another 81,000 refugees arrived in Palestine between 1936 and 1939. On the eve of the Second World War, Jews accounted for a third of the country's population. As ever increasing numbers tried to flee Europe, it was only a question of time—a few years at most—before Palestine would have a Jewish majority. The British government explored the possibility of resettling large numbers of European Jews in its vast empire, but administrators stationed in those colonies chosen for the plan unanimously rejected it.

Making sure that Jews did not become a majority in Palestine had become unofficial British policy in the late 1930's. It was made official with the publication, in May 1939, of a White Paper, which set a limit of 15,000 Jewish immigrants annually to Palestine over a five-year period. After that, any further influx of Jews would have to be approved by the Palestinian Arabs. These dispositions contradicted the spirit of the Balfour Declaration, which was intended to create a haven in Palestine for persecuted European Jews. To those seeking such a haven, it seemed a bit late in the game to change the rules. Indeed, Jews everywhere had come to think of Palestine as the one country which would not refuse entry to the victims of anti-Semitic violence. In this they were sadly mistaken. Great powers always act in accordance with their own interests, and it was no longer in Britain's interest to protect the Jews. When the Jewish Agency tried to smuggle refugees into Palestine, Britain replied by suspending all Jewish immigration for ten months—a most critical period during which the noose tightened further around the Jews of Europe. A more graphic demonstration of Jewish weakness in world politics can hardly be imagined.

British historians have rationalized the White Paper as being necessary to ensure Arab support in the forthcoming war with Nazi Germany. Yet it remained in effect even after the Allied victory in 1945. The Labour government under Clement Attlee pursued a similar policy in Palestine. In any case, an Anglo-German conflict was hardly a foregone conclusion in May 1939. The decision of Prime Minister Neville Chamberlain to guarantee Polish independence two months earlier was not intended to provoke war. It was basically a grandstand play, made to ward off attacks by members of his own party, such as Churchill and Duff Cooper, as well as the opposition Labourites, who accused the government of having chosen dishonour by appeasing Hitler. The prime minister had no intention of going to war over Poland. He had not even consulted the Poles before announcing his guarantee (nor the French, who would have to do most of the fighting). Besides, Britain had no land army to speak of; only one division was ready for battle in the spring of 1939. So in retrospect, Britain's hasty guarantee of Poland's independence—not its territorial integrity—seems quite reckless. Chamberlain did not see it that way. He hoped that it would somehow give Hitler pause, so that an honourable settlement of Germany's land claims on Poland could be negotiated.

The White Paper had not been drafted with Europe in mind. It was intended to secure the British sphere of influence in the Middle East. Britain obviously did not want to antagonize the Arabs any more than she had already done in taking Turkey's place as the dominant power in the region. Since all Arab governments opposed—at least officially—the Zionist plan for a Jewish state in Palestine, Britain had to oppose it also. More than that, British experts on the region saw Palestine as a land bridge linking Egypt with the other Middle Eastern countries under British domination. The White Paper provided for Palestinian independence by 1949—presumably as a British protectorate, like Transjordan. Just how a nominally sovereign Arab Palestine was expected to cope with a Zionist nation of one-third its total population was not explained in the document, whose authors had probably given no thought to the question. What is clear, in any case, is that Britain had no use for a Jewish state in Palestine, because such a state would be truly independent and not subservient to British policy in the region. So Britain sought to prevent the Palestinian Jews from becoming a majority. The Balfour Declaration and the subsequent mandate had allowed Britain to gain control over Palestine. The White Paper was designed to perpetuate that control. Seen in the light of British imperial tradition, the White Paper was not a reversal of the Balfour Declaration, but its continuation.

It is a tribute to the basic decency of the British people that a policy as self-serving as this one had to be justified in moral terms. The foundations for such a moral argument had already been laid in a book published in 1938 and entitled, *The Arab Awakening*. It was written by George Antonius, an Egyptian scholar living in

Britain, who had led the Arab witnesses at the 1936 royal commission. He first reminded his readers just how much Britain owed to the Arabs. The Arab uprising against the Ottoman Turks in 1916, he maintained, had enabled British forces to conquer the Middle East. Recent scholarship has cast doubt on the military significance of the Arab revolt; but in 1938, thanks in no small measure to T. E. Lawrence, it was still taken very seriously. Having helped Britain, the Arabs would not take kindly to British support of a Jewish state in their midst. Antonius did recognize that European Jews had to find refuge somewhere. 'The treatment meted out to Jews in Germany and other European countries,' he wrote, 'is a disgrace to its authors and to modern civilization, but posterity will not exonerate any country that fails to bear its proper share of the sacrifices needed to alleviate Jewish suffering and distress. To place the brunt of the burden upon Arab Palestine is a miserable evasion of the duty that lies upon the whole of the civilized world.' His argument had great persuasive force in 1938, as it has even today. In British political and journalistic circles, *The Arab Awakening* was widely quoted in defence of the 1939 White Paper.

Events in Europe, meanwhile, moved with amazing rapidity. Far from bringing Germany and Poland closer to negotiating with one another, the British guarantee drove them farther apart. The Polish government took it as permission to remain obdurate, while Hitler raised the ante, claiming still more Polish territory. The signing, on 23 August 1939, of a non-aggression pact between Nazi Germany and the Soviet Union signaled that an attack on Poland was imminent. Britain and France would have to oppose Hitler militarily in order to honour Chamberlain's ill-conceived commitment to Polish independence. Yet they hesitated. It was more than forty-eight hours after the Nazis invaded Poland that a dejected prime minister announced to the House of Commons that, in view of Hitler's failure to withdraw his forces, Britain was at war with Germany. But it was a phoney war, not a real one. On 7 September 1939, bombers of the RAF made their first sortie over Germany, dropping ten million propaganda leaflets. They read in part that the war was entirely unnecessary and that Britain was ready to make peace with any German government that could be trusted. This thinly disguised appeal for Hitler's overthrow had no tangible effect, and the Phoney War in the West continued for another six months.

Military action to enforce the provisions of the White Paper, however, was swift and decisive. On 2 September 1939, a coastal patrol vessel of the Royal Navy fired on the *Tiger Hill*, a ship that was landing 1,400 illegal Jewish immigrants from Poland, Czechoslovakia and Romania on a beach in Tel Aviv. Two Jewish refugees were killed. They were the first casualties of British arms in the Second World War.

Chapter VIII

THE UNSPEAKABLE

EVEN BEFORE THE OUTBREAK of war in September 1939, the Jewish masses of Central and Eastern Europe were caught in a vise. With few exceptions, they could not leave because hardly any country was willing to take them. Not only were they unwelcome in the West—particularly in the United States and Canada—but Palestine was now closed to them as a result of British policy. This basic fact helps put into its proper perspective the role of Germany in what was to follow. Anti-Semitism has never been a specifically German phenomenon. Prior to the Second World War, the worst slaughter of Jews had been committed by Ukrainian cossacks in the mid-seventeenth century. Modern French writers made a greater intellectual contribution to anti-Jewish ideology than did their German counterparts, and Tsarist Russia furnished Hitler with a moral justification for killing Jews: the myth of a universal Jewish conspiracy. Some historians are fond of quoting Luther's diatribes against the Jews as if they were uniquely German in character. Luther was the only founder of a major Christian sect to advocate physical violence against the Jews, and his more vicious writings did find an occasional place in Nazi propaganda. But there is no evidence that German Lutherans as a group have ever been more anti-Semitic than other Christians. Hitler himself was a Catholic.

Even among committed Nazis, anti-Semitism did not always seem to merit high priority. In 1934, a resourceful American sociologist named Theodore Abel wrote to long-time party members, asking them to give their reasons for having joined. He received six hundred replies, which formed the basis of his book, *The Nazi Movement*,[1] published in 1938. Of these, only forty

---

[1]2nd ed.; New York: Atherton Press, 1966.

percent mentioned the Jewish question at all, and a few expressed embarrassment over its place in party doctrine. One contributor wrote, 'I got the impression that they [the Nazis] incited to war, and I resented their blind hatred of the Jews. Even after I joined the party, I did not see eye to eye with it on the Jewish question.' Another recalled: 'I felt that I belonged to these [Nazi] people. Only their statements about the Jews I could not swallow.' If even some Nazi militants found anti-Semitism distasteful, it is a safe assumption that most ordinary Germans did not fully share Hitler's animosity toward the Jews. In the parliamentary elections of 6 November 1932, with unemployment at an all-time high, some two million Germans who had previously voted National-Socialist turned against the movement out of disgust with its verbal and physical excesses. Nazi representation in the Reichstag declined from 230 seats to 196. It was precisely because Nazism seemed to be losing momentum that Hitler was invited to preside over a new cabinet that included only two other Nazis. Von Papen and the other old-line conservatives assumed—mistakenly, as it turned out—that they could control him.

Just as Hitler's accession to power was improvised, so was his policy toward the Jews. His anti-Semitism, like that of his contemporaries, was not altogether logical. On the one hand, he considered the Jews to be the source of all evil—vermin, as Nazi propaganda tried to depict them. This line of reasoning would, in theory, lead directly to their extermination. But Hitler was not merely a theoretician. He claimed to understand history, which had been his favourite subject in school, and saw the Jews throughout the ages as destroyers of civilizations. As a student of history, he assumed that he could weaken other countries, particularly the Western democracies, by dumping Jews onto their shores. Expulsion was his initial policy; only when it was no longer feasible did he turn to mass murder.

Expelling the Jews from Germany, where they had lived for centuries, was no easy task. Their nearly complete integration into German society made it difficult to uproot them. On assuming power, the Nazis began by excluding Jews from positions of influence, such as teaching, journalism and the arts. Those in the liberal professions were next. Last came factory- and shop-owners, whose businesses were taken over by Nazis one by one. In this regard, the Hitler regime followed mediaeval European tradition, which valued the Jews for their economic utility. The Jews resisted the imposition of such liabilities stoutly, and some managed to delay it for several years. Those who had served in the First World War as front-line combatants obtained exemptions simply by showing their citations to the proper authorities. The Nazis were astounded to discover how many patriotic Jews there were in Germany. Another problem for the regime was defining exactly who was a Jew. Originally, the Nazis sought to include everyone who had one Jewish grandparent; but this brought in too many Germans, including some party members, into the net. So they eventually settled on the criterion of two Jewish grandparents.

Eliminating marriages and sexual liaisons between Jews and Gentiles was a Nazi priority. Both were prohibited under the Nuremberg racial statutes of 1935. Behind the pseudo-scientific racism used to justify such segregation, the Nazis were genuinely fearful that the Jewish partner in such unions would exercise a dominant moral influence in the couple. In this, they were not mistaken. The German-Jewish author Lion Feuchtwanger examines just such a mixed marriage in his 1933 novel, *The Oppermanns*, which depicts a bourgeois Jewish family in Berlin just before and after the Nazi takeover. The young Berthold Opperman, whose mother is not Jewish, nonetheless considers himself a Jew and is perceived as such by his bullying Nazi teacher. The public bonfires in 1933 of books by Jewish authors and those presumed to be under the influence of Jews further attest to the Nazis' fear of Jewish moral and cultural influence.

The Hitler regime refuted its own claim that the Jews were a race by forcing them to wear a yellow star once the war began. Although the Israelites of Biblical times were in all probability a Semitic people, centuries of proselytism had brought millions of Indo-Europeans—or Aryans, as the Nazis liked to call them—into Judaism. Had the Jews really been a race, they would not have needed a distinctive badge in order to be recognized. The yellow star was itself a carryover from the high Middle Ages, when the church commanded Jews to wear yellow insignia on their outer garments. The church used it to impose segregation on the Jews, so as to preserve Christians from Jewish influence. The Nazis had the same object, except that they did not stop at segregation. That their prime phobia was the integrated Jew can be seen in a Nazi propaganda film of 1939 entitled, *The Eternal Jew*. One sequence first shows Jews wearing beards, sidecurls and broad-brimmed hats. Upon those images are then superimposed others of the same people with their hair cut, clean-shaven and hatless. This was meant to show that, with a few minor cosmetic changes, even the most observant Jew could pass for a Gentile. So viewers were warned to be on their guard. The Nazis, like other anti-Semites, saw themselves at war with Jewry. As in all wars, the enemy was expected to wear a uniform. When he does not, the rules of modern warfare allow the opposing army to put him up before a firing squad. One of the things that vexed the Nazis most was that the Jews had largely abandoned their uniform and were no longer instantly recognizable.

It took nearly six years for Germany to reduce its Jews to pariah status. In Austria, the process lasted a mere six months—partly because the Nazis had greater experience, but mainly because they enjoyed the widespread support of ordinary people. No sooner was Austria annexed to the Reich than its Jewish inhabitants were deprived of all civil rights. As crowds of Viennese stood by laughing, the Jews of the capital were subject to various forms of public humiliation, such as having to clean the sidewalks with toothbrushes, as a sign of their inferior position. During the war, Allied propaganda often referred to the 'rape' of Austria by Nazi Germany. It was not a rape. It was not even a seduction. No woman ever threw herself into her lover's arms with more passion than the Austrian people, as they welcomed their native son, Adolf Hitler. For the *Führer* was an Austrian, by birth and by education. He did not even bother to take out German citizenship until 1930, and then only under pressure from anti-Nazi parties. It was in Austria that he had learned to hate the Jews.

The future leader of Germany grew up in a society where Catholicism and imperial grandeur complemented one another.

Judaeophobia has always been strongest in Christian societies that feel themselves threatened. The expulsion of the Jews from Spain followed a centuries-long struggle with the Arabs. Similarly, Catholic Austria was repeatedly threatened by the Turks, who besieged Vienna in 1683 and receded from Europe only gradually thereafter. Unlike Spain, Austria did not expel its Jews. They were tolerated, along with the other subject peoples annexed in the eighteenth and nineteenth centuries, as long as they remembered their place. By the late nineteenth century, however, the economic ascension of the Jews, plus the national stirrings of the Slavic minorities, led to a growing xenophobia among Austrians. An anti-Semitic party flourished in Austria as it never had in France or Germany. By 1900, one of its leaders, Karl Lueger, was elected mayor of Vienna. But he did not persecute the Jews, since they enjoyed the protection of Emperor Franz-Josef.

When the dual monarchy of Austria-Hungary was broken up in 1918, the Austrians had to endure chronic unemployment and a pervading sense of insecurity. Austrian Catholics were aghast at seeing a Jewish Communist, Béla Kun, briefly assume power in neighbouring Hungary just after the First World War. Even after his overthrow, they continued to feel threatened by Russian Bolshevism. Their only consolation was the fading memory of an imperial past. Hitler's Reich gave them the chance to recapture it, and many became enthusiastic Nazis. Even though Austria accounted for less than a tenth of greater Germany's total population, it was to furnish a fifth of the Nazis who participated directly in the 'Final Solution'—the official euphemism for the mass murder of Europe's Jews.

Another Catholic country which saw itself as a rampart against barbarism was Poland. The siege of Vienna by the Turks was lifted only after the Polish king, John Sobieski, intervened at the head of his army. Over the centuries, the Poles came to think of themselves as the defenders of Catholicism against other invaders from the East, the Russians. As a result of the Allied victory in 1918, Poland was revived as a political entity, but its population was only sixty percent Polish. Germans formed the largest national minority, with over three million inhabitants; others included Ukrainians, White

Russians and Lithuanians. The 3.3 million Jews of Poland had led their separate existence for centuries. After the resurrection of Poland, many Jews, particularly in the larger cities, decided to adopt the Polish language and culture. Their efforts at national integration were viewed with incredulity and even suspicion by most Catholic Poles. Open hostility erupted in 1935, as the Depression, plus the rise of Soviet power under Stalin, caused many Poles to turn against their Jewish neighbours. Jews were accused of taking jobs that rightfully belonged to Polish Catholics and, at the same time, of being in league with the Russian Communists. They were barred from the civil service, the army and nationalized industry, while being subject to a rigorous quota system in the universities. Anti-Jewish violence increased, as the police usually looked the other way. The few Jews who managed to enter university were often set upon by their fellow students. Others were attacked on the streets, in their shops, or on leaving the synagogue. From 30 January 1933, the date of Hitler's accession to power, to 8 November 1938, there were far more acts of physical violence against Jews in Poland than in the Third Reich.

By 1938, the situation in Poland had deteriorated to the point where thousands of Polish Jews sought refuge in—of all places—Germany. The Nazis regularly arrested these unfortunates, packed them into trucks, and shipped them back across the border. Among those expelled was the family of a Jewish youth living in Paris, Herschel Grynszpan. On receiving a letter from his parents describing their ordeal, Grynszpan bought a pistol and headed directly for the German embassy. There, he demanded to see the ambassador on what he termed urgent business. He was ushered into the office of a third secretary, Ernst Vom Rath, who, it was revealed later, was not an anti-Semite. Grynszpan fired several shots at Vom Rath, who died of his wounds in hospital. The 17-year-old assailant was promptly arrested by the French police.

Hitler and the Nazi hierarchy could not possibly have foreseen that an anguished Jewish youth in Paris would some day kill one of their minor diplomats. But Vom Rath's murder was the signal for the SA, the Nazi storm troopers who had been the party's Pretorian guard in its early days, to organize a wholesale pogrom of the Jews still remaining in Germany. The storm troopers had been cast aside and many of their cadres assassinated in July 1934. They were no longer necessary once Hitler had attained power, and their revolutionary slogans frightened the German upper classes. Now, they believed, had come their chance to regain their former status. In the night of 8-9 November 1938, the SA vandalized and looted Jewish shops, set fire to synagogues throughout the country and beat up—often killing—hundreds of individual Jews. The broken glass of the shop windows gave this brutal pogrom its name: *Kristallnacht.*

That the Jews were still allowed to engage in retail trade at this late date shows that they still possessed some economic usefulness. German insurance companies pleaded with the government to stop the violence, since most Jewish merchants were insured against vandalism. An *ex post facto* decree excused the insurers from having to pay any claims to their Jewish clients. Thus vanished the last vestige of civilized behaviour toward the Jews in Nazi Germany. Now even the contracts that they had signed with Gentiles, such as leases and consignments, were worthless. Without the protection afforded by contract, the Jews of Germany could no longer earn a living. Their only hope was to leave while they still had a chance.

The Moment Of Truth

On 30 January 1939, Adolf Hitler made a speech to commemorate the sixth anniversary of his accession to power. It was a long, rambling discourse, the kind dictators like to make, secure in the knowledge that they will not have to face questions from the opposition. After extolling the achievements of his regime, he turned to foreign affairs. The German nation, he maintained, wished to live in peace with Britain, France and the United States, despite the efforts of Jewish and non-Jewish propagandists to push these countries into war with Germany. He defended the expulsion of Jews from the Reich, claiming that it was necessary to free the German people from what he called Jewish cultural domination. Rhetorically, he asked why, in other nations which claim to value the Jews so highly, 'their settlement should be refused with every imaginable excuse'. Then the *Führer* turned prophet, as was his custom. 'If the international Jewish financiers in and outside Europe should succeed in plunging the nations once more into a world war, then the result will not be the Bolshevization of the earth, and thus the victory of Jewry, but the annihilation of the Jewish race in Europe!' The very idea that Jewish financiers were out to spread Bolshevism throughout the world seems to have surprised no one. Hitler's tedious rantings against the Jews were too familiar by then to cause any raised eyebrows.

After the Jews of Europe were nearly annihilated in the Second World War, this particular segment of Hitler's speech was widely quoted to prove that he had already planned the genocide. But if we pause for a moment to explore the nooks and crannies of the dictator's twisted mind, it becomes evident that he initially had no specific plans for the Jews or anyone else. Rather, he relied on intuition, just as he surmised—correctly—that a general war in Europe would eventually pit Nazism against Bolshevism. Yet less than eight months after Hitler made his infamous prophesy, Nazi Germany and the Soviet Union signed a non- aggression pact. Both parties were essentially buying time. Hitler used it to dispose of Poland and, once his generals felt ready, to conquer Western Europe. Only when Germany had fully digested these gains did he turn his attention eastward once again. His talent for improvisation never served him better.

In similar fashion, Hitler took advantage of the opportunities that were offered him to deal with the Jews, as they fell under his control. Great as was his gift for prophesy, he had no way of knowing, in January 1939, just how war would come about or whether Germany would win. The thought of exterminating the Jews had come to him in 1922, as he confided to fellow Nazis: 'When I take power, I shall have rows of gallows built, on the Marianplatz in Munich, for example. Then the Jews will be hanged one after another...until Germany is finally rid of them.' In fact, nothing of the sort took place. On assuming power, Hitler did not have Jews hanged publicly. That would have caused revulsion within Germany and given his regime a bad name abroad. Instead, he opted for expulsion, a policy to which he adhered as long as it had any chance of success. The last country to admit Jewish refugees as a matter of official policy was the Dominican Republic, which began to resettle some 6,000 German Jews early in 1940. After the fall of France in June of that year, Hitler proposed to deport all the Jews in Nazi-occupied Europe to the French island of Madagascar. That this policy was serious is indicated by the shipment of several thousand German Jews to concentration camps in southern France in preparation for their embarcation to the French colony. It was abandoned in the face of a British naval blockade, which grew tighter as the war progressed. The German Jews interned in southern France were eventually sent eastward—to Auschwitz. As the Nazis strengthened their hold on most of continental Europe, random killings of Jews increased. But the policy of mass murder was adopted only after the Soviet Union was invaded. This brought all 3.3 million Jews of Poland, plus over a million more to the east, under Nazi control. There was no longer any other country to send them to. So they were simply exterminated.

Even today, more than fifty years after the event, it still seems impossible to examine dispassionately what Churchill has called the greatest crime in history. Liberal Gentile historians in the West, following the verdict of the Nuremberg trials, mention it in passing to show how evil the Nazis were. A typical Jewish approach is that of Lucy S. Dawidowicz, whose book, *The War Against the Jews*,[2] takes Hitler's phobias and German anti-Semitism as its starting points. The exhibits in most Holocaust memorials similarly begin with Germany, as if hatred of the Jews were somehow limited to that country. Yet if the Germans alone had been responsible for the genocide, Jewish fears would have dissipated following Germany's crushing defeat in 1945. Instead, Jews in general continue to worry about a renewal of anti-Semitism, even though Germany has since lost the capability—and the desire—to wage another world war. In

---

[2]New York: Holt, Rinehart and Winston, 1975.

the absence of any coherent explanation for the genocide, a review is in order as to what made it so unique.

The campaign against the Jews was war at its most total: no effort was spared to ensure their utter destruction. In several instances, they proved useful as slave labour for Germany's war production. Nonetheless, the Nazis preferred to kill them, even though this meant having to divert precious manpower and rolling stock from strictly military operations. By 1944, when it became obvious that Germany was going to lose the war, the roundup of Jews for the death camps actually accelerated. When the Nazis occupied Hungary on 23 March, their first official action was to locate and deport that country's Jewish population. A clue to this remarkable determination in the pursuit of evil can be found in a speech that Himmler made to the SS in October 1943, urging them on to even greater efforts. Not only Jewish men, he said, but also Jewish women and children must be killed, 'so that no Jews will remain to take revenge on our sons and grandsons'. Since then, the Jews have not taken revenge against Germany, for the simple reason that revenge is not part of their value system. But Himmler thought it was. He may have been influenced, as was Hitler,[3] by the traditional Christian interpretation of 'an eye for an eye and a tooth for a tooth'.

As for the *Führer* himself, his principal grievance was not with the British ('democratic idiots', as he called them) or with the Americans. Even the vast military offensive against the Soviet Union was, in Hitler's mind, subordinate to the wider struggle against Bolshevism, which he viewed as merely the latest manifestation of an age-old Jewish conspiracy. The Allied powers, each in its own way, were fighting German expansionism. The German people, after applauding their army's initial victories, found themselves in an increasingly defensive posture, especially as aerial bombardment by the British and Americans intensified. But the Nazi leaders were focused on a moral and cultural struggle against what they regarded as the corrupting influence of world Jewry. Since it

---

[3] See below, pp. 176 and 261.

took precedence over all others, even the Jews' economic usefulness was overlooked.

Judaeophobia had existed in the West for centuries, but not until the Second World War was it allowed to reach its logical conclusion. Previously, European Jews had been protected against popular wrath by the aristocratic rulers, to whom they paid special taxes for such protection. But Hitler was no aristocrat. 'I am the unknown soldier of the last war,' he liked to remind his followers. (To this the great English historian A. J. P. Taylor added sardonically, 'Unfortunately not buried.') The Austrian corporal who became dictator of greater Germany was a common man, with his common prejudices, and lacking the sense of balance and proportion that normally characterized those who had been born to rule. His coming to power was proof that the aristocratic classes of Germany had failed. They had led the German people into war in 1914, confident of a quick, easy victory. After a four-year war of attrition ruined the country, they sued for an armistice dictated by the Allies, leaving the problem of economic recovery and reparations payments to the inexperienced German republicans. When the economy finally collapsed in 1930, they sought to regain power, using Hitler as their tool. Their tactic amounted to a declaration of political and moral bankruptcy.

European Jews, accustomed to dealing with a more traditional sort of political authority, were largely unprepared for the tidal wave that was about to engulf them. Their first reaction was to flee, but where could they go? Armed resistance was effective only in conjunction with other military operations against the Nazis. This was true not only for the Jews but for other underground fighters. The French resistance was primarily an information-gathering agency throughout most of the war. Its members did not begin to fight effectively until the Allies landed in Normandy in June 1944, and then only in the immediate theatre of operations. When the *maquisards*, as they liked to be called, mounted an independent assault against the German army in the Vercors a month later, they were annihilated. For their part, Jews fought ably as members of Soviet partisan groups operating behind the German lines, as long as the Red Army kept them supplied with the necessary munitions.

Independent Jewish revolts against their Nazi oppressors, such as the Warsaw ghetto rising of April-May 1943, showed extraordinary courage, but were inevitably suicidal. In the end, the most effective form of Jewish resistance was subterfuge, in the form of forging identity cards and ration books. This practice was most common in Western Europe and allowed many Jews to survive until the liberation. To succeed, it required the complicity of benevolent Gentiles, who were not often easy to find.

The Nazis made every effort to hide from the Jews what was in store for them. They spoke of resettlement in the East and of forced labour, but never of extermination. The process came about in stages; and at each one, the victims usually cooperated, in the hope that their condition would improve. Identification was the first stage. It was facilitated by the records meticulously kept by Jewish communal organizations throughout Europe. Once the Jews were identified, they were segregated from the rest of society by being ordered to wear a yellow star. Those who opposed assimilation into the Gentile majority welcomed this move; it would, they believed, make Jews conscious of their heritage. When the Jews of Central and Eastern Europe were then ordered out of their homes and into ghettos, many were relieved. They saw the ghetto as protection against the random violence to which they had been increasingly subjected. The penultimate stage of their tragedy was deportation to the East. Here too, most victims went willingly. They were starving and had been promised a loaf of bread each for their journey.

When the Jews of Eastern Europe were crammed into ghettos, the Nazis appointed Jewish councils (*Judenräte*) to govern them and to select candidates for deportation. The role of these councils has been justly condemned by several authors, notably Raul Hilberg, professor of political science at the University of Vermont, whose book *The Destruction of the European Jews*,[4] exposed in great detail the workings of such collaboration. By choosing the victims, the Jewish notables made the Nazis' work that much

---

[4] Revised ed.; New York: Holmes & Meier, 1985.

easier. Could they have done otherwise? Some in fact did. When the Nazis ordered the *Judenrat* of Siauliai to hand over a contingent of Jews, the council members offered themselves instead. At Radom, 4,700 Jews out of a total of 30,000 survived the war—a remarkably high proportion for Poland—because the *Judenrat* found work for them in a local munitions factory. Such examples of heroism and enterprise were, unfortunately, the exception rather than the rule. In most cases, the Jewish leaders in Nazi-occupied Europe allowed themselves to be deluded into collaborating with their oppressors. A centuries-old tradition of respect for established authority was not easy to break. One could always rationalize that by yielding up the aged and the infirm, precious time was gained for the rest. Unable to bribe the Nazis with money or valuables, the Jewish councils attempted to bribe them with people. But the Nazi death machine was too efficient; it kept demanding more victims.

The wartime ghettos were a Nazi creation, a half-way house between prewar Jewish society and the death camps. Within their narrow confines, Jews were forced to live as many as twelve to a room, without adequate food or sanitation facilities. The Jewish leadership, both within the councils and without, did what it could to make their life not only bearable, but meaningful. Schools were established, including a music academy in the Vilna ghetto. Newspapers, literary clubs and even theatre groups helped maintain morale. There were regular religious services and even *matza* for Passover. The Nazis usually tolerated such activities as a means of keeping their victims pacified until the final roundup. The Jewish organizers hoped that by promoting culture, they could give their people something to live for until they were liberated by the Allied armies. Unfortunately for most, the Allies arrived too late. Yet the Jews never gave up hope. Tens of thousands arrived at Auschwitz carrying musical instruments or valuable books in their meagre baggage.

Once the victims were packed into freight cars for their final destination, they could do little to defend themselves. Their apparent passivity has led to the unfair accusation that they went to the gas chambers like sheep to the slaughter. It is perhaps useful in this connection to recall that some two million Soviet prisoners of war died in captivity. These were strong, healthy young men who had been trained to fight. Yet they eventually succumbed to the inhuman treatment inflicted upon them by the Nazis. By the time the Jews arrived at Auschwitz and other death camps, most were already weakened by starvation and disease. Their ultimate act of resistance was to get out news to the rest of the world about what was happening to them. By August 1942, the governments of Britain and the United States were faced with the truth about Hitler's 'Final Solution'.

War Politics As Usual

In 1944, a professor of social work at the University of Buffalo named Uriah Zevi Engelman published a one-volume essay on Jewish history, which has yet to be equalled for its sweep and insight. It was called *The Rise of the Jew in Western Society*,[5] and its thesis was reflected in its title. Jews have improved their position in the West, the author explains, because democracy grants them equal rights under the law. The United States certainly fitted that description. American Jews had equal access to all public services, notably education. During the war, they received the same ration coupons as everyone else and were inducted into the armed forces on an equal basis with Gentiles. They were not segregated while in uniform, as were black conscripts, nor were they herded into internment camps, like Americans of Japanese ancestry. Perhaps most important, they participated fully in the prosperity created by the rapid increase in war production. The Second World War helped promote their economic and social progress.

American Jews held Franklin Delano Roosevelt in great esteem—not so much for what he actually did for them (which was precious little), but for his vision of society. Roosevelt was the first president to popularize the notion that the United States was a nation of immigrants. When this high-born Episcopalian addressed the Daughters of the American Revolution as 'fellow immigrants', he

---

[5] New York: Behrman, 1944.

warmed the hearts of Jews throughout the country. Actually, of course, neither the president nor his elite audience was descended from immigrants. Their ancestors had chosen to live in America not to emulate the native peoples, but to establish their own society, with its particular language, laws and customs. They were not immigrants, but settlers. The president probably knew enough American history to distinguish between the two. But he was not expounding history; he was playing politics. And American Jews loved him for it. Even more than other children of immigrants, they needed to be reassured that they were as American as anyone else because they alone, among all religious or ethnic minorities, had no 'old country' to look back on with nostalgia or pride.

Not all Americans, however, were ready to accept Jews as compatriots. In particular, there was an active Nazi movement in the United States. It was composed of German immigrants, plus native-born Americans who wished to establish a Hitler-type regime in their own country. To counteract Nazi influence at home, the Warner Brothers studio produced a film called *Confessions of a Nazi Spy* in 1939, just as membership in pro-Hitler organizations reached its peak. Based loosely on a minor espionage case tried the previous year, in which several Americans of German ancestry had been found guilty of passing military secrets to the Reich, the film went on to portray a vast Nazi fifth column set to destroy American democracy from within. In one scene, a New York-based Nazi leader, played by Paul Lucas, makes a violent speech to his followers, pledging to destroy the Constitution and the Bill of Rights. In real life, American Nazis would never have thought of openly attacking such quasi-sacred national institutions; they preferred instead to denounce Jewish influence in the United States. Yet nowhere in the film is anti-Semitism even mentioned. Most of those involved in its production were Jews, and they knew that any such allusion would only attract more sympathy for the Nazi cause.

Confessions of a Nazi Spy was a box-office success and nearly caused a diplomatic incident between the United States and Germany. Its effect on American public opinion was far-reaching, extending beyond the Second World War to the Cold War, when the Nazi fifth column was replaced in public discourse by Communist subversives. But it did not make Americans any more hospitable toward the persecuted Jews of Europe. On the contrary, xenophobia in the United States actually increased in 1939 and 1940, as simple-minded people assumed that any European refugee, whether Jewish or Gentile, was a potential spy.

Roosevelt understood popular feeling better than most. He was a canny politician who kept his ear close to the ground. Although this position did not usually allow for a high moral stance, it did enable him to be returned to the White House for an unprecedented third term in 1940. Following *Kristallnacht*, there was an immediate outpouring of sympathy among Americans for Jewish refugees; even Henry Ford proposed that the United States welcome them. But Roosevelt did not budge. 'We have the quota system,' he explained to the press. To express his disapproval of the pogrom, the president had the American ambassador in Berlin recalled. There were no further official protests or gestures of support for Hitler's victims. When war broke out in Europe, the refugee question receded even further in the consciousness of most Americans. As ever more Jews sought to leave Europe, their admission into the United States was effectively blocked. By mid-1940, the State Department adopted a policy of deliberately delaying immigration visas for qualified Jewish applicants. Nazi propaganda was quite adept at portraying a war against Hitler as a war for the Jews. Roosevelt tried very hard, especially after his re-election in 1940, to win support in Congress and among voters generally for the Allied cause. He did not want to give the impression that the Jews would in any way benefit from this policy.

The United States entered the European conflict following Hitler's gratuitous declaration of war on 11 December 1941—four days after Pearl Harbor. Nazi Germany made no surprise attack on American territory, as Japan had done; nor was it in a position to threaten the the U. S. mainland. So ordinary Americans, and in particular those being drafted into military service, could be excused for wondering why their government should give immediate priority to the European theatre of operations. Surely it was not, as the Nazis claimed, because Roosevelt was under the thumb of the Jews. To give American servicemen convincing reason for risking their lives on foreign battlefields, the War Department produced a series of short films entitled, *Why We Fight*. The first episode, *Prelude To War*, won an Oscar for best documentary in 1942. It depicted the Nazis as being the enemies of all religion, not merely of Judaism. The tribulations of German pastor Martin Neimöller, who had been placed under house arrest for opposing the Hitler regime, were given greater prominence than those of the Jews.

In similar fashion, the Hollywood entertainment industry avoided the Jewish question in its fictional war sagas. Typical of these was the 1944 film, *Destination Tokyo*, which is set on board an American submarine in the Pacific. At one point, the sailors begin to talk among themselves about why they enlisted. The most moving reason is given by a young man of Greek origin, played by the Jewish actor, John Garfield. He explains that he joined up because the Nazis had shot his uncle, a university professor in Athens, for his democratic political views. The ordeal of Europe's Jews, which by 1944 had been reported by the American press, was completely overlooked.

Just as war propaganda in the United States sought to avoid any reference to the Jews, so the Nazis made repeated appeals to the Americans' own anti-Semitism in order to dampen their fighting spirit. One particular leaflet, which was dropped repeatedly by the Luftwaffe over American positions in Italy, depicted a fat, ugly man with a hooked nose and protruding ears sitting on a bed next to a voluptuous young woman in her underwear. The accompanying text explained that he had been plying her with furs and jewelry—presumably the only way a Jew can ever seduce a woman. The American troops were warned that while they huddled shivering in muddy foxholes, Jewish war profiteers back home were stealing their wives and girlfriends. Such crude caricature does not seem to have affected the soldiers' morale. The opposing Germans were 'Krauts', and you had to shoot them before they shot you. Even so, military and political planners in Washington had to be careful not to give the impression that the United States was fighting for the Jews.

When Jews in the United States raised the question of the ongoing genocide with their Gentile compatriots, they were usually cut off with the rhetorical question, 'Don't you know there's a war on?' Some nonetheless persisted in bringing the matter to public attention. A rally on the theme 'Stop Hitler Now!' was held in Madison Square Garden in New York on 1 March 1943. It drew 22,000 people, with another 15,000 listening to the proceedings outside through loudspeakers. The principal orators were Jewish leaders, who denounced Roosevelt's inaction in offering help to Hitler's victims. Rabbi Stephen Wise of New York put the matter clearly when he pleaded: 'We are told that the best way to save the Jews is to win the war, but what hope is there that victory will come in time to mean survival of European Jews?' With the 1944 presidential election approaching, Roosevelt momentarily bowed to Jewish pressure and announced a conference of senior American and British officials in Bermuda to discuss what was still called officially 'the refugee question'. In Britain, the House of Commons voted a resolution calling for 'immediate measures on the most generous scale compatible with the requirements of military operations for providing help and temporary asylum for refugees'. The Bermuda Conference took place on 19-29 April 1943. It accomplished nothing beyond proposing to create a refugee camp in French North Africa, and even this very modest proposal was not implemented. The British delegates were especially loath to rescue what one of them termed 'millions of unwanted persons'. Any European Jews saved from Hitler's crematoria might eventually make their way to Palestine, thereby upsetting Britain's Middle East policy.

No public clamour led to the suggestion that the extermination camp at Auschwitz be bombed by American warplanes. The idea had originated early in 1944 with a few Central European rabbis. Their American colleagues entrusted some secular Jewish leaders, such as Nahum Goldmann, with the task of presenting it to the War Department and the British military mission in Washington. They met with an immediate refusal: the proposed target was not a military objective. Beyond this stated reason was the plain fact that American public opinion would never tolerate such an operation. Had a single American bomber been hit on the way to Auschwitz and its crew forced to bail out, anti-Semites in the United States would have been given an easy opportunity to denounce the entire war effort as part of a Jewish plot. Without a broad national consensus, civilian and military morale could suffer. The very nature of American participation in the European conflict precluded taking any military action to save Hitler's chief victims.

As the war drew to a close, the possibilities of saving European Jews increased, just as there were fewer European Jews to save. Political pressure from American Jews led to the creation of the War Refugee Board in January 1944. Funded largely by private (i. e.: Jewish) donations, the Board allowed for the temporary resettlement in areas liberated by the Allies of civilians fleeing Nazi persecution—both Jewish and Gentile. Just where they would find a permanent home was left in abeyance until the war's end. There was little chance that the United States, with its infamous quota system, would take in more than a handful. Canada and Australia pursued an even more restrictive immigration policy, while the Latin American nations felt that they had already done their bit to provide refuge for stateless Jews. The only community in the entire world that was ready to accept them was the *Yishuv*, the Jewish national home in Palestine. But it was not sovereign and therefore had no control over immigration.

The provisions of the British White Paper remained in force throughout the war. Churchill, despite his pro-Zionist views, left the Palestine question to the Foreign Office as he busied himself with military strategy in his underground war room. So the Royal Navy zealously repulsed ships carrying Jewish refugees bound for Palestine, despite the obvious fact that they had nowhere else to go. Neutral Turkey had allowed them passage through its seaports but refused to take them back. Several unseaworthy vessels sank in the eastern Mediterranean after having been turned away by British warships, with the total loss of their human cargo. A few managed to slip through the blockade and landed several thousand clandestine immigrants in Palestine, where they were provided with forged papers by the Zionists. On balance, however, British efforts to exclude Jews from Palestine were successful—so much so that by May 1944, 31,000 places in the White Paper's quota of 75,000 were still unfilled.

The rationale behind enforcing the White Paper was that, without it, a revolt would break out in the entire Arab world. But even as the Royal navy continued to turn back refugee ships, the Arabs remained hostile to Britain throughout the war. The Egyptian government sought closer relations with Fascist Italy and Nazi Germany until the British High Commissioner in Cairo summarily dismissed Egypt's prime minister in 1943. Pro-Axis feeling remained high among the younger army officers, such as Gamal Abdel Nasser and Anouar El Sadat, less out of sympathy for Fascism and Nazism than because they wanted Britain to quit Egypt. The situation was even more tense in Iraq, where a group of army commanders deposed the pro-British government in May 1941 and made overtures to Nazi Germany. Agitation among the Arabs of Palestine broke out in sympathy with the Iraqi coup. Both revolts were quelled by British arms before Hitler could provide military assistance to the insurgents. But the message was clear: the Arabs wanted Britain out of the Middle East, irrespective of the White Paper. In the event, Britain was forced out of its Arab protectorates in the mid-1950's. Whether the restrictions on Jewish immigration to Palestine actually helped the British war effort will forever remain a moot question.

Britain had no difficulty in obtaining American sanction for its Palestine policy. On 11 April 1944, a meeting of senior British and American diplomats was held at the Foreign Office in London to elaborate a common policy on the Middle East. In the chair was Sir Maurice Peterson, Undersecretary of State for Foreign Affairs, who expressed his government's concern over 'Zionist agitation in the United States and the desirability that this be kept in hand during the war'. The Foreign Office, like many subsequent British historians, labeled a Zionist anyone who sought to rescue the persecuted Jews of Europe. But instead of discrediting Zionism as they so obviously intended to do, the architects of British Middle East policy succeeded in making it acceptable to Jews at large, even those who felt quite at home in Western society. By 1944, most American Jews were convinced that only a sovereign Jewish state could offer permanent refuge to Hitler's chief victims. Thus did Zionism, which had been a minority current in Judaism until the Second World War, enter its mainstream. The American diplomats present at the meeting heartily concurred with their British colleagues. Wallace Murray, director of the State Department's Near East division, recalled that his country's military leaders had persuaded Congress to delay the passage of pro-Zionist resolutions until the war's end. Foiled in Congress, American Jewish leaders prodded Roosevelt, who was facing yet another presidential election in November 1944. He obliged them in March with a public statement expressing the hope that the doors of Palestine be opened to 'hundreds of thousands of homeless Jewish refugees'. Later that year, he allowed somewhat reluctantly that, yes, he did support the plank in his party's platform that favoured unlimited Jewish immigration into Palestine. The president knew that he would have to deal with this issue until after the war. Perhaps luckily for him, he died before it came up again.

What Did It All Mean?

When British soldiers liberated the Belsen concentration camp in the spring of 1945, they were appalled at what they saw: piles of decaying corpses lying outside and a few thousand emaciated survivors agonizing in the filthy barracks. BBC reporter Richard Dimbleby, who was accompanying the troops, blurted into his microphone: 'Now I know why we went to war in 1939!' This curious telescoping of events indicates that he did not know in 1939 why Britain went to war. It also implies that the Allies were fighting for justice and morality. The Nuremberg war crimes trials in 1946 pursued the moral argument still further. They were designed in part to avoid a repetition of the strident dispute in the 1920's as to which side had been responsible for the First World War. This time there would be no doubt: Germany alone stood acccused of having planned and executed the carnage of 1939-1945. To drive home the issue of Nazi guilt, the prosecution compiled mountains of evidence on the mass murder of European Jews, estimating the total number of dead at 5.7 million. Here was conclusive proof that the Hitler regime was absolutely evil, and that the victorious Allies had been justified in demanding its unconditional surrender. The

Nuremberg trials ended debate on the Nazi genocide before it could even begin.

Throughout the newly liberated countries of Western Europe, popular revulsion at the recent reign of right-wing terror led initially to a Christian revival. It was especially active in France, where hundreds of idealistic young men rushed to join the priesthood in the early postwar years. They were disillusioned not only with Fascism, but with the democracies' feeble response to it. To the extent that Christian thinkers faced the problem of Auschwitz, they concluded that it was simply one more manifestation of man's evil nature. Christians must therefore redouble their efforts to save humanity from original sin. In Germany, the British, French and American armies of occupation encouraged religious activities as a means of filling the moral void left by the Hitler regime. With American support, Christian Democratic parties were founded in Germany and Italy in order to counter another movement that had benefited from the Axis defeat: Communism.

Amid the harmonious expressions of belief that Christianity was the antidote to totalitarian ideology came a discordant note, which at first was barely audible. It was sounded by the French historian Jules Isaac, whose wife and daughter had been killed by the Nazis. He had been saved by the priest and pastor of a provincial town, who had taken turns hiding him in their respective churches during the war. To pass the time, Isaac read all the books in his hosts' libraries. He was a secular Jew who had been a senior official in the French ministry of education before the war. As such, he was hardly prepared for what he discovered in the devotional texts written by both Catholic and Protestant theologians: an outpouring of abuse against the Jews and Judaism. What upset him most was the accusation of deicide. A careful reading of the Gospels convinced him that only a small fraction of the Jewish religious leaders had a hand in Jesus's death, which in any case had been decreed by the Romans. He published these findings in 1946 in a book entitled *Jésus et Israël*. (Israel in this case referred to the Jewish people, not the state.)

Immediately after its publication, Isaac's book created a controversy in French intellectual circles. The author found himself engaged in a running debate with Catholics, who denied that there was any causal connection between Christian teachings and anti-Semitism. He answered them in 1951 with a new, well-documented study entitled *Genèse de l'antisémitisme* ('The Birth of Anti-Semitism'), which described the hostility of the early church toward the Jews. It was based largely on the works of two Protestant authors: James Parkes, an Anglican minister, whose book, *The Conflict of the Church and the Synagogue*, had appeared before the war, and the *Verus Israel* of Marcel Simon. Isaac appealed to Christians to abandon their anti-Jewish clichés and to accept Judaism as a legitimate faith. His writings made a positive impression on Pope John XXIII, who managed to have some of the more hostile references to Jews deleted from the Catholic liturgy.

Jules Isaac's solitary campaign to eliminate the more egregious anti-Jewish elements in Christian teaching aroused little interest among Jews generally, and barely touched those who could not read French. In the immediate postwar period, their attention was focused on getting on with everyday life after the recent trauma, on choosing sides in the nascent Cold War (a heart-wrenching decision for those who still believed in socialism), and on supporting the Zionist efforts to create a Jewish state in Palestine. Few were interested in a dialogue with Christianity, which from past experience promised to be a monologue, with Christians trying to convert the Jews. Eliminating religious hostility toward Jews and Judaism seemed to be at best a long-term approach. It would not bring the millions of murdered European Jews back to life, nor would it help the survivors in their daily relations with non-Jewish society.

To the extent that Jews in America and Europe had one common concern, it was not Christianity, but the new State of Israel and its precarious position in the world. Over the years, this concern led back to the Nazi genocide. The first memorial to Hitler's Jewish victims, *Yad Vashem*, was created in Israel, just outside Jerusalem. In the Diaspora, Jewish campaigners for Israel increasingly referred to the genocide in their fund-raising efforts. Do not give Hitler a posthumous victory, they would say, through indifference to the only country in the world which will always accept Jewish refugees.

The Six-day War of June 1967, served to fuse in Jewish consciousness the Nazi massacres and the fate of Israel. For the first forty-eight hours of the fighting, there was a total blackout on news from the front. Israel had been at war previously, the latest conflict being the Sinai campaign of 1956. On that occasion, the Jewish state had sided with Britain and France against a common enemy: Egypt. This time Israel was alone, having to fight at least two countries, Egypt and Syria, and possibly even a third, Jordan. Given the confidence shown by the Arabs, some of whom vowed to throw the Jews into the sea, it seemed to many as though a new Jewish tragedy might be in the offing. After the blackout was lifted and Israel emerged victorious on all three fronts, the French philosopher and political analyst Raymond Aron, himself the very personification of a culturally assimilated Jew, explained why emotions in the Diaspora had run so high. 'The victory was Israeli; the defeat would have been Jewish.'

As a direct result of the Six-day War, a new term entered the Jewish vocabulary: Holocaust, with a capital H. The first use of this expression in connection with the Nazi genocide had appeared in 1943, as Polish Catholics watched from afar the destruction of the Warsaw ghetto. It was revived by some Jewish writers in 1957, but did not gain currency for another ten years. Previously, the accepted terms had been genocide or mass murder. These had been used by the Nuremberg tribunal and the United Nations. But there have been other genocides and mass murders in the twentieth century. The massacre of 1.5 million Armenians by the Turks during and immediately after the First World War was the earliest. Some five million Kulaks were starved to death by Stalin in his drive to collectivize Soviet agriculture in the 1930's. More recently, the Khmers Rouges massacred two million Cambodians whom they suspected of preferring the old regime. The Jews were looking for a name that would set their tragedy apart from the others. Unfortunately, they made a poor choice of words. A holocaust, in its original Biblical sense, is a burnt-offering, a sacrifice made to atone for one's sins. Ever since the Pharisees assumed undisputed religious authority after the destruction of the second Temple, there have been no holocausts in Judaism.

The religious connotation makes the use of the word Holocaust especially disturbing. That a just and merciful God should desire the sacrifice of six million peace-loving people, including a million children who could not yet distinguish right from wrong, is morally unacceptable. Yet there are many Jews today, most of them militants of the far Right, who see the tragedy as some kind of divinely ordained punishment. The Jews of Europe had strayed from the Torah by shaving their beards, by violating the dietary code, by profaning the Sabbath and by trying in other ways to imitate Gentiles. The genocide was their reward. This belief finds its most perfect expression in the outburst of a Hasidic rabbi, who, accompanied by a few disciples, stormed into a discothèque in west Jerusalem one Friday evening and shouted at the women (but not the men) present: 'Whores! Whores! It is because of you that there was a Holocaust.'

Even those who reject divine will as an explanation for the tragedy claim to see a causal connection between the fact that Hitler took power in Germany and that German Jews were the most thoroughly integrated of any Western society. The assimilated Jews were the first to suffer, so goes this reasoning; therefore assimilation was to blame. Jews are warned not to assimilate lest a similar tragedy befall them. But a closer look at the facts reveals this argument to be totally specious. As it happened, a slim majority of German Jews managed to survive by emigrating, while 90 percent of Polish Jews perished. Not all Jews in Poland were religious, but only a few were as integrated into Gentile society as were their coreligionists to the west. So one could plausibly argue that the unassimilated Jews suffered the most.

Taking this analysis a step further leads to the conclusion—unpalatable, but unavoidable—that the Jews of Europe could have all been saved from the gas chambers had their grandparents been baptized. In their assiduous quest for Jews, the Nazis went back only two generations because they could go no further. Even today, as the average life expectancy continues to increase, hardly anyone knows who his great-grandparents were. Seen in this light, the problem is not that so many Jews were assimilated, but that their assimilation was incomplete. Obviously, no believing Jew can accept such an argument, since it makes a mockery of all Jewish existence since the time of Abraham. Yet it is no less logical than the widely accepted view that the root cause of the tragedy was assimilation.

To delve into the meaning of the Nazi genocide, we must bear in mind that it was done **to** the Jews, and not **by** them. Rather than studying the victims of this crime, we should examine its authors. Who were the assassins, and what possessed them to act as they did? Let us begin with Hitler. He was born to Catholic parents (his mother was especially devout) and grew up in a Catholic environment. At the local primary school, he received religious instruction as part of the regular curriculum. The Catholics and anti-Semites in the Austrian parliament had succeeded in restoring Catholic education to public schools in February 1894, when Hitler was five years old and about to enter first grade. Throughout his adult life, he was registered as a Catholic for tax purposes, even after becoming chancellor of Germany. In 1941 he told General Gerhard Engel, 'I am still a Catholic and will always remain so.' Hitler decreed that German schoolchildren recite a prayer at the beginning of each school day. He was never excommunicated.

Hitler's vision of the Jews was derived directly from Christianity. As Nazi party leader, he made a speech in Munich on 12 April 1922 (published in the *Völkischer Beobachter* on 22 April 1922) in which he defended Jesus as the greatest enemy of the Jews. 'My feeling as a Christian points me to my Lord and Saviour as a fighter.' Hitler recalled that 'as a Christian and as a man, I read the passage which relates how the Lord finally gathered His strength and made use of the whip to drive the usurers, the vipers, and cheats from the temple. Today, 2,000 years later, I recognize with deep emotion Christ's tremendous fight for this world against the Jewish poison.' Roman civilization, he added, 'was driven to destruction by the Jewish people.' And now that the German nation has taken its place, the Jews want to destroy Germany as well. But he, Adolf Hitler, will oppose them, just as Jesus did. 'As a Christian, I owe something to my own people.' He advised his followers to attend the Oberammergau Passion play in order to understand the Jews' evil nature. This speech and the subsequent article, entitled

'In Behalf of Christ', can be found in English translation in a collection of speeches edited by Gordon Prange under the title, *Hitler's Words*.[6] They are replete with allusions to God and to divine providence. Hitler's Christian bias is also evident in his speech of 30 January 1939, in which he referred to the 'Old Testament vengeance' of the Jews. 'I believe that I am acting in the sense of the Almighty Creator,' he explained. 'By repelling the Jews, I am fighting for the Lord's work.'

Not only Hitler, but Nazi ideology as a whole was inspired by Christianity. The connection between the two is explained by Claus-Ekkehard Bärsch, a German professor of political theory, in his masterful study of Joseph Goebbels entitled, *Erlösung und Vernichtung* ('Salvation and Extermination').[7] The Nazis simply took the Apocalypse of the New Testament and applied it to their own times, with the Jew in the role of Satan. This is not to say that the Nazis were devoutly religious, but simply to note that their inspiration came from Christian tradition. All were raised in Christian families and were given a Christian education. Adolf Eichmann's father was a Protestant minister; Rudolph Hoess, the commandant of Auschwitz, had enrolled in a Catholic seminary as a youth in the hope of becoming a priest. Not all Christians became Nazis—far from it; but without Christianity, Nazism would have been unthinkable.

Much has been written about the responsibility of the Catholic church, and especially that of Pope Pius XII, in the genocide. This issue was first raised by Roosevelt, who in 1943 tried to get the Vatican to condemn anti-Jewish atrocities publicly. The Pope, sensing that the American president wished to use him for propaganda purposes, remained silent. Yet it is not so much Pius XII who merits reproach, as the age-old tradition that led to his election. When the College of Cardinals met, early in March 1939, to choose a successor to Pius XI, its members were well aware that the late Pontiff's open criticisms of the Hitler regime had caused serious

---

[6]Washington: American Council on Public Affairs, 1944.

[7]Munich: Boer, 1987.

difficulties for the church in Germany. So the prelates played it safe and chose Eugenio Pacelli, who had been Papal nuncio to Berlin and was said to be on good terms with Hitler. In so doing, they renewed the church's established practice of courting secular power.

'The powers that be are of God,' wrote the apostle Paul. The election of Pacelli as Pope indicated that the powers that be included Hitler, who was then the most powerful figure on earth. He used that power to murder millions of innocents, without any serious opposition. A few individual Christians did what they could to save Jews from the slaughter. Most simply acquiesced, including the clergy, high and low. The leaders of Vichy France enacted anti-Jewish legislation without any prompting from Berlin. By excluding Jews from French civil society, they made the Nazis' work that much easier. Racial purity was not their aim; they sought to preserve their Christian heritage, as they saw it. So did other Europeans who delivered their Jewish compatriots to the Nazis. The Western democracies, which refused to accept more than a token contingent of Jewish refugees, similarly expressed Christian-inspired prejudice against them. Such pervasive hostility, transcending state boundaries and even oceans, illustrates the essential meaning of the genocide: in Hitler's reign, Christianity was weighed in the balance and found wanting.

Chapter IX

PICKING UP THE PIECES

IN THE NAZI DEATH CAMPS, more was lost than human lives. The German-Jewish synthesis, which had fostered the development of Judaism within a dynamic and relatively open society, failed to survive the onslaught of right-wing populism. The aristocratic order on which the Jews formerly relied for protection had collapsed, and the civil rights granted to them in the nineteenth century proved to be revocable by an unscrupulous tyrant. Those who had hoped that emancipation would establish a new *modus vivendi* were cruelly disappointed. Others, such as the Hasidim, who had chosen to withdraw from society, fared no better. All were faced with the consequences of their own minority status and lack of power. Into the void left by the destruction of established Jewish society in Central and Eastern Europe came Zionism. Alone among the various Jewish factions that had survived the disaster, the Zionists had a programme, one that could be enacted without delay.

During the war, the Zionist leaders recognized that they could no longer rely on Britain to help further their goal of a sovereign Jewish state in Palestine. David Ben Gurion had told his followers to fight the war as if there were no White Paper and the White Paper as if there were no war. With Germany defeated, the Zionists could turn their attention fully to the White Paper. The Arabs, on the other hand, lost much of their political leverage: any possibility that they might join the Axis vanished along with the Axis itself. As for Britain, its status emerged from the war somewhat diminished; it was no longer the indispensable ally of the United States on all occasions.

Further altering the power relationship was the new American president, who was less Anglophile than his predecessor. Harry S Truman had already made public his opposition to the White Paper, in a brief address to the Senate on 19 May 1939: 'The British government has used its diplomatic umbrella again, this time on

Palestine. It has made a scrap of paper out of Lord Balfour's promise to the Jews.' Truman then read into the record an article which had appeared in the *Washington Post* the previous day, comparing Britain's Palestine policy to its appeasement of Hitler at Munich. No pressure from some obscure Jewish lobby had prompted the senator from Missouri to take this stand, which in any case had no immediate political effect. He was simply expressing his own views on the subject.

Over the years, a myth has circulated to the effect that the West allowed a Jewish state to be created in order to salve its conscience for having done so little to save the Jews of Europe. This moralistic view of history hardly befits Truman, whose conscience was clear on the Jewish question, as on all others. It might have applied to Roosevelt, had he survived the war. Shortly after the Yalta conference in February 1945, the ailing president received Ibn Saud, king of Saudi Arabia, on board an American warship lying at anchor in the Nile. Turning on his legendary charm, Roosevelt asked his royal guest for suggestions on how to deal with the Jewish remnant of Hitler's former empire. Ibn Saud answered directly: 'Give them and their descendants the choicest lands and homes of the Germans who had oppressed them.' When Roosevelt objected that the Jews would prefer Palestine to the country which had persecuted them, the king grew more insistent. 'Make the enemy and the oppressor pay; that is how we Arabs wage war. Amends should be made by the criminal, not by the innocent bystander. What injury have Arabs done to the Jews of Europe? It is the "Christian" Germans who stole their homes and lives. Let the Germans pay.'

Roosevelt did not press the point, but he knew instinctively that the Palestine question would be put to the world by the Jewish survivors of Nazism. Had there been no survivors, had the Nazis completed their grizzly task of exterminating all the Jews of Europe, the subject of Jewish immigration to Palestine might not have been raised. But such was the speed of the Allied advance in the final months of the war that those who were next in line for the gas chambers won a stay of execution. They, along with other victims of Nazi persecution, became known as 'Displaced Persons', or

DP's, in the bureaucratic jargon of the time. Having lost their homes and families, they had nowhere to go and continued to vegetate in the very same camps into which the Nazis had herded them. Truman, whose personal motto was 'The Buck Stops Here', did not evade responsibility on this issue. On 22 June 1945, he commissioned Earl G. Harrison, the American delegate to the Intergovernmental Committee on Refugees, to report to him on the conditions in the camps and to propose ways of alleviating the misery of the DP's. In itself, this was a humanitarian gesture. What followed, however, involved Britain and had the effect of a political bombshell.

On 24 June 1945, just two days after having given Harrison his assignment, Truman wrote to Churchill, asking that Britain lift its restrictions on Jewish immigration to Palestine. After Churchill was replaced as prime minister by Labour Party leader Clement Attlee, Truman repeated his request on 31 August, calling specifically for the immediate admission of 100,000 Jewish DP's to what was still a British mandate. At that time, the number of Jews actually in the camps was closer to 50,000. More were to arrive, as they came out of hiding or exile; but Truman's figure was then clearly exaggerated. It had been supplied by the Jewish Agency, and the president simply accepted it without further verification. Just why he should have followed the Zionist lead on this matter is still a mystery. With Congressional elections more than a year away, the Jewish vote in the United States could not have been a factor. The most logical explanation is Truman's own deep-seated opposition to the White Paper. Admitting 100,000—or even 50,000—Jews to Palestine would effectively undermine it.

The coming to power of the Labour Party in July 1945 gave comfort to Zionists in Britain and throughout the world. Labour had consistently opposed the White Paper and, at its latest annual meeting in May of that year, had reiterated its support for a Jewish national home in Palestine. As party leader, Clement Attlee was associated with this position. Privately, however, he had serious reservations about Zionism and often told his closest confidants that, in his view, 'the Jews are a religion, not a race or a nation'. This is a curious statement, coming as it did from the leader of a party whose Jewish members, from the theorist Harold Laski to the humblest voter in London's East End, were for the most part non-observant and even atheistic. Actually, the Jews are neither just a religion nor just a nation, but something in between: a historical community loosely held together by a common strand of memory. Like most other people, they do not enjoy being defined by strangers; and this is one reason why so many Jews who have no desire to emigrate to Israel have, at one time or another, supported the Zionist cause. Attlee's perception of the Jews was, from a left-liberal point of view, rather flattering—as if they somehow transcended ordinary social or ethnic categories. It is shared even today by many well-meaning people who find the concepts of nationality and race too confining to express the human condition in all its fullness.

But it is not policy. The fact that Christians are a religion has not prevented them from founding over fifty states—some more religious than others—where Sunday is the official day of rest and Christmas a national holiday. Similarly, Muslims—also a religion—constitute a sovereign majority in some thirty states. The Jews worldwide are not, by generally accepted standards, a nation; but the Jews of the *Yishuv* most certainly were. This is why neither Attlee, nor George Antonius nor Ibn Saud could resolve the question of Palestine. They could oppose further Jewish immigration to the mandated territory, but they could not find a proper place for the Jews who were already there. The Palestinian Jews were not interested in becoming another ethnic minority in an Arab state; they already possessed all the attributes of a nation, save one: political sovereignty. The *Yishuv* had its own schools and hospitals, its own political factions and, in a somewhat rudimentary form, its own army. Above all, its members shared what is known in French as *le vouloir-vivre collectif*—the desire to live together as one people. Preoccupied as they were with Arab nationalism, the British tragically underestimated that of the Palestinian Jews.

Compounding Britain's difficulties was the fact that nearly all the Jewish DP's in Europe wished to join the *Yishuv*. The Harrison report, which Truman received late in August 1945, described in stark detail their living conditions, which were hardly better than under the Nazis. In the Bergen-Belsen camp alone, some 23,000 inmates (90 percent of them Jewish) had died since the liberation. The others had to survive largely on a diet of black bread which provided only 1,200 calories a day. Lack of proper clothing left some with no choice but to don the uniforms of their former captors. 'For reasons that are obvious and need not be laboured,' Harrison wrote, 'most Jews want to leave Germany and Austria as soon as possible.' Very few wished to return to their countries of origin, and then only to look for surviving relatives. 'The life which they have led for the past ten years, a life of fear and wandering and physical torture, has made them impatient of delay. They want to be evacuated to Palestine now, just as other national groups are being repatriated to their homes.' Truman concurred. In his letter to Attlee, he pressed for 'the quick evacuation of as many as possible of the non-repatriable Jews, who wish it, to Palestine'.

In his reply to Truman's letter, Attlee objected to placing the Jews 'in a special racial category at the head of the queue'. This, he claimed, would be 'disastrous for the Jews' by appearing to favour them among the many groups of Displaced Persons. Harrison had already anticipated this argument. 'Refusal to recognize the Jews as such,' he wrote, 'has the effect, in this situation, of closing one's eyes to their former and more barbaric persecution, which has already made them a separate group with greater needs.' In other words, the Jews were already at the head of the queue. Hitler had put them there. To alleviate their misery, Attlee suggested transferring some 35,000 to refugee camps in North Africa, but not to allow into Palestine more than 1,500 a month from the unused quota of the White Paper. For Ernest Bevin, the former trade union leader whom Attlee had chosen as Foreign Secretary, the problem was simple. If the Americans sought to put 100,000 Jews into Palestine, he told a Labour Party meeting in June 1946, it was 'because they did not want too many of them in New York'.

Bevin's jibe touched a raw nerve, angering many Americans, both Jewish and Gentile. But it contained a powerful element of truth. Truman reacted to the speech by trying to persuade Congressional leaders to permit the entry of 50,000 Jewish DP's into the United States. He ran into a wall of opposition. The American legislators, many of whom were on record as supporting the establishment of a Jewish state in Palestine, knew their constituents' feelings far too well to risk defeat at the polls by allowing a throng of destitute Jews to enter their own country. Anti-Semitism was still a political force in the great American republic, where the needs of returning war veterans received far greater consideration than those of former concentration camp inmates. What Bevin apparently did not understand was that his argument reinforced the Zionist contention that Jews needed a home in Palestine because they were not welcome anywhere else.

The Zionist Campaign

Meanwhile, the problem of the Displaced Persons grew steadily worse, as more stateless Jews gravitated to the camps. Bevin was convinced that the solution lay in their integration within Europe. Any hopes for an accommodation of this kind were dashed in the spring of 1946, when some 120,000 Polish Jews who had found refuge in the Soviet Union during the war returned to Poland. They were greeted with a pogrom, whose authors feared that the returning exiles had come to spread Communism. Polish Communists did nothing to prevent this outrage, hoping thereby to discredit their rightist adversaries. Several hundred Jews perished; the rest fled to Germany, mainly to the American zone of occupation, where the DP camps were already bursting at the seams. Within a year after the war's end in Europe, the number of Jewish DP's reached 250,000. Overcrowding, short rations and daily taunts from the surrounding German population drove them to despair. They would surely have ridiculed Bevin's suggestion that they become better integrated as a minority in Europe. They were tired of being a minority. They wanted out; and for nearly all of them, out meant Palestine.

The Jewish Agency was quick to help. It organized the refugees' clandestine passage out of Germany and Austria to Trieste and other Adriatic ports. From there, a motley fleet of recently-acquired vessels, most of which were fit only for coastal transport, carried them toward Palestine. Toward, rather than to, for the Royal

Navy lay waiting and intercepted most of the refugee ships once they entered the three-mile limit. From May 1945 to May 1948, nearly 70,000 Jews were thus smuggled out of Europe. The British caught 51,500 and interned them in Cyprus. The rest managed to join the *Yishuv* as illegal immigrants. Inasmuch as they were under the constant threat of deportation, those who were in decent physical condition (they had to be reasonably fit in order to make the trip under such arduous conditions) were naturally drawn to Jewish underground organizations.

It had been an axiom of British policy that the Jews of Palestine would never revolt. Only the Arabs had to be mollified. In a report to Attlee dated 10 July 1946, the British chiefs of staff warned of a 'general Arab rising, more serious and more widespread than in 1936' if more Jews were allowed in. But it was from the Jewish side that the trouble came. Attacks by the *Hagana* on British military installations usually inflicted only property damage. Those by the paramilitary *Irgun*, led by a former soldier in the Polish army named Menachem Begin, were often directed at British personnel. Its operatives wore many disguises and easily found shelter among the Jewish inhabitants. British attempts to weed them out and discover their secret stores of arms were generally inept. Worse, the repeated searches and identity checks so harassed the Jewish masses that they became increasingly sympathetic to the terrorists. It was the Irish experience all over again. In the escalating spiral of violence and repression, Britain's hold on Palestine steadily weakened.

On 22 July 1946, the *Irgun* struck its most telling blow against British authority in Palestine. A team of its agents slipped into Jerusalem's King David Hotel by the service entrance and, after subduing the guards inside, left seven milk cans containing high explosives near the offices of the Mandatory secretariat and military headquarters. The *Irgun* later claimed that it had warned the British a half hour earlier by telephone to clear the building; but if such a warning was in fact given, it was not heeded. Some eighty employees of the secretariat—British, Arab and Jewish—were killed and about seventy others seriously wounded. The official Zionist leadership disavowed the action. Truman was outraged and confided to Secretary of State James F. Byrnes that such terrorism could only delay a solution to the Palestine problem. In Palestine itself, the British military commander, Lieutenant-general Evelyn Barker, issued a written order to his troops to avoid all social and business dealings with the Jewish population. Such measures, he explained, 'will be punishing the Jews in a way the race dislikes as much as any, by striking at their pockets and showing our contempt for them'.

Dastardly though it was, the King David raid achieved its purpose, which was to make the British tire of administering Palestine. Barker's intemperate language is ample evidence of their growing weariness and sense of frustration. In the Arab world, Britain's stock fell sharply. The Arabs reasoned that if the Jews could blow up the mandatory's headquarters with such apparent ease, then perhaps Britain was no longer in control of the situation. More important was the reaction in Britain itself. In a parliamentary debate held on 31 July and 1 August 1946, Churchill rose to ask whether, by spending so much money and effort on Palestine, the government was not weakening the British Empire as a whole. On 23 October, he proposed that Britain 'lay our Mandate at the feet of the United Nations Organization'.

The prime minister was naturally reluctant to follow Churchill's advice. He did not want to give up the mandate, but American, Arab and Zionist pressure was making it increasingly untenable. Finally, at a cabinet meeting on 14 February 1947, it was decided to invite the United Nations to make a preparatory study of the Palestine question, so that it could be discussed at the session of the General Assembly scheduled for September. Technically, Britain was not abandoning the mandate, but merely consulting the world body as to how it could best be carried out. Placing the Palestine question before the General Assembly was bound to reinforce Britain's position—or so the Foreign Office believed. Even if the United States managed to get most European and Latin Americans countries to favour dividing Palestine into a Jewish and an Arab state, so went the argument, the Soviet Union would never go along. Opposition by the Soviet bloc, plus the Arab and other Muslim countries, would prevent any partition scheme from obtaining the necessary two-thirds majority. The United Nations would then turn to Britain for leadership in this field just as its predecessor, the League of Nations, had done. The tactic seemed flawless.

In answer to Britain's request, the General Assembly of the United Nations met in special session on 28 April 1947 to set up an *ad hoc* committee on Palestine. The Arab delegates immediately introduced a resolution calling for termination of the mandate and a declaration of Palestinian independence, but it was defeated by 24 votes to 15, with 10 abstentions. So far Britain seemed to be having its way. Then came a most unpleasant surprise for the Foreign Office. The Soviet Union, which had repeatedly condemned Zionism as a form of petty bourgeois nationalism and had long sought to curry favour with the Arabs, suddenly changed its stance. On 14 May 1947, Andrei Gromyko, head of the Soviet delegation, announced to the General Assembly that his country might support partition. The Zionist case was not without merit, he said, recalling that during the recent European war, no Western European country had been able to protect its Jewish population. This, he reasoned, 'explains the aspiration of the Jews for the creation of a state of their own'. The Soviet Union would prefer a bi-national Palestinian state in principle; but if such a configuration proved to be impossible in light of deteriorating relations between Arabs and Jews, then two separate states, with adequate guarantees for the minority in each, might be the only solution. The definitive Soviet position would not be made known until the committee presented its report. It was clear, in any case, that the Kremlin could no longer be counted on to oppose partition as a matter of course.

Further contributing to Britain's discomfiture was the work of the United Nations Special Committee on Palestine, or UNSCOP for short. From the outset, Arab intransigence tilted its members in favour of partition. Unable to hear from the Palestinian Arabs, who boycotted its proceedings, the Committee met with various political leaders of existing Arab states. Their collective position on the ethnic composition of a united Palestine was presented by the foreign minister of Lebanon, who said that all Jews who had entered the country since the Balfour Declaration would be considered illegal immigrants. This meant that the vast majority of Palestinian Jews, including many who were native born, could be deported at the whim of an Arab government.

What emerged from the hearings was that there were too many Jews for the Arab position to be accepted—too many to be treated as a protected minority in an Arab Palestine, and too many straining to get in. The Zionists made certain that the members of UNSCOP regarded the two groups of Jews as aspects of a single problem. They invited the Committee to visit the DP camps and learn firsthand where the inmates wanted to go. Then an aging Chesapeake Bay ferry, originally known as the *President Warfield* and renamed *Exodus 1947*, was loaded with refugees and bound for Palestine in June. It was a skillful bit of staging, but the people on board were not actors; they genuinely wanted to settle in that turbulent country. The mandatory power acted true to form. Before the rusting vessel could dock at Haifa, it was boarded by British troops, who used force to evacuate its 4,500 passengers. Three Jews died in the scuffle; another two hundred were wounded. The rest were loaded onto another ship for transport to Hamburg. As the Cyprus internment camps were already filled to capacity, they were sent to DP camps in the British zone of Germany.

The drama did not end there. When the ship carrying the survivors of the *Exodus* tied up at the small harbour of Port-de-Bouc, near Marseilles, for refueling, the French government offered them asylum in France. Only a handful accepted; the others remained in their hot, cramped quarters and insisted on being taken to Palestine. This was national self-determination writ large, and the members of UNSCOP could not fail to be impressed. The Zionists had won a moral victory, which was soon to be translated into a political one: having bungled the *Exodus* affair, Britain could no longer transfer DP's to Germany. And more refugee ships were on their way to Palestine.

By then it was obvious that the mandate had outlived its usefulness. A consensus developed within UNSCOP that the Jews had as much right to a Palestinian state as the Arabs. So a partition plan was devised late in August 1947. It gave the coastal plain and most of the Negev to the Jews, while the Arabs retained Judaea and Samaria, plus most of Galilee. International corridors were to join the two states, with Jerusalem under United Nations control. This was an awkward solution, but the Zionists accepted it after some discussion. All Arab countries rejected partition, as did Britain. The Attlee government was well aware that the British protectorate in Egypt would soon be called into question. It saw Palestine as a fall-back position. An independent Arab state would require British help, just as Transjordan did, to create a proper economic infrastructure and an army. In return, it could be counted upon to lease military bases to Britain. So the Foreign Office worked for rejection of the partition plan in the General Assembly. It was caught short, however, by events within Palestine.

Israel Creates Itself

Before the United Nations General Assembly could reconvene in November 1947 to deliberate on the UNSCOP report, the ongoing battle between Jewish insurgents and the mandatory power in Palestine had already reached its bloody climax. In July, three members of the *Irgun* were hanged for having raided the Acre prison and freed over two hundred inmates, including some Arabs. The *Irgun* retaliated the following day by killing two British sergeants whom it was holding hostage. This 'execution' shocked decent people everywhere, not least within the Zionist movement itself. The normally placid *Economist* of London echoed public sentiment when it asked plaintively: 'Why should British soldiers continue to be exposed to this kind of killing? Why should the British community bear the cost?' Taking its cue from the general disenchantment, the Attlee government announced, late in September, its intention to withdraw British troops and civil administration from Palestine, just as had recently been done in India. This was intended to be a strategic pullback rather than total retreat. Britain still hoped to retain influence—and more importantly, military bases—in Palestine.

The resulting vacuum was filled only partially by the United Nations. The delegates from 58 countries, assembled in a converted skating rink that bore the somewhat facetious name of Lake

Success, were deeply divided over the Palestine question. Thanks to American and Soviet support, the UNSCOP resolution favouring partition could count on a slim majority. Britain remained officially neutral, while the Arab and Muslim states strongly opposed it. They drew into their camp two clients of the United States: Greece and Cuba. As several other states were undecided, a two-thirds majority necessary to carry the resolution was initially far from assured.

To obtain it, American Jews put pressure on some of the smaller countries. They deluged the Firestone Tire and Rubber Company with letters threatening to boycott its products unless Liberia, where Firestone had extensive plantations, voted for partition. A telephone call from Harvey Firestone, the company's CEO, to the president of Liberia brought that country into line. Similar pressure was exerted by Adolf Berle and other influential American Jews on Haiti. France, on the other hand, was a major power and therefore less tractable. The head of the French delegation to the United Nations, Alexandre Parodi, feared that his country's remaining interests in the Middle East could be at risk if he voted for partition. He did not take kindly to a hint by New York financier and longtime presidential advisor, Bernard Baruch, that France might lose American economic aid if it did not support the resolution. Only a last-minute telephone call from Weizmann to former French premier Léon Blum managed to swing France's vote. Neither Baruch nor Blum was a Zionist; both were intensely devoted to their respective countries. Yet at this particular juncture, they felt it necessary to promote some kind of Jewish state in Palestine.

The partition resolution was adopted on 29 November 1947 by 33 votes to 13, with 10 abstentions. The two superpowers were largely responsible for its passage; pressure from the Jewish Diaspora also helped. In the scramble for votes, the role of the Palestinian Jews has often been overlooked. The *Yishuv* had its own small diplomatic corps, ably led by Moshe Shertok (later: Sharett) and Abba Eban, who persuaded several vacillating delegates, such as the ambassador from Iceland, to support partition. Passage of the resolution gave international recognition to the idea that a Jewish state in Palestine was legitimate, but it did not create that state. No outside force could do that. Sovereignty over the Jewish areas of Palestine could be established only by the Jews already living there.

Immediately after the partition vote, Palestinian Arab irregulars launched a series of attacks on Jewish settlements. A so-called 'army of deliverance', composed of volunteers from several neighbouring countries and funded by the Arab league, joined in the fray from bases in Syria. Britain responded to this offensive by advancing its departure date to 15 May 1948 and by informing the Arab Higher Committee in Jerusalem of its schedule for evacuating military bases and police stations. The Arabs had only to occupy them in order to establish control over the entire country. The British authorities were less cooperative toward an advance party of United Nations observers who arrived in Palestine in January 1948. These diplomats were housed in an unventilated basement in Jerusalem and left to find their own food and water. To the Palestinian Jews, whose insurrection had cost the lives of several hundred British soldiers and police, the mandatory authorities remained implacably hostile. *Hagana* fighters were disarmed whenever they were discovered, and the embargo on arms shipments to the Jews remained in force—even as the Arab states, which continued to receive British weapons under existing contracts, intensified their military operations.

The renewed fighting in Palestine dashed hopes that partition could be accomplished without violence. The State Department was especially perturbed, now that partition was increasingly perceived around the world as an American plan. Since it was not self-executing, the Near East specialists in Washington felt free to abandon it altogether. On 19 March 1948, Warren Austin, head of the American delegation to the United Nations, announced to the General Assembly that the United States now favoured U. N. trusteeship for Palestine. Truman, who learned about Austin's pronouncement only through newspaper accounts the following day, was taken aback. Only a day earlier he had reassured Weizmann that he still favoured partition. The president privately accused his diplomatic corps of having 'pulled the rug from under me' and added: 'I am now in the position of a liar and a dou-ble-crosser.' When questioned about the new American policy at a press conference on 25 March, he defended it lamely, saying that trusteeship was merely a temporary measure designed to prevent further bloodshed.

The Zionists were greatly distraught, fearing that trusteeship could nullify their efforts to create a Jewish state in Palestine. They need not have worried, for the new American proposal (which had originated with Britain) had no chance of succeeding. For one thing, it was opposed by the Arabs. For another, it would have necessitated sending American troops to Palestine. This was clearly a political impossibility. What land forces Truman still had at his disposal, in the wake of their precipitous demobilization after World War II, were now needed to confront the Soviet Union in Central Europe. Worse, trusteeship under the auspices of the United Nations would perforce entail Soviet military participation as well, thereby allowing Moscow to gain a foothold in the eastern Mediterranean. A diplomatic solution had foundered on the shoals of Arab opposition. The fate of Palestine would have to be decided by armed conflict between the two contending parties on the ground.

In April 1948, the Jewish forces in Palestine took the offensive against Arab adversaries who were superior in number but who lacked a unified command. The Jews were not particularly unified either. Although the *Hagana* made up the bulk of their combatants, smaller groups such as the *Irgun* were still in operation. Some of the heaviest fighting was along the road between Tel Aviv and Jerusalem. It remains for Israeli historians to determine whether keeping that road open was worth the great cost in human lives. From a purely military standpoint, it might have been wiser to give some more depth to the coastal area, so as to make it more defensible. But Jerusalem has always had a mystical attraction for Jews, even the secular Jews who had founded the *Yishuv*. It figures in the Zionist anthem, *Hatikva*, and has had a nearly uninterrupted history of Jewish habitation. To leave all of Jerusalem to the Arabs was unthinkable. It was on the road to Jerusalem that the *Irgun* committed the worst atrocity in the entire Jewish struggle for Palestine. On 8 April 1948, it murdered some 250 Arab civilians, mostly women and children, in Deir Yassin, a village from which several attacks on Jewish convoys had been launched.

Deir Yassin will forever remain a blot on the Israeli escutcheon. Yet it did initially serve a military and political purpose. Not only was the road to Jerusalem kept open, but the Arabs in the Jewish areas of Palestine began to flee in droves. A few Jews, such as the mayor of Haifa, pleaded with them to stay. But such was the panic created by the massacre and Arab radio propaganda exploiting it, that some three hundred thousand Arabs left Jewish-held territory within weeks. Another five hundred thousand fled the areas that were annexed by Israel as the war progressed. Most Jews were glad to see them go. Some provoked their departure by knocking on the doors of their homes at night and warning them that they would be killed if they did not leave within twenty-four hours. In the State Department and the Foreign Office, the existence of a large Arab population in the Jewish zone of Palestine had constituted one of the principal arguments against partition. This argument no longer carried much weight.

By 15 May, the date set for the official British departure from Palestine, the Jewish forces were not only holding their own, but were advancing on most fronts. This fact helps explain why the State of Israel, which was officially proclaimed on 14 May, was recognized the same day by the United States. Truman was strongly influenced by his personal advisor, a young lawyer from Saint Louis named Clark Clifford. At a White House conference on 12 May, Clifford argued that a Jewish state was going to be established anyway. It would be better for the United States to recognize it immediately and 'steal a march' on the Soviet Union. He rejected the contention that the Arab oil-producing states would retaliate by refusing to sell to the United States. 'The fact of the matter is that the Arab states must have oil royalties or go broke.' Recognition of the Jewish state, he added, was consistent with American policy since the presidency of Woodrow Wilson and would help strengthen the United Nations. Truman recognized the State of Israel shortly after six PM Washington time on 14 May. It was *de facto* recognition. The first state to recognize Israel *de jure* was Guatemala that same evening, followed by the Soviet Union a few minutes later. The American arms embargo to both sides in

Palestine remained in effect, thus obliging Israel to rely on newly-Communist Czechoslovakia for most of its weaponry.

Opponents of recognition, such as Secretary of State George C. Marshall and the British Foreign Office, accused Truman of pandering to the Jewish electorate. The president himself gave credence to this view shortly after assuming office in 1945. During a meeting with American ministers to several Middle Eastern countries in November, he explained his position on Palestine tersely: 'I'm sorry, gentlemen, but I have to answer to hundreds of thousands who are anxious for the success of Zionism. I do not have hundreds of thousands of Arabs among my constituents.' Such remarks need not be taken at their face value. Truman knew that the State Department strongly opposed Zionism and found in the Jewish vote a convenient pretext for doing what he intended to do in the first place. He had opposed British policy in Palestine since 1939 and believed that the Jews had a right to a state there. From the time he proposed that Jewish DP's in Europe be allowed to emigrate to Palestine, his policy led logically to diplomatic recognition of Israel. Truman's endorsement of a permanent refuge for persecuted Jews may be compared to his support for civil rights: he felt that both were necessary, regardless of the political consequences. His modest civil rights program did him no good politically. It brought him no new black voters and antagonized most southern whites, who favoured a splinter party, the Dixiecrats, in the presidential election of 1948. The southern blacks, who stood to gain the most from civil rights legislation, could not give the president any tangible support because they were largely disenfranchised.

Similarly, Truman did not derive any political benefit at home by recognizing the State of Israel. The Jewish vote did not fall into his lap because American Jews have never been one-issue voters. In 1948, they were preoccupied with the same questions of national interest that affected their Gentile compatriots. These included farm subsidies, inflation, the Taft-Hartley labour law and the incipient Cold War with Russia. In New York, which had the largest concentration of Jews—and the largest number of electoral votes—in the country, the Jewish electorate was deeply divided. Nearly half favoured Henry A. Wallace, who had been Secretary of Agriculture and then vice-president under Roosevelt and now led a splinter party called the Progressives. Wallace drew many Jewish voters because he opposed Truman's hard-line policy toward Moscow. A small minority of New York Jews voted for the Republican presidential candidate and Governor of the State of New York, Thomas E. Dewey. Truman received less than 50 percent of the Jewish vote in New York and lost the state. Jews outside New York exerted little domestic political influence and even less in foreign affairs. The leading American Zionist was Rabbi Abba Hillel Silver of Cleveland, an ardent supporter of Senator Robert A. Taft. In the Senate, where he was majority leader since 1946, Taft regularly spoke in favour of Jewish statehood, accusing the president of inconsistency on this issue. His pro-Zionist stance did him little good politically, since he failed to win the Republican nomination for president. Dewey, who also tried to outbid Truman for the Jewish vote by supporting the Zionist programme unreservedly, fared little better: he lost the election.

In the final analysis, the creation of the State of Israel had little to do with American domestic politics. It was mainly the work of its Jewish inhabitants, whose sense of common purpose was never so much in evidence as when they repelled their Arab adversaries. But military victory alone did not establish a sovereign Jewish state in Palestine. The government of Israel first had to assert its authority over the country's Jewish population. It did so on 28 May 1948, when the *Altalena*, a ship chartered by the *Irgun*, arrived in Tel Aviv with 900 men and a cargo of munitions on board. The government insisted that the arms be turned over to the Israeli army. When the *Irgun* leaders refused, Ben Gurion ordered fire to be opened on the ship, which sank with the loss of its cargo and fifteen lives. A month later, all Jews under arms had to swear allegiance to the State of Israel, and the *Irgun* ceased to exist as a separate force. The recently-founded Jewish commonwealth was now fully sovereign.

A New Synthesis

No sooner was the State of Israel established than it began to admit the Jewish DP's who had been awaiting entry since 1945. They arrived even as the fighting with Arab armies was still under way. After the war ended in an uneasy armistice in 1949, more Jewish immigrants flooded in, this time from Arab countries, where they were accused of constituting a Zionist fifth column. At this writing, there are hardly any Jews left in the Islamic world, with the exception of Morocco, whose king, Hassan II, has maintained the tradition of the great mediaeval caliphs and continues to protect his remaining Jewish subjects. The departure of over a million Sephardic Jews from countries where they had lived for centuries, even millenia, ended a long tradition of mutual tolerance between Judaism and Islam. Throughout the Middle Ages and well into the modern period, rabbis regarded Christianity as idolatrous, because of its use of statues and other graven images to inspire faith. They always recognized Islam as monotheistic, however, even if they did not endorse all its moral tenets. Thus a Jew could convert to Islam if threatened with death and not be guilty of idolatry. One who accepted baptism, on the other hand, became an apostate and was forever banished from the Jewish community. Similarly, classical Islam considered the Jews to be the 'People of the Book' and extended to them far greater tolerance than did Christianity.

In traditional Islamic society, Jews and Christians alike were allotted an inferior social status to that of Muslims, while enjoying the ruler's protection. But the ruler's power to protect anyone diminished along with his political authority, which was undermined by the growing European domination of the Islamic world in the nineteenth century. A delicate balance, which had assured Jews of protection as long as they knew their place, was being upset: impressed by European culture and technology, the Jews of Islam tended to forget their inferior place in society. In Algeria, they gladly accepted the French citizenship offered to most of them (but not to the Arabs) in 1870. Elsewhere in North Africa and the Middle East, they were able to improve their social and economic position by attending the schools of the *Alliance Israélite Universelle*. Arab envy fed upon French anti-Semitic tracts in Arabic translation. For the Arabs, the ultimate humiliation was the creation of a Jewish state in what they considered to be the 'domain of Islam'.

The mass exodus of Jews from Arab countries, coming only a few years after the destruction of the Jewish communities of Central and Eastern Europe, left the United States as the principal heir and successor to Diaspora Judaism. Returning Jewish war veterans were the spearhead of a movement to win full acceptance for Jews in American life. Having served their country overseas, they refused to accept the discrimination that had been inflicted on their parents. The G. I. Bill of Rights, which enabled demobilized service personnel to pursue higher studies at public expense, did more than any other single measure to break down the quota system that had formerly excluded qualified Jewish students from many American universities. Once married and in the process of raising families, Jewish war veterans tended to join a synagogue. In most cases, it was Conservative, since they had grown accustomed to the Conservative ritual in the armed services. Jewish chaplains deemed it to be the most acceptable to the greatest number. Synagogue membership greatly increased in the postwar years and reached its peak in the early 1950's. By then, being a Jew in the United States had become politically acceptable—part of the belonging system, by which every loyal American was expected to visit the house of worship of his or her choice. Attending religious services was widely encouraged in the news media and political discourse as an excellent way of opposing 'Godless Communism', which seemed to be very much of a threat in those days. President Eisenhower set the example, as he went to church regularly with his wife Mamie, in full view of press photographers. Synagogue affiliation gave American Jews an opportunity to reaffirm their patriotism and allowed them to find a place in the new suburban society that developed after the war.

The entry of Jews into the American religious mosaic did not give them any particular influence over foreign policy. When Israel joined with France and Britain in a military campaign against Egypt in October 1956, the vast majority of American Jews sided with Israel. They considered its lightning thrust into the Sinai peninsula to be justified in view of previous Egyptian provocation, notably the blockade of the Straits of Tiran. President Eisenhower, who was running for re-election, condemned the action publicly and forced the British and French to end it. Israel eventually withdrew from the Sinai, but obtained free passage through the Straits. American Jews, most of whom voted for Eisenhower's Democratic opponent, Adlai E. Stevenson, were reduced to the role of spectators in this drama. Eisenhower had such a commanding lead in the public opinion surveys that he could win without the Jewish vote.

Throughout the following decade, Jews in the United States concentrated most of their political activity not on support for Israel, but on the civil rights movement at home. Idealistic Jewish students from the North joined the Freedom Riders who went south to end racial segregation. Some of these young Jews were killed by vengeful Southern whites. The Jewish establishment supported the movement by urging Congress to pass laws abolishing discrimination in jobs and housing. The motives of the older, wealthier Jews were not entirely altruistic. By helping to eliminate discrimination against Negroes (as they were still called), they also eliminated it against themselves. With the passage of equal-rights legislation in the early 1960's, the infamous N. J. A. ('No Jews Allowed') on many real estate listings disappeared. In fact, such laws probably benefited Jews more than blacks, only a few of whom could afford to buy expensive suburban homes or join country clubs that had formerly been restricted to white Protestants. By 1967, American Jews had clearly arrived.

The Six-day War in June of that year proved to be a cataclysmic experience not only for Jews in the United States, but for those throughout the Diaspora. At the prospect that the State of Israel might be destroyed, all Jewish opposition to Zionism vanished overnight. The American Council for Judaism, which had campaigned against the creation of a Jewish state in the 1940's out of concern that Jews might be accused of divided loyalties, simply disbanded. Many of its leaders contributed to the Israel Emergency Fund. By far the most remarkable demonstration of sympathy for Israel took place in France, where even the most secular and apparently assimilated Jews rallied publicly to the defence of the Jewish state. French academics were astonished to see colleagues, whose Jewish origins had been well hidden until then, suddenly blossom into Zionists. But no Frenchman was more shocked at this open and spontaneous outpouring of support for Israel, than the President of the Republic, Charles de Gaulle. He had publicly warned Israel not to launch a pre-emptive strike against its Arab neighbours, and he fully expected his loyal Jewish subjects to follow official policy. When they did not, he vented his well-controlled rage by calling the Jews 'an elite people, sure of itself and domineering'. For more than a generation, de Gaulle had personified French resistance to Nazism. His anti-Jewish slur proved—if proof was still needed—that the war against Hitler had never been a war for the Jews.

Despite the wrath of this republican monarch and a crescendo of anti-Israel pronouncements from French intellectuals, the Jews of France did not abandon Zionism. Their community had grown from 300,000 just after the Second World War to nearly 700,000 and was now the largest in Western Europe. Most of this increase was due to the influx of Jews from North Africa, particularly Algeria, which had become independent in 1962. These Sephardic Jews were not immigrants in the sense that earlier Ashkenazic arrivals had been. They already spoke French—for most, it was their first language—and had no Yiddish accent to be ashamed of. Their very numbers made assimilation into the older, largely secular Jewish community of France almost impossible. Many had relatives in Israel. Zionism made it easier for them to affirm their own Mediterranean Jewish identity.

As a direct result of the Six-day War, Israel became the focal point of Jewish existence. Jews throughout the Diaspora rallied to Zionism in many ways: by buying State of Israel bonds, by visiting Israel regularly, by sending their children to Israel for an extended stay in the hope that they might learn some Hebrew and become proud to be Jewish. Whenever Israel was attacked in the Western press, Diaspora Jews would dash off letters defending it. Such attacks became increasingly frequent after Israel's spectacular military victories in the Six-day War. Formerly cast in the role of David, the Jewish state now appeared to many Western journalists and intellectuals as a hulking Goliath, which seemed to threaten peace and stability in the Middle East. The Palestine Liberation Organization was suddenly thrust into the public view. Its leader,

Yasser Arafat, received a thunderous ovation at the United Nations, when, clad in a military uniform and carrying a pistol, he addressed the General Assembly on 13 November 1974.

In his speech, Arafat characterized Israel as a colonialist construction, which would have to be excised along with other relics of Western imperialism. This meant that Israel would have to disappear in order to make room for a Palestinian Arab state. In its covenant, which was not amended until 1996, the PLO had already laid down the principle that the Jews, being the adherents of a 'heavenly religion', have no right to a state of their own anywhere on earth. Arafat's repeated appeals to international public opinion were apparently based on the widely-held misconception that Israel had been created by outside forces. Therefore, the same forces could presumably undo the Jewish state. It took him nearly twenty years to realize that if he was ever going to create an independent Palestine, he would have to deal directly with the Israelis.

The PLO was able to pursue this quixotic policy of trying to wish Israel away because it received generous subsidies from Saudi Arabia and other Persian Gulf states, whose incomes rose along with the price of oil. Western, especially American, profligacy with that precious commodity had led to a worldwide shortage, which coincided with the third conflict between Israel and Egypt, the Yom Kippur war of October 1973. The Arab oil-producing states declared an embargo on those countries which aided Israel, notably Holland and the United States, and raised prices for all others. Throughout the West, Israel and its Jewish supporters were widely held responsible for the oil crisis, a feeling aptly expressed by a bumper sticker then seen on American highways. It read: 'We need oil, not Jews.'

When Israel invaded Lebanon in the summer of 1982, its standing in the West fell to an all-time low. Presented to the Israeli people and parliament as a limited operation intended to protect northern Galilee from PLO bombardment, the campaign had in reality very different objectives: the destruction of the PLO as a military and political force, and the establishment in Lebanon of a Maronite Christian regime favourable to Israel. In keeping with these goals, Israeli defence minister Ariel Sharon had his troops let

Christian phalangists into the Sabra and Chatilla refugee camps near Beirut, where they wantonly killed hundreds of unarmed Palestinian civilians. Under pressure from the opposition, the government of Menachem Begin instituted a commission of inquiry, which severely blamed the Israeli military commanders for having allowed the tragedy to occur. Few other democracies would have been so forthright in admitting their errors; a public opinion poll in Israel itself revealed that sixty percent of those questioned viewed the Lebanese venture as a gross blunder. But Western journalists and intellectuals were not in the mood to make fine distinctions: they castigated Israel as a whole, calling into question its very right to exist. Some detractors even compared the Jewish state to Nazi Germany.

The reaction of the Diaspora Jews to this slander was to rally around Israel once again. Since signing a peace treaty with Egypt in 1979, the Jewish state was more secure than ever militarily. In the years immediately following, however, a series of terrorist attacks was launched by some Palestinians and their Western sympathizers against Jewish targets in Europe—synagogues, schools and restaurants. Scores of innocents were killed, including a nineteen-month-old baby in Berlin. The disease of terrorism is best treated through its symptoms; it abated as security improved. The effect of these outrages on the Jews of the Diaspora was, in any case, counterproductive: rather than being cowed, they drew even closer to Zionism. Further contributing to their sense of solidarity was a torrent of abuse against Israel in the Western media. For French secular philosopher Alain Finkielkraut, such blatant hostility was derived from Christianity, which had reverted to accusing the Jews of deicide. The Palestinians had become the Christ-people and Israel, the Jew among nations.

By contrast, the Jewish lobby in the United States, officially known as the American-Israel Public Affairs Committee, was not given to intellectual speculation. To counteract propaganda directed against Israel, it pressed Congress with renewed vigour to approve military aid for what it called 'the only democracy in the Middle East'. American aid to Israel was not, in fact, gratuitous: the Israelis earned it by supplying the Pentagon with the latest Soviet weapons captured from Syria. Yet Washington's apparent generosity was widely attributed to the machinations of the Lobby, whose leaders urged American Jews to make even greater financial contributions in order to ensure Israel's security.

In their collective zeal to rush to the defence of Israel, Diaspora Jews sometimes failed to notice that the world was changing. In the fall of 1982, the price of oil began to decline, thereby weakening the political influence of Saudi Arabia and the other Gulf producers. The Cold War came to an abrupt end in 1989 with the opening of the Berlin Wall. Not wishing to risk a new confrontation with the United States in the Middle East, Soviet premier Gorbachev drastically reduced arms deliveries to Syria. In the winter of 1991, an American-led coalition, which included some Arab states, effectively neutralized the military power of Iraq. The Gulf War, whose land operations lasted four days, was fought primarily to prevent the vast oil reserves of Saudi Arabia from being annexed by Saddam Hussein. Although Israel did not participate in the fighting and remained stoically passive while Iraqi missiles rained on Tel Aviv, it emerged from the ordeal stronger than ever. The defeat of Iraq had eliminated the only remaining threat to its military security.

Now that the survival of Israel was assured, the Jews of the Diaspora suddenly found themselves without a cause to drum up support for. What then was to be their common purpose, if any? Not unnaturally, they were most reluctant to deal with this question.

Chapter X

AN END TO PHOBIAS

TO GET SOME IDEA of the remarkable progress made by Jews in recent decades, let us return briefly to 1945. The liberation found the Jewish remnant of Western Europe in a state of collective shock. Even those Jews who could return to their homes knew that no one wanted to hear about their recent ordeal. So they pushed it back in their memories. They tried to be as inconspicuous as possible as they took up the thread of their prewar existence. Four years of Nazi propaganda had left their mark; one could never tell just how anti-Semitic one's neighbours were. Some European Jews thought it best not to have their male offspring circumcised so that they might be less vulnerable. Across the ocean, Judaeophobia was still rife. A public opinion poll taken in the United States in 1942 revealed that Americans considered Jews to be the third greatest danger to humanity, just after the Japanese and Germans. A Canadian survey of 1946 placed Jews in second place among undesirables, just behind the Japanese and several places ahead of the Germans. In Palestine, the provisions of the White Paper remained in force; the *Yishuv* seemed powerless to change them.

Some fifty years later, a Jewish state, whose citizens have had to fight several wars to assert their independence, has replaced the faltering British mandate. Since the end of the Cold War, Israel has won diplomatic recognition from many quarters—even the Vatican. It may yet live in peace with its Arab neighbours. Less noticeable, perhaps, is the decline of anti-Semitism in the West. Despite occasional acts of vandalism against synagogues or Jewish cemeteries, Judaeophobia has ceased to be a political force. Its fading importance has followed that of Bolshevism. Even as the Soviet Union still dominated most of the Eurasian land mass, fears of a Communist takeover in the West gradually subsided. At the same time, Jews tended to abandon even democratic socialism, which always had more Jewish adherents than the totalitarian variety. They were no longer perceived as the standard-bearers of world revolution. The genocide itself contributed to the decline of anti-Semitism. Even genteel expressions of contempt for the Jews, such as those that occasionally found their way into otherwise innocuous prewar fiction, have gone out of fashion. No respectable person would want to be accused of giving even posthumous aid and comfort to Hitler. Politicians have learned to show due respect for Jews in public discourse or risk general opprobrium. The Reverend Jesse Jackson's reference to New York as 'Hymietown' in 1990 seriously damaged his credibility as a presidential candidate. Anti-Semitism is no longer respectable because educated people have come to understand where it can lead. The State of Israel was the first to recognize the pedagogical value of the genocide—or Holocaust, as it became known. In 1960, Israeli agents kidnapped Adolf Eichmann, the chief organizer of the 'Final Solution', in Buenos Aires and flew him to Jerusalem for judgment. The Eichmann trial served to make young Israelis conscious of their people's recent past and ready to accept the sacrifices, such as military service, which are necessary to maintain the Jewish state.

When applied to Jewish youth in the Diaspora, however, the teaching of the Holocaust has been largely counter-productive, often leading to a total disaffection from Judaism. The lesson of the Holocaust, as interpreted by rabbis and other Jewish community leaders with no formal training in history, is that it can happen again if Jews do not remain united. Appeals for unity serve to muzzle dissent within the Jewish community and to reinforce the authority of its leaders. These are usually men of middle age, who have succeeded in their businesses or professions, but whose knowledge of Judaism is slight. No significant place is allotted to younger Jews, who might otherwise bring new ideas to the community. Brushed aside by their elders, these young people are not easily convinced that disunity was responsible for the genocide. They realize intuitively that the Jews of Europe were slaughtered not because they lacked unity, but because they had no army to defend them. There is still no Jewish army anywhere, except in Israel.

Young Diaspora Jews, tired of being told that they are all potential candidates for the gas chambers, have been leaving organized Judaism in droves. They do not notify their local synagogue of their departure. They just go.

Those who have taken the Holocaust 'lesson' to heart are necessarily militant Zionists. There is simply no other outlet for their fears. If a wholesale massacre of Jews can indeed recur, then Israel must be as strong and as large as possible in order to accept the millions of Jewish refugees who may, some day, have to flee there. In fact, there is no danger of such a pogrom. It cannot take place in Central and Eastern Europe, because there are hardly any Jews left. The largest Jewish community in Western Europe today is that of France, where public opinion surveys show a steady decrease in anti-Semitism since World War II. Only the United States has a Jewish population comparable in numbers to the total killed by the Nazis: about six million. And although Americans are not free from prejudice, they did stop lynching Negroes decades ago. Hardly anyone expects them to start killing Jews.

The one country where another Jewish massacre could possibly take place is, oddly enough, Israel itself. Its high concentration of Jews in a small area makes it an ideal military target. Erstwhile Arab boasts about pushing the Jews into the sea have given rise to such fears; but the only credible danger came from the Soviet Union. If—and this is a very big **if**—the political leaders in Moscow had ever decided to use nuclear weapons against the Jewish state, it could have been blown off the map. To avert such a possibility, the Israeli government decided, shortly after the Sinai campaign of 1956, to build a nuclear arsenal of its own. In recent years, any military threat to Israel has considerably diminished. The Israeli Defence Forces do not currently face the prospect of open warfare with any Arab country, still less with Russia. Their main assignment of late has been to ensure internal security. And although occasional terrorist attacks against Israeli civilians have resulted in great personal tragedy, they do not, in themselves, threaten the integrity of the state.

Unfortunately, the level of paranoia in certain Jewish circles has built up over the years to the point where their members simply refuse to believe that Israel is now secure. Raised on Holocaust stories since their early childhood, they prepare themselves daily for the final combat between good and evil. In their view, the tragedy that befell the Jews of Europe has made all human history meaningless; so it must come to an imminent end. Although Jews are commanded to remember the past for whatever moral lessons it may contain, they tend to deride the study of history in times of trouble. Thus Joseph Caro, author of the *Shulchan Aruch*, forbade the faithful to read history books. These 'tales of war', as he called them, would distract the pious reader from meditating on Holy Writ. Caro was reacting to the great tragedy of his own time: the expulsion of the Jews from Spain. Rigorous observance of all the traditional laws and customs, he believed, would make the Jews acceptable to God, so that, in His wisdom, He would one day send them the Messiah. This radical transformation of the human condition would take place outside the normal course of events. It depends entirely on divine will.

The expulsion from Spain has since been overshadowed by the Nazi genocide. Once again, Jews have largely given up on history. Even those who teach history in universities make no attempt to find any direction in it. Among the less educated, a wave of Messianic fervour has come to dominate religious life. Messianism is the new orthodoxy. After the aborted revolts against Rome, Jews were advised not to place too high hopes in the Messiah's coming, but to go about their daily lives in a spirit of holiness. This is the basic precept of classical Judaism, which has guided and sustained Jews for nearly two thousand years. It is now challenged by a revived Hasidic movement, in particular the Lubavitcher sect, which sees the advent of the Messiah as imminent.

The Lubavitcher Hasidim are ardent missionaries among secular Jews, whom they seek to convert to strict observance. The sooner all Jews return to the Torah, they believe, the sooner they will be redeemed. In contrast to Reform and Conservative Jews, whose birthrate remains low, the Hasidim have very large families. If present demographic trends continue, their particular expression of Judaism could become the norm within a generation or two.

Although it eschews history, contemporary Hasidism is neither other-worldly nor apolitical. The Lubavitch leader, the late Rabbi Menahem Schneerson of Brooklyn, repeatedly warned the government of Israel against making any territorial concessions to the Arabs. He urged the Israelis to seize Damascus in 1967 and to retain Beirut in 1982. His expansionist position was based on a bizarre interpretation of Deuteronomy 20.20, which limits the cutting of trees for building siegeworks. Fortunately for Israel and the Middle East in general, the rabbi's counsel went unheeded. Nor was he successful in preventing the government of Yitzhak Rabin from signing a peace agreement in 1993 with the PLO.

Within Israel itself, there are Messianic elements capable of exerting a powerful influence on government policy. Their earliest spiritual mentor was Zvi Yehuda Kook, the first chief rabbi of Israel, who accepted the reality of a secular Jewish state as a precursor to the kingdom of heaven on earth. Rabbi Kook, who lost several members of his own family in Nazi death camps, sought consolation in the belief that the Messiah would soon come. He advised his followers not to engage in political activity until God gave them a sign. Then came Israel's spectacular military victories in June 1967. Here was the divine portent that Rabbi Kook and other religious Zionists had been so eagerly awaiting. Calling themselves the *Gush Emunim* ('Bloc of the Faithful'), several thousand pitched tents and set up trailer camps in Judaea and Samaria, the occupied West Bank. Their avowed purpose was to welcome the Messiah, whose coming, they believed, would not occur until Jews inhabited all areas of the ancient land of the Bible. Rabbi Kook did not preach violence against the Arabs in the occupied territories, but some of his more zealous followers felt less constrained. In 1983, a group of *Gush* militants threw a grenade and sprayed bullets into the courtyard of the Islamic college in Hebron, killing three Arabs and injuring 33 others. Rabbi Moshe Levinger, who had become the leader of the *Gush Emunim* after having led the first group of Jews to settle in Hebron in 1968, expressed his approval of the bloody deed. 'Whoever did this,' he declared, 'has sanctified God's name in public.'

Even more aggressive is the *Kach* ('Thus') movement, founded by the American-born rabbi, Meir Kahane. Fewer in number than the *Gush Emunim*, Kahane's followers believe that all Arabs must be deported—'transferred' is their current euphemism—from the State of Israel proper and the occupied territories. They are vehemently opposed to the agreement of September 1993 between Israel and the PLO, providing for an embryonic Palestinian state in Jericho and Gaza. In an attempt to abort this project, Dr. Baruch Goldstein, a *Kach* militant, opened fire on Arab worshippers at the Tomb of the Patriarchs in Hebron on 25 February 1994. He killed twenty-nine people and wounded scores of others. The government of Israel was aghast at this barbarous act. Prime minister Rabin excommunicated Goldstein posthumously from the Israeli nation and the Jewish people. But his funeral drew some 600 friends and neighbours, most of whom openly praised the assassin as a righteous man and a hero.

Bloodletting is not new to the Middle East, either in Israel or in Arab countries. What makes the Hebron massacre unique is its amalgam of Messianism and armed superiority. The two had never previously been joined in Jewish history. Earlier Messianic movements, such as the ill-fated risings against Rome, had taken place in periods of Jewish weakness. The current wave, on the contrary, has coincided with the apogee of Israel's military strength. Adding to this explosive mixture is the fact that all Jewish settlers in the occupied territories are permitted to carry automatic weapons. Dr. Goldstein was raised in a militant Orthodox community of Brooklyn, where the Holocaust is relived daily by people who never actually experienced it. When interviewed on Israeli television a few years before the event, he wore a yellow star with the word 'Jew' (in English) embroidered on it and kept referring to the Palestinians as Nazis. At the time, his remarks were dismissed by critics as a mere Freudian slip; but they may have had a more sinister meaning.

If the Palestinians are indeed Nazis, there can be no peace or territorial compromise with them. Did not Roosevelt and Churchill insist in 1943 on the unconditional surrender of the Axis powers? Some wholly respectable Jews, who are not religious fanatics, have equated the PLO with Nazism. Foremost among them is Emil L.

Fackenheim, emeritus professor of philosophy at the University of Toronto, whose book, *The Jewish Return Into History: Reflections in the Age of Auschwitz and a New Jerusalem*,[1] appeared in 1978. Professor Fackenheim categorized Arafat's speech at the United Nations as being Nazi-inspired. (Actually, it was Maoist, both in tone and in content.) He then reminded his readers that the PLO chairman was distantly related to the Mufti of Jerusalem, the leading political and religious figure of Arab Palestine, who had sided with—and been sheltered by—Nazi Germany during the war. Accusations of guilt by kinship are totally out of place in a university and should have been rejected by all fair-minded Jews. Yet Fackenheim's charges against Arafat were not disputed by Jewish leaders, who could not appear to give aid and comfort to Israel's enemies. In view of their acquiescence, is it so strange that Dr. Goldstein confused Palestinians and Nazis? His crime at Hebron was not merely the act of a crazed individual; it reflected the paranoia that has afflicted Jews in general. Perhaps it will give pause to those who use the Nazi genocide as a pedagogical device to instill religious fervour or ethnic solidarity.

The Eleventh Commandment

Out of the Holocaust-Israel nexus has come a new religion, which seems to have won the allegiance of most observant Jews: it is called Jewish self-awareness. Instead of emphasizing one's duties to God and to other human beings, as Judaism does, the current orthodoxy places a higher value on ethnic survival than on ethics. Remember who you are, proclaim its advocates. Do not give Hitler a posthumous victory by abandoning your Jewish heritage. Signs of this doctrine are everywhere, as young Jewish males are pressured into wearing skullcaps all day long—even when playing baseball, although a regulation baseball cap would be more appropriate. Jewish tradition requires the faithful to cover their heads when praying. Older Jews wear a hat or skullcap at all times

---

[1] New York: Schocken Books, 1978.

because they never know just when they will be called into God's presence. The practice of imposing a head covering on the young is quite recent. It appears to have originated at the turn of the twentieth century with a Hungarian rabbi, who thought that a badge of this kind would remind young Jews of their identity. In the late Middle Ages, the Jews of Europe were compelled by ecclesiastical and secular authorities to adopt distinctive dress as a warning to Christians not to mingle with them. Now, it seems, the roles have been reversed. It is the Jews, or at least the most vocal among them, who are afraid to mingle with Christians.

Those who preach the maintenance of Jewish identity as an end in itself have, in effect, issued an eleventh commandment, which bids fair to overshadow the first ten. It reads: Thou shalt not assimilate. For decades, Jews in the West have campaigned to dismantle the barriers that prevented their access to universities, good jobs, clubs, hotels, certain neighbourhoods and places of public recreation. Now that these barriers have come down, they are dismayed to see their children and grandchildren socializing with Gentiles. Of course they want their offspring to succeed in life; and for most, success is predicated on attending the best schools and making the right contacts in order to move up the social and economic ladder. But making the right contacts means meeting with Gentiles, being invited to their homes and—who knows?—even marrying them. The increasing rate of intermarriage has many older Jews worried. They want the best for their progeny, but not at the risk of seeing them turn into perfect strangers. Human procreation has always carried with it an element of selfishness: in accepting the burdens of parenthood, people hope somehow to perpetuate themselves in their children. Jewish parents who have succeeded to the point where they can send their children to college or university are themselves assimilated to some degree. They simply want the assimilation process to be suspended so that they can recognize their own offspring.

Underlying the opposition to assimilation is a fear so pervasive that most Jews dare not express it: the fear of Christianity. Jews hardly ever utter the word: they refer to Christians as *goyim* (Gentiles, anyone who is not Jewish), rather than face the problem head-on. When they denounce assimilation, they do not bother to ask: assimilation to what? They simply assume that all Jews who marry Gentiles (i. e.: Christians) will be drawn to Christianity, or that their children will be. Then centuries of resistance to the dominant religion will have been undone. The Jewish martyrs who died in the Crusades, the Inquisition, the pogroms and the Nazi genocide will have been dishonoured. So will the Jewish grandparents of Christian children who are taught that the Jews killed Jesus. Having endured anti-Semitism at home and witnessed mass murder abroad, older Jews do not wish to be called Christ-killers by their own descendants.

For the Jewish middle class, the most effective way of maintaining one's own Jewish identity and that of one's children, without hindering the family's social and economic advancement, would appear to be Zionism. By making occasional trips to Israel and contributing money to Zionist causes, Jews in the Diaspora can remind themselves who they are and still move freely in the Gentile world. Wearing a skullcap or eating kosher food away from home might cause some raised eyebrows at the workplace or in society, but buying State of Israel bonds conveys a sense of belonging to the Jewish community without jeopardizing one's business or social standing. This is a heritage that successful Jews can pass on to their children. It helps explain why Jewish lobbies in the United States and some other Western countries appear so important. Their actual influence in foreign affairs is doubtful; in 1993, Israeli premier Rabin openly castigated the American-Israel Public Affairs Committee, calling its efforts counter-productive. Yet most Diaspora Jews accept the lobbies as a necessary link between themselves and the Jewish State.

Similarly, the current dogma that postulates the centrality of Israel for Jews everywhere goes unchallenged. This centrality has never been defined precisely, but it is certainly not religious. Only about twenty percent of the Jews in Israel are observant (in Hebrew: *dati*); the rest are secular (*lo dati*). On any given Rosh Hashana, the Jewish New Year and second holiest day in the liturgical calendar, more Israeli Jews can be found at the beach than in the synagogue. A public appearance by Michael Jackson or

Madonna will attract more Israelis, especially the young, than any rabbi. Israel is a democracy, and its inhabitants have a perfect right to spend their leisure time as they wish. But they are not necessarily role models for Diaspora Jews. One does not have to be Jewish to spend Rosh Hashana at the beach or attend a rock concert. For all their love of Western culture, however, the Israelis are certainly not assimilated. The very fact that they speak Hebrew among themselves and are subject to military service helps to reinforce their national identity. Nor is intermarriage a problem in Israel. There may be occasional sexual liaisons between Jews and Arabs, but the two groups are so separate as to make mixed marriages a virtual impossibility. For the Diaspora Jews, Israel is at best a useful symbol of Jewish self-awareness; it is not a transferable reality.

Among Western Jews whose historical conscience is still dominated by the Holocaust, the only certain way to prevent assimilation is to retreat into a self-imposed ghetto. The Hasidic revival of recent years is ample evidence that this option is being taken very seriously. Hasidism is Jewish self-awareness taken to its logical conclusion. Being dressed like an eighteenth-century Polish peasant in his Sunday best with a black frock coat and broad-brimmed hat, even in the dog days of summer, cannot fail to set one apart from the crowd. Of all Jews, the Hasidim are the least likely to become assimilated. Since they speak Yiddish among themselves and eschew secular learning, their children do not attend university and have no opportunity to mix socially with Gentiles. They never intermarry—not even with Jews outside their own community. Other Orthodox Jews who are not as rigidly separatist as the Hasidim nonetheless show them respect because the movement continues to grow. The new Hasidic vogue has effectively reversed the trend to secularism among Western Jews that began in the late eighteenth century. Until recently, most Jews of strict observance were treated with disdain by their secularized brethren, whose economic and social status was usually superior. Now, however, Orthodoxy has taken the offensive. Its followers have regained confidence in themselves.

By contrast, Reform and Conservative rabbis often tend to be yes-men to the Orthodox. They accept the basic premise that assimilation is the greatest danger that Jews face today. Religious instruction in liberal synagogues emphasizes reverence for the past, when Jews had little opportunity to assimilate. Liberal rabbis occasionally extol Yiddish for its cultural role in keeping the Jewish community united. Some like to remind young Jews that their ancestors were ready to die for Judaism. This last contention is patently false, inasmuch as the ancestors in question were immigrants, who had left their native countries to escape martyrdom. Worse, it plays directly into the hands of the Orthodox, since the Judaism that one's ancestors were presumably willing to die for was neither Conservative nor Reform. As for Yiddish, it is still spoken among the Hasidim; but they are hardly an example for the emancipated Jewish youth of today. The myth of a golden age, when all Jews were supposedly pious, serves only to make these young people feel inadequate. They may either leave Judaism altogether or revert to Orthodoxy.

The spiritual needs of Jewish youth receive little attention when the question of intermarriage arises, as it does with increasing frequency. In the United States and France, more than half of all marriages contracted by Jews in the past decade have been with Gentiles. The figure for other Western democracies is not much lower. Until 1980 or thereabouts, most of these unions in the United States (figures for France are unavailable) resulted in a net gain for Judaism, in that the children were raised as Jews. Since then, however, the trend has been reversed: more and more Jewish-Gentile couples are raising their children as Christians or without any sort of religious education. Inasmuch as the vast majority of Jews who intermarry are not Orthodox, the responsibility for such losses must be attributed in large measure to the Conservative and Reform wings of Judaism, which have not been able to keep these young people within the fold. Money is an important factor here. The cost of joining a liberal synagogue is simply too great for many young couples struggling to make payments on their house, car and furniture. In this regard, the missionaries of Lubavitch are more in tune with the needs of Jewish youth. They open small synagogues in run-down neighbourhoods where rents are cheap. It costs nothing to pray there.

At bottom, the decline of Jewish affiliation among mixed couples reflects a serious educational problem. In Judaism, children are deemed to follow the religion of their mother. This means that if the Gentile partner in a mixed marriage is the woman, she must first convert to Judaism if her children are to be considered Jews. With its constant emphasis on the Holocaust and ethnic survival, contemporary Jewish teaching has little to attract converts. And although conversion to Judaism is not necessary for the male partner to a mixed marriage, he still has to be convinced that raising his children as Jews is worthwhile. People marry for the future, not for the past. If all the future seems to hold is more anti-Semitism and perhaps even another genocide, the non-Jewish husband of a Jewish wife may feel that their children should not be exposed to such risks. Finally, the Gentile spouses of Jews cannot be expected to share the guilt complex that is so prevalent in Diaspora Judaism. In the United States especially, Jews feel guilty that they and their families prospered during the Second World War while their brethren in Europe were being gassed. Rabbis know how to play on these feelings: to encourage greater participation in synagogue activities, some have been known to berate their congregants for being 'Marranos in reverse' (Jewish on the outside, Gentile on the inside) or otherwise unworthy of their ancestral traditions. Denouncing assimilation is the modern-day rabbinical equivalent of Christian revivalist preaching against sin. For a convert to Judaism, however, being called a Marrano in reverse is simply insulting.

Further aggravating an already sensitive issue is the refusal of the Orthodox establishment to recognize conversions performed by Reform or Conservative rabbis as valid. This dispute has nothing to do with the course of study given in liberal synagogues for perspective converts. In most cases, it is quite thorough, lasting from a few months to a year. As a result, the new arrivals are often more familiar with the basic tenets of Judaism than their ethnically Jewish spouses. Some Orthodox rabbis, on the other hand, have admitted converts after only an hour or two of cursory instruction. Inasmuch as it is theoretically possible to learn Torah while standing on one foot, they are perfectly within their rights. At issue, then, is not the competence of Reform or Conservative rabbis, but their very status as rabbis. By calling it into question, the Orthodox hope to dominate Jewish institutions in the Diaspora, as they do in Israel. The stakes are high, particularly in France, where religious activity is highly centralized. In 1987, Orthodox militants wrested control of the *Consistoire* from an older, more pliable, Jewish leadership. In the forefront of this power struggle were the Sephardic Jews from North Africa, who had long resented the dominance of the wealthier, more settled Ashkenazic elite. With the help of the Lubavitch movement, the Sephardim played the religious card skillfully and had one of their number, Joseph Sitruk, installed as chief rabbi. Rabbi Sitruk's first target on taking office was intermarriage. His wife warned Jewish mothers over the radio not to invite their Gentile sons- or daughters-in-law to their homes for the Jewish holidays.

This game of religious one-upmanship can only hurt Judaism's chances for renewal. In France itself, there has been a healthy reaction among observant Jews against Rabbi Sitruk's separatist tendencies. Several of his confrères, none of whom can be accused of lacking respect for the Torah, have encouraged their flock to participate fully in the affairs of the republic. The question of intermarriage, however, is still not approached positively. It should be. The Gentiles who marry Jews are obviously not anti-Semitic. They are usually eager to learn about Judaism and therefore represent a heaven-sent opportunity to further its expansion. Any religion, any idea, any set of principles needs to expand if it is not to contract. If Jews are not to become a mere ethnic minority, shriveled and paranoid, they must proselytize. By becoming once again a light unto the nations, they would not only be helping themselves; they would be rendering a precious service to those countless Christians who seek a faith that they can live by. Obsessed by their own recent tragedy, Jews are slow to recognize that, in the past two centuries, all of Western civilization has become increasingly Jewish in thought and action. It is being Judaized in spite of itself. It is being Judaized in spite of Jewish indifference.

Christianity's Predicament

Toward the end of the nineteenth century, a French Catholic named Aimé Pallière discovered Judaism on attending the *Neila*, or closing service of Yom Kippur, at a synagogue in his native Lyons. Although he never formally converted for fear of offending his mother, Pallière lived as a Jew for the rest of his life. His experience was unique in that it allowed him to move freely among Christians and Jews. In 1922, he recounted his spiritual Odyssey in a book entitled *Le sanctuaire inconnu* [2] ('The Unknown Sanctuary'), in which he stated: 'All reforms currently being pursued in Christianity are strictly Jewish in nature.' This tendency, he believed, would lead eventually to 'the Judaization of Christian peoples'. In his conclusion, Pallière was far ahead of his time. The First World War and the totalitarian regimes that it spawned set back the evolution of Western civilization by glorifying armed might and unquestioned obedience to the ruling power. His initial premise was correct, however. Christian thought and practice increasingly resemble those of Judaism.

To understand why, we must recall that Christianity has always been an unstable blend of Judaism and paganism. Its Jewish content is limited to the Hebrew Scriptures, without the rabbinical commentary thereon, which are used primarily as a preface to the Gospels. Pagan elements include the demigod Jesus, whose presumed divine and human parentage closely follows Greek mythology. Christianity is most pagan in its veneration of power, which derives from Paul's letter to the Romans. One of the ways in which the early church curried favour with secular authority was by denigrating the Jewish Sabbath. The Pharisees' prohibition of work in any form on the day of rest was held up to copious ridicule. The social legislation of the Pentateuch, such as the commandment to pay employees every day before sundown, was also pronounced null and void. In the absence of these constraints, workers in the Middle Ages and most of the modern period could be exploited at

---

[2] Paris: Rieder, 1926.

will. European peasants, who until the French Revolution were mostly serfs, effectively worked seven days a week.

The increase in productivity brought about by the industrial revolution made possible a gradual decrease in working hours. By 1900, thanks to trade union pressure, the forty-eight hour work week was the norm in most Western countries. For the first time in their history, Christian workers could enjoy a full day of rest. Increased leisure time, along with improved hygiene and wide-spread literacy, led over the years to a modification of religious and moral values. Christianity has always been a salvific faith; it promises a reward in the afterlife to those who follow its precepts. For the downtrodden peasants of mediaeval Europe, the prospect of being received into heaven was the only way out of their misery. Life on earth, with its succession of wars, plagues and famines, was wretched and terribly short. Those who did not die in infancy could expect to last on average twenty-five years. Everyone had to prepare for death, and only the church could offer eternal salvation. But as life expectancy increased in the nineteenth and twentieth centuries, preparing for the hereafter became less important. Giving some meaning to one's earthly existence gradually took precedence.

European anti-Semites blamed the Jews for this change, which tended to sap traditional authority. Charles Maurras, who founded the neo-royalist movement, *Action Française,* late in the nineteenth century, voiced his hatred of 'Hebraic thought and all the dreams of justice, of happiness and of equality it drags in its wake'. Judaism does, of course, try to promote these ideals, and Maurras paid it an inadvertent compliment in attributing their growing acceptance to Hebraic thought. But their real proponents in the West were the philosophers of the eighteenth-century Enlighten-ment, whose disciples included the authors of the American Declaration of Independence. When, in 1776, these brash colonists held as self-evident that all men are created equal and are entitled by right to life, liberty and the pursuit of happiness, they were flying in the face of traditional morality. Their ebullient optimism was grounded in the scientific discoveries of the age, plus the fact that they lived in a new country, where land was cheap and individual opportunity seemed boundless. With the economic gains brought about by industry, these American ideals spread throughout Europe and rocked the established order to its very foundations. European Jews were not directly responsible for the newly-accepted belief in human progress, but they rode the wave with undisguised enthusiasm.

The two World Wars and the Cold War have shown that progress does not flow in a straight line and that material gains do not necessarily bring about an improvement in human nature. As a result, the positivistic atheism of the late nineteenth century has all but vanished. But aside from a brief revival in the mid-twentieth century, traditional Christianity continues to lose adherents. Its message of salvation has little appeal in our own time. Now that people live longer, they tend to concentrate on life on earth, rather than pray for admittance into heaven. As for hell, it was made obsolete by Auschwitz. There, and in the other death camps, the Nazis created a hell on earth that surpassed in horror anything that Christian theology could ever devise. As fewer and fewer Christians believe in hell, the question naturally arises: what is there to be saved from?

Another casualty of the twentieth century is the apostle Paul's assumption that the powers that be are of God. The mediaeval alliance of throne and altar worked to the benefit of the church only as long as secular power was weak. When Philip the Fair of France had Pope Boniface VIII kidnapped in 1302, this advantage was lost forever. From then on, Western Catholicism became subservient to the state, as Eastern Orthodoxy had always been in Russia. The overthrow of the Tsarist regime in 1917 dealt the Russian church a blow from which it never fully recovered. The Catholic church, in turn, lost much of its moral credibility when it tried to court Hitler by choosing Eugenio Pacelli as Pope. Since then, the advent of nuclear weapons has obliged some of the more perspicacious Christian philosophers to reconsider Paul's maxim. Can secular rulers, all of whom are necessarily fallible, really be trusted with the Bomb?

The Cold War has shown just how illusory power can be. After amassing a nuclear arsenal capable of destroying all of humanity several times over, one of the superpowers simply disintegrated. The other has won a Pyrrhic victory at best. With no rivals beyond its borders, the United States now has to address itself to internal problems which cannot be solved simply by building more bombs. Rampant crime, widespread drug addiction, soaring medical costs and decaying public education are issues that defy recourse to armed might. The crusade against 'Godless Communism' was organized Christianity's last attempt to regain some of its former influence. Now that the West has won by default, the established churches are weak and directionless. Their clergy have been able to maintain the allegiance of the faithful only at the local level, by getting involved in economic and social issues—such as unemployment, drugs and the breakdown of family life—that affect the entire community. These brave priests and pastors recognize, at least tacitly, that most Christians today prefer to improve their lives on earth, rather than merely to await salvation after death.

With the decline of organized religion has come a rise in the disorganized kind. Millions of lost souls have come to seek in the person of Jesus what they cannot find in the mainstream churches: a guide for living. They campaign for mandatory school prayer in the hope that it will prevent their children from becoming drug addicts and/or contracting AIDS. People who call themselves 'concerned Christians' appeal to Jesus to restore traditional family values, even though he himself scorned them. A French psychiatrist, Dr. Pierre Solignac, has denounced Catholicism's negative attitude toward sex in a book entitled *La névrose chrétienne*[3] ('The Christian Neurosis'). His solution is to rely on Jesus, who never married, for what little guidance he might have to offer. As more and more Christians turn away from their respective churches, they turn to Jesus under the mistaken impression that he, rather than Paul, was the founder of Christianity. No one ever told them otherwise.

For Judaism, the renewed interest in Jesus presents a danger because Christians tend to view him in opposition to the Pharisees. They fail to realize that any attack on the Pharisees is an attack on

---

[3] Paris: Editions de Trévise, 1976.

the Jews, since all Jews—at least all who have any religious convictions—are Pharisees. By exalting Jesus in the spirit of Christian tradition, his followers inevitably denigrate Judaism. They set back not only the cause of human understanding, but their own social progress as well. Christian apologists have long ridiculed the Pharisees in order to make Jesus appear nobler by comparison. One of their favourite targets is the rabbinical debate, which opens the *Betsa* tractate of the Talmud, as to whether it is permitted to eat an egg that has been laid on the Sabbath. As is usual in such academic exercises, the rabbis agree to disagree: the school of Schammai allows one to consume the Sabbath egg while that of Hillel forbids it. Jesus himself showed no interest in the question. When viewed in the larger perspective of human experience, this apparent hair-splitting has little to do with eggs, but is instead an object lesson in social justice. The egg laid on the Sabbath can be seen as a symbol for all goods produced in violation of laws protecting workers. Thus a modern Jew would ask: is it authorized to buy toys made by political prisoners in China or rugs woven by young children in India? The answer in both cases, based on the Talmudic text, would seem to be 'No'. When they mock Jewish legalism, Christians do themselves a disservice by delaying justice for all working people.

The irony of all this is that the values sought by most Christians nowadays are Jewish values. Dr. Solignac would find in traditional Judaism a powerful antidote to the sexual neuroses fostered by Christianity. Pious Jews do not glorify sex as pagans did, nor do they encourage sexual licence. But they praise God for life's joys and consecrate the Sabbath by having sexual relations with their spouses on Friday night. The family values which so many Christians wish to restore are those of Judaism, which commands parents to teach its precepts to their children. But in order to understand Judaism, Christians must first come to terms with the Pharisees, whose aim was—and is—to infuse all aspects of daily life with holiness. Jesus, although educated as a Pharisee, was so eager to see the kingdom of heaven arrive that he brushed aside the sanctity of work and the family. By venerating him,

Christians are blinded to the very moral values they so fervently seek: those of Pharisaic Judaism.

Aimé Pallière was right: all reformist tendencies in Christianity are Judaizing. His compatriot Charles Maurras was likewise correct in stigmatizing as Hebraic the current striving for justice, equality and happiness. Perhaps the greatest tribute ever paid to Judaism by a Christian was that of the English historian, Arnold Toynbee. Trained in the classics, Toynbee admired the unity of the Graeco-Roman world, where a healing balm of universal culture kept the quarreling nations of the Mediterranean basin at peace with one another. He tended to despair of contemporary Europe, where tribal passions had led to two World Wars in his own lifetime. Toynbee was the only historian of his generation actively to seek a meaning in history. He believed that Western civilization must find some spiritual unity or face moral decadence and eventual self-destruction. He viewed Judaism as a disruptive, separatist force, which seemed to prevent the achievement of that unity. For him, the Jews were a tribal relic and Judaism a 'fossil' of ancient Syriac civilization. But Toynbee was always ready to learn. Under pressure from his Jewish critics, he studied Judaism and Jewish history. Toward the end of his life, he reversed himself completely. Christianity had lost its way; the unifying force necessary to halt the decline of the West would have to be Judaism. The historical role of the Jews was to convert all of humanity to their religion. Toynbee died in 1975 before he could develop this concept further, and the Jews have yet to take him up on it.

Chapter XI

THE WAY FORWARD

OUR PRESENT CENTURY has witnessed a colossal abuse of power: two World Wars, a suicidal arms race, rampant pollution and medical overkill are all indications that science has given man more power than he knows how to use. The most extreme abuse of power took place at Auschwitz, where modern technology was utilized to destroy Jewish lives as efficiently as possible without disturbing the existence of others. Science in the sole service of political and economic authority has largely discredited secular humanism. To be a humanist, one must first believe in human beings, in their capacity for self-improvement. But as man threatens daily to destroy himself, it has become very difficult to believe in him. Similarly, the Hitler genocide seriously undermined Jewish belief in a just, compassionate God who created man in His own image. Liberal Judaism has been especially hard hit, since it postulates that a new age of moral, as well as material, progress began in the eighteenth century. Auschwitz represents, at the very least, a giant step backward. But the answer to that tragedy cannot be found in the apocalyptic frenzy that led to the Hebron massacre of February 1994. Dr. Goldstein might not have committed that crime had he read (re-read?) the Yom Kippur prayerbook, which mentions the abuse of power as one of the most grievous sins that all Jews must atone for. Having experienced (or at least witnessed) the most extreme abuse of power by the Nazis, Jews must exercise restraint now that they have emerged from power-lessness. The Rabin government in Israel clearly understood the limits of power, even if some religious Zionists do not.

The great stumbling block to an understanding of the Jewish relationship to power and to the Gentile world as a whole remains Auschwitz. There is simply no way of getting around it. But to speculate on what God had in mind when He allowed six million European Jews to be murdered is fruitless. Nor is it at all salutary to drum Holocaust stories constantly into the heads of young people. Revelations about the genocide did initially have a beneficial effect among Gentiles by demonstrating that Jews are not nearly so powerful as was once claimed. Their effect on Jews has been less positive. If the Holocaust continues to dominate Jewish con-sciousness, Jews will be reduced to the status of guests at their own funeral. Judaism commands its followers to choose life, not death. Auschwitz should not be relived vicariously, but overcome, so that Jews and Gentiles alike may once again work for human progress. To overcome that greatest of horrors, we must first try to understand its place in history.

Auschwitz marked the beginning of the end of the Christian era by putting Christianity's moral failure into sharp relief. At issue is not that Pope Pius XII remained silent as the Nazis rounded up Jews for extermination or that the Vatican helped Adolf Eichmann find refuge in Argentina after the war. These policies, though deplorable in themselves, are incidental to the core of the problem: namely Christian teaching on the Jews and Judaism. All those who participated, directly or indirectly, in the Nazi genocide were baptized Christians and derived their hatred of the Jews from Christianity. Hitler's contention that Judaism encourages vengeance was based on the traditional Christian misinterpretation of 'an eye for an eye'.[1] The so-called 'Holocaust deniers,' those who claim that it never happened and who call it a Jewish hoax, seek to absolve Christianity of all blame. The Jewish response to such slander has been to build more Holocaust memorials and to have courses on the Holocaust included in the public school curriculum. But these efforts, like so many others, are subject to the law of diminishing returns: more is not always better. There is a real danger that Gentiles will tire of hearing about the sufferings of the Jews—all the more so since Jews can hardly be said to suffer today. The Jews never had a monopoly on martyrdom; other

---

[1] See below, p. 261.

peoples have been tortured and slaughtered, although not always in the pursuit of an exalted ideal. Are the school curricula to be cluttered with all the atrocities that have ever befallen humanity? Jews recognize the causal connection between Christian teaching and Auschwitz. Since 1945, they have attempted, with fair success, to have some of the more egregious anti-Jewish references removed from Christian liturgy and teaching. In response to Jewish grievances, the Catholic church eliminated the prayer for the 'perfidious Jews' from the Good Friday service in 1965. Twenty-eight years later, the Lutheran assembly in the United States officially repudiated Luther's anti-Jewish diatribes. Little by little, these symbolic reforms will trickle down to the Christian masses. They represent a step in the right direction, but only a small one. And further steps may well prove impossible. There is a point beyond which Christians cannot reform their religion without subverting it entirely. If they were to recognize the true nature of the Pharisees, for example, the entire Jesus story as presented in the Gospels would lose its traditional meaning. The official catechism of the Catholic church continues to propagate the myth of the Pharisees as the enemies of Jesus. Its authors have surely read the latest scholarship on the subject. They must be aware of the valiant efforts in the 1950's of a French priest, Father Paul Démann, to tone down the anti-Jewish bias of Catholic teaching. Yet the calumny continues to be repeated—not out of ignorance and probably not through conscious malice, but in order to shore up the church's sagging moral position.

The Swiss Protestant theologian Karl Barth issued a percussive reminder to Jews that their Band-Aid approach to Christianity will not work. Throughout his ministry, Barth opposed both Nazism and anti-Semitism. Yet he referred to Judaism since the year 70 as 'the Synagogue of death', whose continued existence alongside the church is 'an ontological impossibility, a wound, a gaping hole in the body of Christ'. In his view, 'the Jews of the ghetto...have nothing to attest to the world but the shadow of the cross of Jesus Christ which falls upon them'. Here the ghetto is used to designate those Jews who remain loyal to Judaism, which Barth, following traditional church teaching, has declared obsolete. However offensive such remarks may be to Jews, they are nonetheless entirely logical: Judaism and Christianity cannot coexist forever. If Judaism is still valid, it has no need of a successor.

At some point, the Jews will have to recognize this fundamental opposition and take up their mission to the Gentiles, and to Christians in particular, where they left it centuries ago. They may find inspiration in the writings of Theodor Herzl, the founder of modern Zionism, who attributed anti-Semitism to a decline in their power to assimilate. Individual Jews, from Spinoza to Trotsky, have exerted a powerful influence on Western thought and action, but not always in a specifically Jewish sense. As the West continues its largely unconscious process of Judaization, the Jews should recognize this trend and engage once again in active proselytism. In the words of Tunisian-born French philosopher Albert Memmi, it is time to 're-open Judaism to the nations'. Failure to do so would be an abdication of the role assigned to the children of Israel in the Covenant. What were they chosen for, after all, if not to enlighten others? Now that official anti-Jewish persecutions have ceased in the West, Jews have no excuse to hide their light under a bushel. The Jewish mission is not primarily a task for the Israelis; they have a country to look after. Their relations with the West are confined largely to diplomacy and tourism, neither of which is propitious for religious teaching.

Re-opening Judaism to the nations falls to the Diaspora Jews, however ill-equipped they may be for such a daunting task. They alone live in daily contact with a Christian majority. If they so wish, mixed marriages can be turned to Judaism's advantage by helping it to expand. Jewish assimilation into Western society could then be dealt with in the same forthright manner as was the Hellenization of Jews some two thousand years ago: through education. All education, and not least Jewish education, must prepare young people for the real world if it is to be fruitful. For most Jews, this world is predominantly Christian. Therefore, young Jews must learn about Christianity and how to counter its anti-Jewish bias. Thus forearmed, they will be able to mingle with Christians with confidence and answer their religious arguments convincingly. When it comes time for marriage (more than half will be engaged to non-Jews), these well-informed young people will be in a position to lead their fiancés to Judaism. Even those who marry other Jews can benefit from such an educational program, since it will direct them to the future rather than to the past.

Renewed missionary activity presents many advantages for contemporary Judaism. It would eliminate some of the morbidity left in the wake of the genocide. It would help combat anti-Semitism at its source; every Christian who converts to Judaism is one less potential anti-Semite. It would allow honest Christians to discover a religion that emphasizes life rather than death. It would effectively end the current domination of religious affairs by the Hasidic fringe and its allies. Even more important, proselytism would give new vitality to Jewish life and thought, which until recently were dominated by fears that the State of Israel might not survive. By seeking converts, Jews would have to explain Judaism to others, and therefore to themselves. This process is already taking place in many mixed marriages. A study entitled *Intermarriage and the Jewish Future*, which was commissioned by the American Jewish Committee in 1979, revealed that when the Gentile spouse converts to Judaism, the resulting family life is more consciously Jewish than among endogamous couples. 'In the conversionary marriage, Jewish identity is not merely asserted; it is acted upon.'

A dynamic, expansive Judaism would then help the Jews free themselves from the siege mentality that has afflicted them for centuries. They began to adopt a defensive posture when Constantine forbade conversions to Judaism within the Roman empire. Although they continued to proselytize throughout the Middle Ages, the Jews of Europe felt themselves to be under siege, as outright persecution—in the form of Crusades, oppressive taxation and expulsions—became more intense. The ghetto offered some protection: it was their fortress, but also their prison. Official emancipation, while conferring upon the Jews the same legal rights as other citizens, did not liberate them totally: even when not confronted by the full force of anti-Semitism, they were still under pressure from Gentile society to justify their distinct identity. This was a virtually impossible task. To the committed Christian, Judaism was obsolete, having been superceded by Christianity. To the atheist, all religion was obsolete. Neither could fathom why Jews, once admitted into civil society, chose to remain Jews. The very fact that many of them sought to hide their Jewish origins and assimilate altogether indicates that the emancipation process was incomplete.

To make it complete, Jews in the liberal West have attempted to win acceptance for themselves as Jews, and not merely as loyal citizens. Their most concerted effort was in Germany during the first three decades of the twentieth century. The intellectual and spiritual leaders of German Jewry recognized that to win acceptance for themselves, they had to win it for Judaism. Through legal action and adult education, they made remarkable progress—until the advent of Hitler. Since then, the German-Jewish approach of trying to influence the Christian majority has fallen into disrepute. The tragedy of the Nazi period has revived a siege mentality that ought to have disappeared with the ghetto itself. Jewish ethnocentrism has been reinforced, as if Jews were consciously trying to adopt the Nazis' own definition of them. The Hasidim are especially zealous in this regard. Their steadfast refusal to marry outside their community is in total conformity with the Nuremberg laws, which forbade intermarriage. Their distinct attire and general appearance make them a most visible minority. No one could ever accuse them—as the Nazis accused culturally assimilated Jews—of trying to infiltrate Gentile society by adopting Western dress and speech.

In historical terms, Hasidism leads inevitably to a dead end, from which only the Messiah can extricate its adherents. Although the Lubavitch movement does proselytize actively among Jews, no Hasidic sect has evinced the least interest in approaching Gentiles. The Hasidim have tacitly agreed not to be a light unto the nations. In their view, the *goyim* are incorrigibly anti-Semitic anyway; so why bother to influence them? Yet there is much evidence to suggest that anti-Semitism is in general decline. Not only do public opinion surveys lead to this conclusion, but the very increase in mixed marriages shows that old prejudices are being overcome. Most Christians who marry Jews have already freed themselves of their society's anti-Jewish bias. If the *goyim* are not all visceral anti-Semites, then perhaps they are worth cultivating.

Seen in this light, the failure of the German-Jewish approach was not that it was inherently flawed, but that it was not given enough time to succeed; Hitler cut it short. Inasmuch as there is no Hitler on the horizon nowadays, the pioneering efforts of the German Jews to instruct Gentiles in the truth about Judaism may safely be resumed throughout the Diaspora. The great Leo Baeck, shortly after emerging from a Nazi concentration camp at the end of the Second World War, urged a renewal of Jewish missionary activity. It was ignorance of Judaism, he argued, that engendered anti-Semitism. Rabbi Baeck's proposal was made over fifty years ago, but has yet to win general acceptance. Unless Jews prefer to abdicate all responsibility for the future of humanity and leave everything for the Messiah to sort out, they have every reason to take up their traditional role as educators. In so doing, they may be able to extricate themselves from a debilitating survival mode, into which they have been locked by centuries of Christian domination.

From Survival to Life

Ever since the early Middle Ages, the Jews managed to survive in Christendom by being economically useful to the sovereign, on whom they depended for their protection. This arrangement was satisfactory to both parties until the Crusades, when many rulers proved incapable of protecting their Jewish subjects. As the Jews were forced out of agriculture by the feudal system and out of the handicraft trades by the guilds, their economic utility diminished. In order to pay the special taxes imposed on them, many took up money lending, which made them hated even more by the populace. Those who had no money to lend were reduced to a bare subsistence. By the eighteenth century, some Jewish communities in Europe were so destitute that they threatened to become a burden to society. Enlightened Christians, such as the Austrian

Emperor Joseph II and Abbé Grégoire, sought to make the Jews more productive by allowing them to enter all trades and professions. The resulting emancipation was based less on humane considerations than on utilitarian grounds. The Jews were still expected to be useful; their usefulness now extended to society as a whole and not merely to the crown.

They still required some form of protection. Even after the Napoleonic reforms ensured equal rights under the law for all citizens, Jews continued to regard the sovereign as the court of the last resort, their ultimate protector. Centuries of survival as a minority group had taught them to recognize where the real power lay. European society of the late nineteenth and early twentieth centuries was still organized into well-defined classes, dominated by a landed aristocracy whose origins went back to the Middle Ages. With the sole exception of France, where the bourgeoisie assumed power in stages from 1870 to 1900, the political and social elite of all the great European powers was recruited largely, if not entirely, from the nobility. For the Jews of Central Europe, the reality of aristocratic power was demonstrated at the turn of the century, when Karl Lueger, an avowed anti-Semite, was elected mayor of Vienna. He was unable to do any serious harm to the city's Jewish inhabitants because they enjoyed the protection of the Austrian emperor.

The old nobility was discredited as a result of the First World War, creating a power vacuum throughout Central and Eastern Europe. Having failed to achieve victory, it lost prestige as a military caste. The first country to oust its aristocratic rulers was Russia, where the war effort had been frightfully mismanaged from the start. As the inexperienced Russian bourgeoisie proved incapable of ending the conflict, it was replaced in short order by the Bolsheviks. With the Allied victory in 1918 came more social upheaval, this time in Central Europe. There, the aristocrats stepped aside, but discretely aided the bourgeoisie in crushing those leftist contenders who tried to profit from the collapse of the old order. But the bourgeois politicians did not maintain their hold on government for very long. They were so frightened by the spectre of Communism that, one by one, they yielded power to movements of the totalitarian Right. In Italy, a series of violent strikes prompted the propertied classes to leave the government to Mussolini in 1922, even though his Fascists had won only seven percent of the seats in parliament.

Fascism drew its strength from those millions of poor and lower-middle class people whose sacrifices for the war effort had not brought them the material and social benefits that the old-line politicians had promised. Being Catholic, they could not support socialism because of its anti-religious bias, which seemed even more menacing now that atheistic Communists had taken power in Russia. The Fascists were political rebels, but they respected many of the country's established institutions, notably the church. Italy's small but prosperous Jewish communities gave their loyalty to the Fascist regime until, under pressure from Nazi Germany, it enacted discriminatory legislation in 1938. Despite this aberration, Italians in general have proved to be remarkably resistant to the anti-Semitic virus that infected much of Western society in the twentieth century. Few expressed interest in *The Protocols of the Elders of Zion*; and when a new translation appeared in 1937, Italian book dealers refused to stock, and Italian newspaper editors declined to review, that infamous forgery. Unlike many other Europeans, Italians see no historical connection between Christianity and national grandeur. They know that their country reached the pinnacle of its glory under pagan Rome and that the advent of Christianity brought no new gains. As a result, they are little inclined to attribute Italy's occasional triumphs to divine providence or its reverses to dark, satanic forces. Mussolini, the son of a leftist schoolteacher and himself a former socialist, was not an anti-Semite.

Hitler was a different piece of goods altogether. In the Middle Ages, he would have been an anonymous figure among the millions of downtrodden, ignorant people whose anti-Jewish prejudice often vented itself in collective rage, but who had no power. Public education and military service in the First World War helped turn this little man into a monster. One problem with Hitler was that he had learned to read and write. Had he remained illiterate, he could never have risen in politics. Instead, like all other Austrian children in the late nineteenth century, he went to the local primary school. There, as part of the regular curriculum, he learned catechism, as well as a particularly chauvinistic version of history, which was designed to turn schoolchildren, especially the boys, into loyal subjects of the state and willing conscripts for military service. This semi-educated son of a minor customs official was too poor to be a bourgeois and too proud to identify himself with the proletariat. As part of the German army, which he joined as a volunteer in 1914, Hitler found the sense of belonging that he so desperately needed.

Under Nazism, the centuries-old Judaeophobia of the European masses became official policy. The little man now held absolute power, evicting the aristocratic elite that had formerly protected the Jews from his hatred. Hitler put an end to the traditional policy of allowing the Jews to survive because of their economic usefulness. He did not consider them to be particularly useful; and in a sense, he was right: they certainly had nothing to contribute to the new Nazi order. In the three generations since their full emancipation, German Jews, like those of other Western countries, had undergone a remarkable social transformation. The first generation rose from the marginal existence of its forebears to engage in retail trade and manufacturing. The newly-prosperous Jews typically left these thriving businesses to their eldest sons, while the others studied law or medicine. The third generation branched out into journalism, teaching and entertainment. By 1933, German Jews were greatly over-represented in those professions, such as publishing and the cinema, which tended to influence people's view of the world about them. The Nazis, while allowing Jewish businessmen to survive for a few years, regarded Jews in the media as subversive of traditional values and ruthlessly eliminated them.

The West's refusal to accept more than a limited number of Jewish refugees from Hitler's Europe was based on similar considerations. Albert Einstein and a score of nuclear physicists, who were either Jewish or married to Jews, were gladly accepted by the United States for their future utility. The vast majority of Europe's Jews, however, were refused asylum because no one could find any use for them. They were perceived, at best, as ambitious upstarts who would usurp other people's jobs or, at worst, as carriers of Bolshevism. Lacking a protector and unable to convince anyone of their usefulness, they were simply not allowed to survive. The survival equation, on which the Jews had relied for centuries, was no longer operative.

Since then, the State of Israel has offered hope for millions of Jews who wish to begin a new life, free from the disabilities of the past. Yet even Israel has, at various times, required protection from the great powers, in return for being useful to them. The Soviet Union supported the partition of Palestine and recognized the Jewish state *de jure* in order to reduce British influence in the Middle East. For a time, Stalin entertained the idea of using Israel, whose early political leaders were socialist, as a means to spread Communism throughout the region. In 1949, the Soviet embassy in Tel Aviv had a staff of fifty—far more than was necessary for such a small country. Moscow's relations with Israel cooled after the Jewish state gave tacit support to American policy in the Korean War. Then it found a new patron, France, which in the mid-1950's was engaged in a bloody civil war with the Algerian insurgents. Not only was Israel useful to France as a counterweight to the Arab nationalism represented by Egyptian President Nasser; it also provided a convenient testing ground for a new generation of French weapons, such as the *Mystère* jet fighter and the AMX-13 tank, both of which were sold to Israel in large numbers. In return, the French helped the Jewish state build its first atomic bomb. After de Gaulle turned against Israel in 1967, it received the protection of the United States, to which it supplied the latest Soviet-made weapons captured from Egypt and Syria, plus valuable intelligence reports on Soviet activities in the region. Now that the Cold War has ended, Israel will have to become useful to its Arab neighbours, by offering them economic cooperation and technical assistance.

In the Diaspora, survivalism has not yet disappeared and, in some instances, has undergone an amazing revival. Its most striking manifestation is in Antwerp, where a busy Hasidic community of diamond cutters and merchants enjoys special police protection in return for its particular contribution to the city's economy. With the mayor's blessing, the Hasidim of Antwerp have re-created a mediaeval *juiverie*, completely separated from the rest of the city except for commercial transactions. Not all Jews, however, wish to cut themselves off from Western culture, especially since their own participation in that culture increases year by year. Jewish writers, musicians, teachers, journalists and entertainers are far more numerous and active than the small Jewish population in the West would seem to warrant. Like the Jews in pre-Hitler Germany, those in France, Britain, the United States and several other Western democracies are leaving the retail trades and manufacturing for more intellectual pursuits. As a result, their economic usefulness to Gentile society has greatly diminished. Will that society continue to tolerate them?

To ensure continued tolerance, established Jewish organizations have relied largely on the Holocaust to remind non-Jews what can happen when a minority is denied its basic rights. In the United States especially, the selling of the Holocaust to the public at large—through films, museums and academic programmes—has been quite successful. But to sell a product to Americans, one must first sanitize it and present it in a neat package. Thus, toilet paper is promoted as 'bathroom tissue', and deodorants are given the title of antiperspirants, whose main purpose, it seems, is to control 'wetness'. Jewish public relations experts in New York and Hollywood have done a similar job on the Holocaust, with the result that its historical specificity has been almost totally obscured. They know that Gentiles, and especially Christians, will not buy their product if it makes the consumer feel the least bit dirty. But if the Holocaust was just another example of man's inhumanity to man, it can have no particular meaning for Jews; and Gentiles may eventually tire of it.

Underlying the cult of the Holocaust is the Jewish will to survive. But survival by being economically useful to others is no longer a valid option. Not only are Jews less useful than they once were, but they can no longer count on established authority to protect them. In this regard, the example of Vichy France is especially relevant. Marshall Pétain was not a rabid populist like Hitler, but a frightened conservative. In the summer of 1940, he took it upon himself to sign the decrees which deprived all French Jews, including the home-born, of their basic rights as citizens. Thus excluded from the nation, they were easy prey for the Nazis and their French sympathizers. Perhaps this was to be expected. The French monarchy had already violated Charlemagne's promise of protection to the Jews by expelling them in 1394. The republic proved incapable of defending itself in 1940; so it was in no position to defend its Jewish citizens. As power continues to shift in a world where tradition has lost all meaning, Jews have nowhere to turn for their protection. Their continued survival is increasingly problematical; they have no choice but to live.

To live means to take control over one's own existence, to act on events rather than being acted on by them. For the Jews of the Diaspora, who are a small minority everywhere, the only way to act on events is by educating the Gentile majority. Eliminating widespread misconceptions about Judaism would be far more effective in the long run than seeking protection against the popular rage that these misconceptions have caused. If Hitler had been taught to take a positive view of Judaism, he could not have become an anti-Semite. There are still millions of ignorant wretches like the young Hitler, whose prejudices are no less strongly held than his. It is in the Jews' own interest to enlighten as many of these people as possible before one of them manages to take power somewhere. The Jews are condemned to educate others. By so doing, they could once again make history—not only as agents for secular change, but in a moral and spiritual sense as well.

Giving History a Meaning

The question of the Jewish role in history is fraught with misunderstanding. The dominant view at present seems to be that of Professor Fackenheim, who sees the State of Israel as the means by which Jews re-entered history, as if they had been absent from it before 1948. But to argue that the Jews can make history only as citizens of a sovereign state is contrary to the Jewish spirit. Long before Benjamin Franklin wrote that the pen is mightier than the sword, Judaism laid stress on education and example, rather than on military prowess. By these means, Jews can act on events without having to depend on political power or armed force. That they have done so is not merely the work of their many artists, musicians and scientists. Their very persistence in Western civilization continually sounds a discordant note that has engendered doubt among Christians. Doubt is the first step toward wisdom. That Western nations have become more tolerant of dissenting opinions and alien cultures in recent years is due in no small part to the Jewish presence. In the past, the Jews have often paid heavily for being different; but to assume that their minority status excluded them from history is absurd.

So what, exactly, has Israel added to the Jewish presence in history? According to Professor Fackenheim, its greatest accomplishment has been to confront what he calls 'the Gentile problem'—a 'teaching of contempt', which he says originated in 'a two-thousand-year-old attempt to theologize the Jewish people out of existence'. This blanket judgment raises some prickly questions. To begin with, the expression 'teaching of contempt' was coined by Jules Isaac, who applied it specifically to Christianity, rather than to non-Jews in general. Fackenheim tacitly admits that the problem is Christian, rather than merely Gentile, by dating it from two thousand years. But has Israel, in fact, challenged Christian teaching on the Jews and Judaism? At most, its existence has made a minor dent in the hoary myth that the Jews were exiled from their land because they had killed Jesus—a myth refuted convincingly by Jules Isaac before the State of Israel was even created. He reminded his readers in 1946 that the Jews had been exiled and their Temple destroyed six centuries prior to the Roman conquest of Judaea. At the time of Jesus, over eighty percent of all Jews already lived in the Diaspora. Isaac himself has done more to set the record straight on this score than the State of Israel, which regularly welcomes Christian pilgrims on Holy Land tours and would not think of offending them. It is not for Israel to challenge Christianity's teaching of contempt, but for the Jews of the Diaspora, who must counter it with the truth about Judaism.

Ultimately, the historical role of the Jewish state would seem to depend on its army, to which Fackenheim gives truly lavish praise. His thesis complements that of Israeli political scientist, Yehuda Bauer, whose essay, *The Jewish Emergence From Powerlessness*,[2] appeared in 1979. Both authors implicitly take armed force to be the prime mover in human events. But it no longer is. The Second World War was the last opportunity for great powers to settle their disputes through military action. Since then, armies do not influence world affairs as they once did: they are hamstrung by the very destructive power of the weapons at their disposal. No one understands this better than the Israelis, most of whom recognize that despite their awesome military strength, which includes a well-developed nuclear arsenal, they cannot suppress Palestinian civilians in the occupied territories forever.

One of the most persistent difficulties confronting the State of Israel since its inception is that its sovereignty has not been fully recognized. It has not been recognized by the rejectionist Arabs who refer to it as 'the Zionist entity' and claim that it will last no longer than the Latin kingdom of Jerusalem founded by the mediaeval Crusaders. It has not been recognized by the many Western journalists, intellectuals and politicians, who love to deliver lectures in morality to the Israeli government. It has not been recognized by those Diaspora Jews—who do not vote, pay taxes or do military service in Israel—but who nonetheless insist that it retain all the land annexed in 1967. Never did the State of Israel

---

[2]Toronto: University of Toronto Press, 1979.

affirm its sovereignty with greater effect than when its diplomats began secret negotiations with representatives of the PLO in Oslo during the summer of 1993. Neither the United States nor the European Union, both of which had repeatedly urged Israel to make peace through open diplomacy, took an active interest in these meetings. And despite numerous obstacles, not the least of which was the Hebron massacre, the two sides have managed to create the conditions in which a Palestinian state can exist in peace with Israel.

By admitting publicly that the Palestinians have a right to a state of their own in the occupied territories, the Rabin government reaped many tangible political benefits. These include diplomatic relations with the Vatican and a trade agreement with China. In return, Israel has had to abandon the Messianic ideal of annexing all of the Biblical promised land. The fact that the Jewish state is not totally Jewish (it contains an important and growing Arab minority), and that it does not encompass all of Palestine, should prompt Jews everywhere to reflect on its true role in history. In addition to giving new life to the Hebrew language, Israel has proved that the Jews are not parasites, that they can live and work together as a viable and progressive society. Jews and righteous Gentiles can only wish it well. On a spiritual plane, however, the redemption that so many Diaspora Jews expected from the State of Israel has yet to materialize. Yitzhak Rabin chose to deal with the Palestinian question politically. He thus continued a tradition of compromise set by his Zionist predecessors Weizmann and Ben Gurion, who accepted the partition of Palestine. As Israeli novelist Amos Oz has rightly reminded us, one makes peace with one's enemies, not with one's friends. The infant State of Israel was quick to establish diplomatic relations with Britain, which had tried since 1939 to prevent its coming into being. The peace treaty with Egypt also indicated a willingness to overcome past enmity. But politics alone cannot bring Jews or the rest of humanity to a golden age. Deprived of the wholly Jewish state that they have so ardently desired, the Zionists of the Diaspora will have to seek redemption elsewhere—within themselves.

To do so, they and other Jews must examine Auschwitz in historical, rather than in providential, terms. The genocide was no more a sign that God had abandoned the Jews than was the Israeli victory of 1967 a sign that He had redeemed them. Any rabbi seeking God's presence in military action would do well to remember the use that early Christians made of the Roman victory over a rebellious Judaea. They took the destruction of the second Temple and the Jewish commonwealth as proof that the Jews had been rejected by God. Actually, however, Rome's military triumph on that occasion simply marked the high-water mark of its power. Decline began to set in immediately thereafter. Similarly, the Nazi genocide effectively undermined the church's reliance on secular power that began with Paul's letter to the Romans. Christianity has lost much of its credibility ever since. Seen in this light, Auschwitz belongs to Christian, even more than to Jewish, history. To help Christians shake off the baneful tradition that led to this tragedy, Jews should not point an accusing finger at them and insist that they modify their religion so as not to offend Jewish sensibilities. It would be wiser to appeal to their intelligence, instead of their sense of shame (if any), and explain what Judaism really is.

If the Jews are ever to correct the frightful misconceptions that led to the Nazi genocide, they must take an optimistic view about humanity and about history itself. The very idea of being a light unto the nations implies that the nations are capable of seeing the light, that they are intrinsically good and not evil—that moral, as well as material, progress is possible. After two World Wars and the numerous crimes against humanity that have marked the outgoing century, it is tempting to give up on man and to assume that history has no meaning. In universities, the study of history has become increasingly fragmented, as scholars turn out a steady stream of learned papers intended solely for other specialists. The magisterial syntheses of earlier years, accessible to a far wider audience, are not being renewed. A sense of progression has been lost.

And yet E. H. Carr was right: history is progress; if not, it would hardly be worth studying. Unfortunately, the heavy hand of ancient and mediaeval tradition, with its emphasis on military force, has prevented Western civilization from converting much of its material gains into moral advance. At times it seems as though the benefits of modern science have been offset, if not outweighed, by its destructive power. Not applied science, but education has been the prime cause of human self-improvement. This is why the Renaissance and the Enlightenment have given the West its most sustained periods of faith in humanity. To take a small example: until the mid-eighteenth century, visiting an insane asylum with the purpose of making fun of the inmates (often poking them with canes or umbrellas to laugh at their pained reactions) was considered a proper Sunday afternoon's entertainment for respectable people in England. Then, for no apparent reason, such excursions went out of fashion, never to return. The English simply got it into their heads that it was no longer fun to torment other human beings. This particular illustration does not prove that moral progress is inevitable, merely that it is possible. Once society begins to regard the mentally ill as fellow citizens endowed with certain basic rights, it may yet show similar consideration for the foreign-born and for those of other races and religions.

Belief in human progress cannot be based solely on past events. Rather, it is derived from the simple fact that all human beings aspire to some form of happiness. Every political or social movement that has ever challenged established authority stems from this fundamental desire. Human happiness is impossible without an essential moral order which can protect the weak from the strong. The entire thrust of history is centered on the search for such an order. Judaism, whose legal system has precisely this purpose, gives religious sanction to individual happiness. It considers life to be worthwhile in itself, and not merely a vale of tears that all mortals must cross in order to enter paradise. In Deuteronomy 24.5, a newly-married man receives a one-year dispensation from military service and civil chores so that he may bring happiness to his wife. Rabbis have interpreted this prescription to include sexual pleasure, as being the right of every married woman. It is easy to dismiss the Biblical text as having been designed merely to further the population growth of a harassed people that had just escaped from slavery. Judaism has always taken it to mean that all human beings are entitled to happiness, men as well as women.

The Biblical statute and the interpretations thereon go beyond the American Declaration of Independence, which recognizes the right of everyone to pursue happiness. (Since 1776, Americans seem to be pursuing it in all directions.) Judaism stipulates that everyone has a right to attain happiness—a more exalted ideal. But happiness, in the Jewish sense, is not to be confused with the kind of instant gratification that television and mass advertising have accustomed us to: it requires work and self-discipline. Hence all the commandments which appear in the Pentateuch and are elaborated on by rabbis. Their purpose is to enable each individual to find a proper balance in life. That Charles Maurras, perhaps the most intelligent of all anti-Semites, begrudged Judaism its dreams of happiness is thoroughly understandable. He regarded them as subversive of established authority, which relies ultimately on force to maintain itself. In this, he was perfectly right. All of human history is a struggle between coercive force and the right of individuals to find happiness in harmony with their fellows. The failure of modern ideologies, such as Marxism, stems from their pretension to know a short cut to universal happiness through the use of counterforce. Whenever a revolutionary party has seized power, as in the Russia of 1917, it proved to be every bit as oppressive as the aristocratic tyranny it replaced, if not more so.

There is no short cut. Human happiness cannot be achieved by a simple transfer of power. Nor is it directly related to purchasing power—the economists' term for spending money. Hillel's maxim that property begets worry (*Avoth* 2.8) is as valid today as it ever was. The modern automobile is a perfect example of what can go wrong when private property is allowed to grow unchecked. No reasonable person would suggest abolishing cars altogether. But when there is no limit on their ownership or use, they pollute the atmosphere, ravage the countryside and destroy cities, creating new social problems and aggravating old ones. Environmental pollution, along with the development of chemical, bacteriological and nuclear weapons, has fundamentally changed man's traditional relationship with nature. Instead of being at the mercy of natural forces beyond his control, man now has the power to destroy the entire planet if he does not discipline himself. As a result, the very notion of prayer has been transformed. In all Western languages, the word prayer is synonymous with request, as exemplified by the farmer who prays for rain during a period of drought. In Hebrew, prayer means meditation or reflection. As human beings learn to accept responsibility for the preservation of our ecosystem, they tend to reflect on their own conduct, rather than pray for divine intervention in nature. Thus, the general, but as yet largely unconscious, process of Judaizing continues.

Its completion depends on the acceptance of divine law, as a necessary reminder that the laws of men are imperfect and can—indeed often do—sanction oppression. Divine law provides the foundation for that moral order which suffering humanity, in its long struggle against ignorance, tyranny and injustice, so ardently desires. The Jewish ideal of moving from point A, the expulsion from Eden, to point B, the Messianic age, is what gives meaning to history. As this progression manifests itself, however slowly, it becomes possible to believe in man, in his capacity for moral improvement. In Judaism, the existence of God is an axiomatic truth; one is not commanded to believe in Him. But to make sense out of history, one has to believe in man, even after Auschwitz. This belief is central to the Jewish challenge. It is the challenge of all humanity.

SUGGESTIONS FOR FURTHER READING

Preface

'Why Be Jewish?' is the concluding chapter of a recently published survey of Jewish moral and religious principles by David S. Ariel, *What Do Jews Believe?* (New York: Schocken Books, 1995). The author reminds his children that Judaism has a glorious past and urges them to work for 'the survival of the Jewish people' (p. 250). In *Why Remain Jewish?* (New York: Hippocrene Books, 1994), David C. Gross urges his fellow Jews to cultivate the recollection of past sufferings. Intermarriage, he fears, will induce amnesia, leaving the victims of Auschwitz without a proper memorial. For British Rabbi Julia Neuberger, the problem is to keep Jewish youth 'attached to the faith and the tribe'. See *On Being Jewish* (London: Heinemann, 1995), p. xv. To this end, she seeks to emphasize the progressive elements in Judaism: its sense of social justice and sexual realism. Unfortunately, these attractive qualities seem to be outweighed by her frequent references to persecutions. More universal in scope and future-oriented is the classic apology of Edmond Fleg, *Pourquoi je suis juif* (Paris: Les Belles Lettres, 1995). This short work was first published in 1927 and therefore contains no references to Auschwitz or Israel. Fleg was sympathetic to Zionism but chose to live as a Jew in the Diaspora. He died in 1963.

The unsettling effect of the Israel–PLO accord, combined with the gradual passing of the Holocaust into history, is brilliantly analyzed by Professor Egon Mayer of Brooklyn college in his pithy article, 'For U.S. Jews, an Age of Anxiety', *New York Times*, 19 September 1993. Such anxiety is felt not only by American Jews, but also by those throughout the Diaspora.

Increasingly, Jewish voices are being raised against making the Holocaust a political issue. In the words of Israeli novelist David Grossman, 'We manipulate it for our own ends', *Die Zeit* (overseas edition), 3 February 1995. His views are shared by Canadian lawyer and constitutional expert Julius Grey, who declared in Montreal: 'I think the Holocaust and anti-Semitism is [*sic*] being used in Israel and the Jewish community to keep people in the fold', *The Gazette* (Montreal), 25 April 1995.

To justify current militancy, religious Zionists often cite Rafael Medoff, *The Deafening Silence: American Jewish Leaders and the Holocaust* (New York: Shapolsky, 1987). The author argues that well-placed Jews in the United States could have done more to save their brethren in Europe, but he utterly fails to prove his point. American anti-Semitism , which reached its apogee during the war, precluded recourse to the pressure tactics he recommends.

For the strident opposition to the late Yitzhak Rabin in Israel, see Amos Elon, 'Israel's Demons', *New York Review of Books*, 21 December 1995, 42-46. The American connection is reviewed by Robert I. Freedman, 'With Blood On Their Hands', *New York*, 20 November 1995, 29-33. Yitzhak Shamir's warning, 'We Are Approaching Another Holocaust', appeared in the *Jewish Press* of Brooklyn on 23 September 1994. Rabin, he claimed, 'cares little, if anything, about our Biblical heritage and G-d-given rights to our land'.

French philosopher Alain Finkielkraut has examined the persistent phenomenon of vicarious suffering among present-day Jews in a controversial essay entitled, *Le juif imaginaire* (Paris: Seuil, 1980). After denouncing the guilt complex that has been foisted on the young, Finkielkraut was virtually excommunicated by his more militant coreligionists in France, some of whom even called him 'an imaginary Jew'.

The situation has not been made any easier by the so-called 'Holocaust deniers', who insist that the tragedy never took place at all. The more the Holocaust is denied, the more Jews tend to dwell on it. Finkielkraut has dealt with this denial in a subsequent work, *L'avenir d'une négation: réflexions sur la question du génocide* (Paris: Seuil, 1982). See also Pierre Vidal-Naquet, 'Vivre avec Faurisson?' in *Les Juifs, la mémoire et le présent* (Paris: Maspero, 1981), pp. 269-272.

The growing tensions between resurgent Orthodoxy and liberalism among French Jews, primarily over the question of intermarriage, are well documented in *Le Monde*, 23 February 1990. When asked for his position regarding conversion to Judaism, the newly-elected president of the *Consistoire*, Benny Cohen, replied coyly: 'I regret that requests for conversion were not more numerous during the war....' Here, vicarious suffering (Cohen was forty years old in 1990) is used to impose religious conformity. In another interview, Alain Finkielkraut disputed the notion that Jews who marry Gentiles necessarily wish to leave Judaism. 'Marrying a non-Jew does not mean abandoning tradition. On the contrary, it demonstrates a desire to carry the message [of Judaism] throughout the world.'

Rabbinical opposition to proselytism is derived largely from a misreading of Jewish history. Thus, Rabbi Emmanuel Feldman, editor of the Orthodox monthly, *Tradition*: 'Conversions to Judaism have not played a major role in Jewish history...' To prove his point, he refers to the *Shulchan Aruch*, which contains only two short chapters on the subject. Yet the *Shulchan Aruch* does not encompass all of Jewish history; it was written in the second half of the sixteenth century—that is, after Judaism, under pressure from the church, had definitively abandoned its missionary vocation. Had Rabbi Feldman gone back to late antiquity, or merely to the High Middle Ages, he would have seen just how vigorous Jewish proselytism had once been. In a formal declaration published in 1935 and reaffirmed in 1946, 1972 and 1984, the Sephardic rabbis of New York and New Jersey have alerted their flock to 'the threat of conversions [to Judaism]'. Yet one of their confrères, Rabbi Marc D. Angel of the Spanish and Portuguese Synagogue in New York, takes a gentler approach. 'Ours must not be a haughty and elite attitude towards would-be converts. We have a moral obligation to convert those who seek conversion, not only for their sakes, but for the sakes of their children.' See Emmanuel Feldman and Joel B. Wolowelsky, eds., *The Conversion Crisis* (Hoboken, NJ: Ktav, 1990), pp. i, 52, 57.

The Jewish obsession with survival can be seen in a profusely illustrated book by Max Wurmbrand and Cecil Roth, *The Jewish People: 4000 Years of Survival* (Tel Aviv: Massada Press, 1976). This is in fact a most competent survey, whose contents do not fully justify its title. In the past 4000 years, the Jews have done far more than merely survive.

Chapter I

An expert summary of Israelitic religion and culture is presented by Sabatino Moscati, Director of the Centre for Semitic Studies at the University of Rome, in chapter VII of his classic, *The Face of the Ancient Orient* (New York: Doubleday, 1962). In his words, 'God has made a pact with Israel; the working out of this pact constitutes history' (p. 237). Moscati's conclusion, in which he explains that the religion of the people cannot be the religion of the state, is pure genius.

More prosaic is the short book by Professor Harry M. Orlinsky of the Hebrew Union College in New York, *Ancient Israel* (Ithaca, NY: Cornell University Press, 1954). This is a largely political account of the Judaean state, its rise and fall, and how these vicissitudes were interpreted by the Hebrew prophets. The author insists that the prophetic message is addressed to all mankind, but he does not examine the possible impact of the Israelites on other societies.

That the Jews have a mandate to act on history is the basic premise of Salo W. Baron, who for many years directed the Jewish history programme at Columbia University. He characterizes Judaism as 'historical monotheism' in the sweeping preface to volume I of *A Social and Religious History of the Jews* (New York: Columbia University Press, 1952). Baron is known for his opposition to what he called the 'lachrymose' version of Jewish history, in which the Jews are cast as mere victims, content to survive. Typical of his approach is this assessment of the confrontation between Judaism and Greek culture: 'The Hellenization of the Jewish masses...turned out to be the chief aid to Jewish propaganda' (I, 188). By contrast, a survey presented by a group of historians at the Hebrew University of Jerusalem under the direction of H. H. Ben-Sasson, *A History of the Jewish People* (Cambridge, MA: Harvard University Press, 1976), devotes a very short chapter to the pre-Christian Diaspora and only a single paragraph to Jewish proselytism.

The progressive and dynamic nature of Judaism in late antiquity can be seen in *Judaism in the First Century* (London: Sheldon Press, 1989) by Hyam Maccoby, a fellow at the Leo Baeck College in London. He gives full credit to the Pharisees for furthering its expansion. Of particular interest is his explanation (pp. 90-93) as to how animal sacrifice evolved from the notion of atonement for sin to that of a gift to God.

The Pharisees were first rescued from general opprobrium through the efforts of an English scholar, R. Travers Herford, whose book, *The Pharisees* (Boston: Beacon Press, 1962), was first published in 1924. He inveighs against the common belief that the Pharisees strayed from the teachings of the prophets, degrading Judaism into organized hypocrisy. 'A greater misreading of history it is scarcely possible to imagine. Pharisaism was the application of prophetic teaching to life, and such the Pharisees understood it to be' (p. 238). Herford, a Unitarian minister, was greatly influenced by Rabbi Leo Baeck, whose pioneering work on the subject has been translated into English under the title, *The Pharisees and Other Essays* (New York: Schocken Books, 1966). More recently, Rabbi Stuart Rosenberg of Toronto has reminded his readers that the Pharisees were the founders of normative Judaism in chapter VIII, 'Appreciating the Pharisees', of his compassionate essay, *The Christian Problem: A Jewish View* (New York: Hippocrene Books, 1986).

An excellent overview of the pre-Christian Diaspora is provided by Jean Juster in his classic study, *Les juifs dans l'Empire romain* (2 vols.; New York: Burt Franklin, n.d.), which was first published in 1914. The author shows the Jews of late pagan antiquity to be active in all trades and professions and generally respected by Gentiles. A more religious slant is taken by Charles Guignebert in *Le monde juif vers le temps de Jésus* (Paris: Albin Michel, 1950). Professor Guignebert, who taught the history of Christianity at the Sorbonne for many years, gives due recognition to Jewish missionary activity in the Diaspora. It reached its peak, he writes, in the middle of the first Christian century (p. 299)—i.e.: sometime after the death of Jesus.

Chapter II

An excellent introduction to the political situation in Judaea during Jesus's lifetime can be found in Doron Mendels, *The Rise and Fall of Jewish Nationalism* (New York: Doubleday, 1992). The author, a professor of ancient history at the Hebrew University of Jerusalem, sees Jesus as being closer to the Pharisees than to the Zealots. He puts the Nazarene's Messianic claims in the context of a popular movement to restore the Hebrew monarchy.

The classic Zionist treatment of Jesus is that of Joseph Klausner, *Jesus of Nazareth: His Life, Times and Teaching* (New York: Macmillan, 1925). The author praises Jesus as a master of parable and notes his popularity in a Judaea on the verge of insurrection. A more recent analysis is that of the Israeli scholar David Flusser, *Jesus* (New York: Herder and Herder, 1969). The emphasis here is on the Jewish sources of Jesus's teachings. André Chouraqui has translated the New Testament into French, using the Aramaic and Hebrew equivalents of the Greek text. The resulting book, entitled *Un Pacte neuf* (Turnhout: Brepols, 1984), gives a decidedly Jewish flavour to the entire narrative.

Of the many attempts to describe the 'historical' Jesus, the most recent is that of John Dominic Crossan, *The Historical Jesus: The Life of a Mediterranean Jewish Peasant* (San Francisco: Harper San Francisco, 1991). Professor Crossan admits that research in the field has become 'something of a bad scholarly joke' (p. xxvii) and then proceeds to follow his predecessors' example by attempting to reconstruct the past.

The French historian Jules Isaac ably refutes the hoary myth that the Judaism of Jesus's day was degenerate, in his plea for tolerance entitled, *L'enseignement du mépris* (Paris: Fasquelle, 1962). This is a sequel to his earlier work, *Jésus et Israël* (2nd edition; Paris: Fasquelle, 1959), in which he emphasizes the Nazarene's popularity among his compatriots and lays the blame for his death on the Romans. Isaac, who developed his ideas on the subject during the Nazi occupation of France, tends to equate the Jewish religious authorities in Roman-occupied Judaea with French collaborators in the Second World War. A more scholarly treatment, though not entirely devoid of emotion, is that of Paul Winter, *On the Trial of Jesus* (Berlin: Walter de Gruyter, 1961). The author leaves no doubt that Jesus was put to death by the Romans for sedition.

In his latest work, *Who Killed Jesus?* (San Francisco: Harper San Francisco, 1995), John Dominic Crossan likewise blames the Romans for the execution of Jesus. His division of the Gospels into historical and unhistorical passages will strike some readers as arbitrary; and his attempt to absolve the Jews of all responsibility, while laudable in itself, may lead Christians to wonder if he is not diminishing Jesus's divinity in the process.

The Jewish opposition to the Nazarene's Messianic claims remains the main sticking point. Milton Himmelfarb compares Jesus to a Hasidic rabbi in his good-humoured essay, 'On Reading Matthew', in *The Jews of Modernity* (New York: Basic Books, 1973), pp. 193-213. Salo W. Baron, after describing Jesus as 'an essentially Pharisaic Jew', soon adds: 'The bulk of the Jews, nevertheless, had to oppose Jesus.' *A Social and Religious History of the Jews*, vol II: *Christian Era: The First Five Centuries* , pp. 67 and 70. There the matter rests; no explanation is given as to why they had to oppose him. A small clue is provided by Rabbi Jacob Bernard Agus in his masterful synthesis, *The Evolution of Jewish Thought from Biblical Times to the Opening of the Modern Era* (London: Abelard-Schuman, 1959). In his view, the Pharisees began to have doubts about Jesus when he refused to give them a sign (i.e.: positive proof) that he was indeed the Messiah. Their opposition to him was a matter not of principle, but of identification. In a well-researched study entitled, *Jesus and the Judaism of His Time* (New York: Polity Press, 1988), Irving M. Zeitlin, professor of sociology at the University of Toronto, sees Jesus's refusal to be the king-Messiah his compatriots so ardently sought as the source of their eventual opposition to him.

Finally, an English scholar, Geza Vermès, has explained the Jewish meaning of the term, 'son of God', in chapter VIII of his popular treatise, *Jesus the Jew: A Historian's Reading of the Gospels* (London: Collins, 1973).

Chapter III

For a reasoned critique of the apostle Paul and his work, see Joseph Klausner, *From Jesus to Paul* (Boston: Beacon Press, 1961), which was originally published in 1943. Here, Paul's ethics and doctrine of submission to political authority are condemned as being totally at odds with Jewish tradition. Yet the author agrees in the end with Maimonides in seeing the religion created by Paul as a necessary step toward the eventual triumph of Judaism. A more sympathetic treatment is that of Richard L. Rubenstein, *My Brother Paul* (New York: Harper & Row, 1972). Rubenstein, a former rabbi, recognizes the apostle's essential Jewishness, even in his break with Judaism. Nearly every Jew has, at one time or another, wanted to shake off the burden of minority status.

A clear introduction to the Jewish religion in Paul's time is presented by George Foot Moore in his widely acclaimed study of 1927, *Judaism in the First Centuries of the Christian Era* (2 vols.; New York: Schocken Books, 1971). Moore, a professor at the Harvard Divinity School, presents Judaism as being charitable and dynamic, effectively laying to rest the myth of its presumed decadence. Another Christian scholar of Judaism, the Anglican minister James Parkes, has taken a somewhat different approach in *The Foundations of Judaism and Christianity* (London: Vallentine, Mitchell, 1960). While recognizing the vitality of Judaism, Parkes sees it reduced to a religion of survival following the Christian takeover of the Roman empire. This may be anticipating somewhat, but it is clear that the abortive revolts against Rome had already necessitated a period of consolidation, which began with Yohanan Ben-Zakkai. His wisdom and sense of political reality are extolled by Jacob Neusner, formerly of Brown University and now research professor of Judaica at the University of South Florida in Tampa, in *First Century Judaism in Crisis* (Nashville, TN: Abington Press, 1975).

That Judaism continued to seek converts after the advent of Christianity is made evident in Rabbi Bernard J. Bamberger's scholarly monograph of 1939, *Proselytism in the Talmudic Period* (New York: Ktav, 1968). Bamberger does not mince words: 'The attitude of the Rabbis, throughout the Talmudic period, was favourable to conversion and friendly to converts' (p. 277). His introduction to the new edition contains a well-documented summary of Jewish proselytism in the Middle Ages. French Protestant scholar Marcel Simon fully recognizes the importance of Jewish proselytism in his exhaustive study of Judaeo-Christian relations, which first appeared in 1947, *Verus Israel* (Paris: de Boccard, 1964). It was the very vitality of Judaism, he argues, that compelled the church to treat it as a redoubtable foe. This theme has also been explored by Marc Saperstein in chapter I of his short but thoughtful book, *Moments of Crisis in Jewish-Christian Relations* (London: SCM Press, 1989).

The Judaizing tendencies of Christians in Antioch and John Chrysostom's reactions to them are examined in Robert L. Wilken, *John Chrysostom and the Jews: Rhetoric and Reality in the Late 4th Century* (Berkeley: University of California Press, 1983). The author notes the vitality of the Jewish community in Antioch and devotes an entire chapter to 'the attraction of Judaism'. See also Marcel Simon, 'La polémique antijuive de Saint Jean Chrysostome et le mouvement judaïsant d'Antioche', in *Recherches d'histoire judéo-chrétienne* (Paris: Mouton, 1962), pp. 140-153. The bishop's own diatribes can be read in French translation as 'Discours contre les Juifs', in volume II of *Oeuvres complètes* (9 vols.; Toulon: Mingardon, 1864).

In a pioneering work first published in 1934, *The Conflict of the Church and the Synagogue* (Cleveland: Meridian Books, 1961), James Parkes postulates a causal relationship between the teachings of early Christianity and modern anti-Semitism. Beginning with the Gospels, the church fathers refined and elaborated on anti-Jewish doctrine until they had created a hermetical system. Jules Isaac expands on Parkes's study in *Genèse de l'antisémitisme* (Paris: Calmann-Lévy, 1956). He sees a fundamental, qualitative difference between the animosity expressed by some pagan writers toward the Jews and the coherent hostility of the church. Moreover, the position of the Jews in the Roman empire—whether social, economic or religious—was materially weakened by the edicts of Constantine.

An excellent survey of Jewish life in the early Middle Ages is provided by Salo W. Baron in volumes III and IV of *A Social and Religious History of the Jews*. As a protected minority, the Jews of Western Christendom and the Muslim world enjoyed several centuries of economic progress and religious development. Inasmuch as Baron prefers to emphasize the positive aspects of Jewish history, his descriptions of the Crusades are all the more poignant. Jacob B. Agus sees the Jews' ability to survive by being useful to the sovereign as a major cause of the popular anger directed against them, in *The Meaning of Jewish History* (New York: Abelard-Schuman, 1963), pp. 255 *et passim*.

Zionism and the Arab reaction to it have elicited interest in traditional Islamic hostility toward Jews; some writers put it on a par with that of Christianity. Mark R. Cohen, professor of Near Eastern Studies at Princeton, sets the record straight in his scholarly monograph, *Under Crescent and Cross: The Jews in the Middle Ages* (Princeton, NJ: Princeton University Press, 1994). The Jews' generally secure place in Muslim society reflected the tolerance shown them by Islamic jurisprudence. Cohen adds: 'Whether their persecution is measured in terms of expulsion, murder, assault on property or forced conversion, the Jews of Islam did not experience physical violence on a scale even remotely approaching Jewish suffering in Western Christendom' (p. 169).

Chapter IV

An excellent source book on mediaeval Jewish life is that of Jacob R. Marcus, *The Jew in the Medieval World* (New York: Atheneum, 1977). The editor wisely extends his documentation well into the eighteenth century, as the Jewish Middle Ages did not end until then. For most Jews, there was no Renaissance. They were catapulted directly into the modern period with little or no time to adjust.

Jacob Katz, professor of Jewish social history at the Hebrew University of Jerusalem, has written a masterful study of Jewish-Gentile relations in mediaeval and early modern Europe under the title, *Exclusiveness and Tolerance* (London: Oxford University Press, 1961). He explains that the rabbis had to soften their initial judgement that Christianity was idolatrous, because more and more Jews were being drawn into business dealings with Christians. Thus, Judaism became more tolerant of Christianity just as the church stiffened its position toward the Jews.

Allusions to Jewish proselytism in the late Middle Ages can be found in Bernard Gui, *Manuel de l'inquisiteur* (2 vols.; Paris: Champion, 1926-27), II, 6-9, as well as the manual drafted for the Spanish Inquisition by Nicholas Eymerich and Francisco Peña, *Le manuel des inquisiteurs* (Paris: Mouton, 1973), pp. 72-89. Baron relates cases of conversions to Judaism in the late thirteenth century in *A Social and Religious History of the Jews*, IX, 23.

A reliable survey of Spanish Judaism, emphasizing intellectual more than social history, is provided by Jane S. Gerber, *The Jews of Spain: A History of the Sephardic Experience* (New York: The Free Press, 1992). Professor Gerber, who directs the Institute for Sephardic Studies at CUNY, is especially persuasive when analyzing the changes brought about by the Christian reconquest. Luis Suarez Fernandez notes the loyalty of Iberian Jews to their secular rulers, whether Muslim or Christian, in *Judíos españoles en la Edad Media* (Madrid: Rialp, 1980). He emphasizes their role as commercial and cultural intermediaries between different Gentile societies. An Israeli educator, Ami Bouganim, has prepared a collection of sources with helpful annotations entitled, *L'or et le feu: le judaïsme d'Espagne* (Jerusalem: Pathways Editions, 1992). Among the annotated source books which allow the non-specialist to gain an understanding of Maimonides and his philosophy, two of the most useful are Jacob S. Minkin, *The Teachings of Maimonides* (Northvale, NJ: Jason Aronson, 1987) and Isadore Twersky, *A Maimonides Reader* (West Orange, NJ: Behrman House, 1972). The first book of the *Mishneh Torah*, which contains many of the philosopher's prescriptions for daily living, has been translated into

French as *Le livre de la connaissance* (Paris: Presses Universitaires de France, 1961).

The prolific British historian Cecil Roth depicts Italian Jews as being invariably pious and hard-working, in his thousand-year survey, *The History of the Jews of Italy* (Philadelphia: Jewish Publication Society of America, 1946). His bias can be explained by the fact that the written records upon which he relies were left by rabbis and other Jewish leaders. When Roth uses outside sources, such as the report of a Gentile physician describing occupational diseases in the ghetto (pp. 374-375), an otherwise glowing portrait of Italian Jewry turns sombre.

For the Messianic craze of the seventeenth and eighteenth centuries, the definitive study is by Gershom Scholem, *Sabbatai Sevi, the Mystical Messiah, 1626-1676* (Princeton: Princeton University Press, 1973). Professor Scholem, the world's leading authority on Jewish mysticism, denies that the movement originated in the 1648 massacres of Polish Jews: Zevi drew his greatest following from the relatively secure and prosperous Jewish communities of Salonika, Leghorn and Amsterdam. This raises the possibility that the general frenzy may have had its origins in the pent-up resentment of Sephardic Jews over their families' expulsion from Spain.

In any event, Messianism and its derivatives proved to be most durable in Poland. The classic story of Polish Jewry, originally written in Russian just prior to the First World War, is that of Simon Dubnow, *History of the Jews in Russia and Poland* (4 vols.; New York: Ktav, 1975). Here we have Jewish history at its most lachrymose—a seemingly endless succession of persecutions, relieved only by an occasional good Polish king, who may have had a Jewish mistress. At least Dubnow's style is vivid, which is more than can be said for that of Bernard D. Weinryb, *The Jews of Poland* (Philadelphia: Jewish Publication Society of America, 1972). This is essentially a reference work, from which causality is largely absent, on the period 1100 to 1800.

The collapse of the mediaeval Ashkenazic system is analyzed with extraordinary insight by Jacob Katz in *Tradition and Crisis: Jewish Society at the End of the Middle Ages* (New York: Schocken

Books, 1971). Increasing pauperism among Polish Jews in the seventeenth and eighteenth centuries weakened their communal organizations and the authority of their leaders. To fill the void, they turned first to Hasidism, then to the belief in secular progress that characterized the Enlightenment.

Chapter V

On Moses Mendelssohn and the German *Haskala*, see the thoughtful study by Michael A. Meyer, *The Origins of the Modern Jew* (Detroit: Wayne State University Press, 1967). It recounts the various attempts made in the late eighteenth and early nineteenth centuries to make Judaism compatible with German society. They all turned around the question: why should anyone of European culture remain a Jew? Jacob Neusner takes a different approach in chapter VII of his essay on the varieties of Judaism, *Self-fulfilling Prophesy* (Boston: Beacon Press, 1987). He sees Reform and its younger cousin, Orthodoxy, as necessary adaptations to the new civil status of German Jews.

Jacob Katz confirms his reputation as an *Auflkärer* in *Out of the Ghetto: The Social Background of Jewish Emancipation, 1770-1870* (Cambridge, MA: Harvard University Press, 1973). Especially perceptive is his assessment of its results, on page 201. The promoters of emancipation 'were unable to create more than a semineutral society where the inferior status of the Jews was ignored by conscious effort rather than eliminated by actual equality'.

For France, the most complete account is that of Arthur Hertzberg, *The French Enlightenment and the Jews* (New York: Columbia University Press, 1968). The political, cultural and economic aspects of the question are carefully examined. Rabbi Hertzberg's conclusion is troubling: he maintains that the same forces which led to emancipation also engendered modern anti-Semitism. A more optimistic note is sounded by Robert Badinter, former French minister of justice, in *Libres et égaux: l'émancipation des Juifs, 1789-1791* (Paris: Fayard, 1989). Even though emancipation has not fully lived up to the initial hopes of its authors, he writes, it nonetheless represents a net gain for all Jews. A collection of documents on Jewish emancipation in France has been published under the title, *La Révolution Française et l'émancipation des juifs* (8 vols.; Paris: EDHIS, 1968). It includes the three prize-winning essays in the Metz literary competition of 1788 and the various petitions from Jews to the Constituent Assembly the following year.

A revival of interest in the Vichy period has led many French Jews to conclude that their own emancipation was a Faustian bargain, in which they were encouraged to abandon Judaism in return for a civil status that was not always honoured. One of the most vocal proponents of this theory is a noted adversary of Alain Finkielkraut, writer Shmuel Trigano, in his bitter polemic, *La république et les juifs* (Paris: Les Presses d'Aujourd'hui, 1982), pp.32 *et passim.*

The uneven progress of Jewish emancipation in Germany is discussed by Reinhard Rürup in *Emanzipation und Antisemitismus* (Frankfurt am Main: Fischer, 1987). The Jews themselves are almost totally absent from this study, which concentrates on the political and intellectual debates on the question. Not all proponents of Jewish emancipation wanted the Jews to be fully equal to other citizens. By contrast, German Jews have their say in an exhaustive source book drawn from the archives of the Leo Baeck Institute in New York by Monika Richarz, *Bürger auf Widerruf: Lebenszeugnisse deutscher Juden, 1780-1945* (Munich: C. H. Back, 1989). In a chronological progression of private letters, diaries and memoirs by unknown German Jews, the reader can follow their economic and cultural achievements until 1933. A statistical table on page 23 confirms this evolution. The initial efforts of the last generation to adapt to the Hitler regime and its eventual decision to leave Germany are also well documented.

The early youth and baptism of Karl Marx are reviewed by Leopold Schwarzschild in *Karl Marx, the Red Prussian* (New York: Grosset and Dunlap, 1958). Marx's role in the evolution of anti-Jewish thought is examined by Julius Carlebach in *Karl Marx and the Radical Critique of Judaism* (London: Routledge & Kegan Paul, 1978). Professor Carlebach recalls the difficulties faced by the Jews of Prussia as they tried to integrate themselves into that stratified society. He denies that Marx was motivated by self-hatred, but admits that his polemics against the Jews helped sustain anti-Semitism on the Left. A good general treatment of anti-Semitism is hard to find. Nearly all books on the subject begin with the premise that the Jews were used as scapegoats for the ills of society. Just why Europeans needed a scapegoat at the end of the nineteenth century, a period of unprecedented economic advance and imperial expansion, is never explained. One author who has done some original thinking on the question is Israeli historian Uriel Tal, in his well-researched monograph, *Christians and Jews in Germany: Religion, Politics and Ideology in the Second Reich, 1870-1914* (Ithaca, NY: Cornell University Press, 1975). He sees anti-Semitism rooted in the fear that society was being deChristianized. Even those anti-Semites who were not believing Christians used arguments derived from Christianity to win adherents to their cause.

Chapter VI

The workings of French Judaism at the time of the Dreyfus Affair are examined in detail by Michael R. Marrus in *The Politics of Assimilation* (London: Oxford University Press, 1971). Professor Marrus, who teaches history at the University of Toronto, suggests that the Jews of France did not mount an effective opposition to the condemnation of Dreyfus because they were culturally assimilated. Yet the unassimilated Jews of Russia did nothing to protest the shameful trial of Mendel Beilis, except to oppose the Tsarist regime itself. French Jews, on the other hand, had to trust in the Republic and rely on its immanent justice, for it offered them the best hope for security and economic advancement. The author's conclusion, in which he recalls that France has not always responded in kind to the loyalty of its Jewish citizens, implies that the Jews of 1894 ought to have known what was going to happen to their descendants fifty years later.

Books on the Dreyfus Affair fall into two main categories: detailed accounts of its judicial aspects or broad denunciations of anti-Semitism as mass hysteria. To understand the political context in which the Affair became a national issue, see François Goguel, *La politique des partis sous la IIIe République* (Paris: Seuil, 1956), pp. 98-109. Professor Goguel, who for many years taught at the Institute for Political Studies in Paris, explains that those who opposed a re-trial were not all anti-Semites.

Of all works on Zionism, none is more complete or more balanced than that of Walter Laqueur, *A History of Zionism* (New York: Schocken Books, 1976). Among its many merits are the causal connection with Jewish emancipation and the author's frank admission that any Jewish state in Palestine would inevitably cause prejudice to its Arab inhabitants. Far less critical is Paul Johnson, who sees Zionism as the spiritual redemption of the Jews. The exchange between Herzl and Count Witte can be found on page 364 of *A History of the Jews* (London: Weidenfeld and Nicolson, 1987).

The efforts of Chaim Weizmann to obtain British support for the Zionist project are recounted in all their minutiae by Leonard Stein in *The Balfour Declaration* (London: Vallentine, Mitchell, 1961). For an explanation of British interests in this matter, see A. J. P. Taylor, *Politics in Wartime* (London: Hamilton, 1964), pp. 112-113.

On the Jews of Russia, Dubnow is as lachrymose as ever—this time with rather more justification. He warmly applauds all attempts, whether through the *Bund* or through Zionism, whereby Jews sought to free themselves from Tsarist tyranny. The quotes from Tsars Ivan IV and Alexander III can be found in volume I, page 243 and volume II, page 379, respectively. A more balanced approach is that of Salo W. Baron, *The Russian Jew Under Tsars and Soviets* (New York: Macmillan, 1964). Baron concentrates on the inner life of the Jewish communities in Russia, but even he cannot ignore the oppressive system under which they had to function. The quote from Nicholas I comes from page 35.

Chapter VII

The over-representation of Jews in radical movements of the Left is analyzed perceptively by Norman F. Cantor in *The Sacred Chain* (New York: Harper Collins, 1994), pp. 273-283. It stems, he writes, from two factors: the strong commitment to social justice within Judaism, plus the inability of the Russian economy (and to a lesser extent, those of some Western countries) to absorb thousands of poor but educated young Jews. A fascinating account of Jewish labour organizations, with particular emphasis on Russia and the United States, is given by Nora Levin, *While Messiah Tarried: Jewish Socialist Movements, 1871-1917* (New York: Schocken Books, 1977). The author never defines what she means by socialist, but it is clear that the common aim of these movements was social justice rather than political power. For the essential Jewishness of Trotsky, see Joseph Nedava, *Trotsky and the Jews* (Philadelphia: Jewish Publication Society of America, 1971).

A sympathetic view of Polish Jewry is provided by Celia S. Heller, *On the Edge of Destruction: Jews in Poland Between the Two World Wars* (New York: Columbia University Press, 1977). Of especial interest are the Polonizing tendencies of many Jews in the larger cities, who took to speaking Polish among themselves in the 1920's. Professor Donald L. Niewyk portrays German Jews of the period as both intellectually vigorous and politically astute in *The Jews in Weimar Germany* (Baton Rouge: Louisiana State University Press, 1980). He defends their essential liberalism and love of country as 'a clear-sighted perception of Jewish self-interest' (p. 199). For the plight of German Jews under Nazi rule, see Wolfgang Benz, ed., *Die Juden in Deutschland, 1933-1945* (Munich: C. H. Beck, 1989). This collection of short monographs shows that the Jewish reaction to Nazism, while varied, was generally intelligent and courageous. The Jews were not blinded by patriotism to the dangers posed by the new regime; their ability to resist was limited only by their political and economic weakness.

The American role—or lack of one—in the Jewish refugee question is the subject of a lively narrative by veteran journalist Arthur D. Morse, While *Six Million Died: A Chronicle of American*

Apathy (New York: Random House, 1967). The author has an excellent grasp of the pre-war period and recalls the efforts of American Jews to resettle the passengers of the *Saint Louis* in Cuba. The statistics on Jewish participation in the United States armed forces are from A. Q. Maisel, 'The Jews Among Us', *Readers Digest* (April 1955), 26-31.

Canada's shameful refusal to accept more than a token number of Jewish refugees from Nazism is the object of a severe indictment by Irving Abella and Harold Troper in *None Is Too Many: Canada and the Jews of Europe, 1933-1948* (Toronto: Lester & Orpen Dennys, 1982). This book is more than a mere denunciation of bureaucratic obstructionism. It exposes the increasing Judaeophobia of most Canadians during the period as well as the inability of Canada's Jewish community, from Samuel Bronfman on down, to influence policy. Although Canadian Jews were more numerous and less assimilated than their French brethren during the Dreyfus Affair, they nonetheless remained completely ineffectual.

Britain's difficulties in carrying out its mandate over Palestine are chronicled by former Prime Minister Harold Wilson in *The Chariot of Israel* (London: Weidenfeld and Nicolson, 1981). The author is extremely critical of the 1939 White Paper and readily quotes those British political figures of the period, such as Labourite Hugh Dalton, who believed that the Jews should be allowed to become a majority in the mandated territory. The question of Arab immigration from neighbouring countries is raised by Fred M. Gottheil, 'Arab Immigration Into Pre-state Israel', in Elie Kedourie and Sylvia G. Haim, eds., *Palestine and Israel in the 19th and 20th Centuries* (London: Cass, 1982), 143-152. This theme is developed further by Joan Peters in *From Time Immemorial: The Origins of the Arab-Jewish Conflict Over Palestine* (New York: Harper and Row, 1984). She notes that the British authorities counted all Arab immigrants as part of Palestine's indigenous or existing population, just as fast as they arrived.

Chapter VIII

Of all the books currently available on the Nazi genocide, one in particular stands out as a synthesis and general introduction: Michael R. Marrus, *The Holocaust in History* (London: Penguin, 1987). The author readily acknowledges that anti-Semitism was not especially virulent in Germany before 1933, and he avoids condemning Jews in Europe or elsewhere for their lack of an adequate response to the tragedy. Unfortunately, the book does not live up to the promise of its title: no indication is given as to the place of the Holocaust in history or its possible meaning for future generations. Israeli political scientist Yehuda Bauer similarly limits his inquiry to the immediate problem in a series of lectures entitled, *The Holocaust in Historical Perspective* (Seattle: University of Washington Press, 1978). The author labours under the misapprehension that 'the Western Allies were fighting for decency, for liberty...' (p. 86).

A total lack of decency toward Hitler's chief victims characterizes the Foreign Office in *Britain and the Jews of Europe, 1939-1945* (London: Oxford University Press, 1979) by Bernard Wasserstein, who now teaches at Brandeis University. Typical of its calculations is this excerpt (p. 248) from a memorandum dated 24 December 1943 by A. W. G. Randall, head of the Refugee Department: 'Once we open the door to adult male Jews to be taken out of enemy territory, a quite unmanageable flood may result. (Hitler may facilitate it!)' According to Tony Kushner, British indifference to the fate of Jews in Nazi Europe was not limited to the Foreign Office, but reflected a widespread hostility toward them. See his article, 'The Impact of British Anti-semitism, 1918-1945', in David Cesarani, ed., *The Making of Anglo-Jewry* (Oxford: Blackwell, 1990).

The efforts (and subsequent failure) of American Jews, such as Rabbi Stephen Wise, to save their European brethren are well documented by Henry Feingold in *The Politics of Rescue: The Roosevelt Administration and the Holocaust, 1938-1945* (New Brunswick, NJ: Rutgers University Press, 1970). Feingold holds the government, not the American people, responsible for lack of action on this issue. David S. Wyman, however, sees the obstructionism of the State Department as being entirely consistent with American anti-Semitism in *The Abandonment of the Jews: America and the Holocaust, 1941-1945* (New York: Pantheon Books, 1984). Wyman, a professor of history at the University of Massachusetts, notes that the Allies did evacuate considerable numbers of non-Jewish Poles, Greeks and Yugoslavs during the war.

For the Jewish leadership under Nazi rule, see the encyclopaedic treatise by Isaiah Trunk, *Judenrat: The Jewish Councils in Eastern Europe Under Nazi Occupation* (New York: Stein and Day, 1977). The main virtue of this work is that it tells what the councils did and not what they ought to have done. Ample evidence of Jewish resistance to Nazism, especially in Western Europe, is provided by Belgian historian Lucien Steinberg in his 600-page book, *La révolte des justes: les Juifs contre Hitler* (Paris: Fayard, 1970).

The London meeting of British and American diplomats on 11 April 1944 is reported in the State Department papers published under the title, *Foreign Relations of the United States, 1944* (Washington: Government Printing Office, 1965), V, 600-604. For Roosevelt's statements on refugees, see the *New York Times*, 10 March and 12 October 1944.

Among those who ascribe the Nazi genocide to Jewish sinfulness is Rabbi Avrohom Berger, whose article, 'The Two Questions Concerning the Holocaust', appeared in the *Jewish Press*, 10 September 1993. When Jews stray from the Torah, God will 'hide His face' from them, and they will fall prey to their enemies. The Jews of Germany were especially negligent. They placed their hopes in German culture, whose 'miserable failure...signaled the bankruptcy and default of the entire secular life-style'.

The tendency to discredit German Judaism is not limited to Orthodox rabbis; it enjoys widespread academic sanction as well. A typical example is Sidney M. Bolkosky, *The Distorted Image: German Jewish Perception of Germans and Germany, 1918-1935* (New York: Elsevier, 1975). Professor Bolkosky, who taught history at the University of Michigan, blames the patriotism of German Jews for their inability to mount an 'organized political opposition' once the Nazis had assumed power (p. 3). Similarly, Enzo

Traverso, a research fellow at the University of Paris-Nanterre, holds that the Jews of the Weimar Republic identified themselves too closely with Germany to perceive the dangers that awaited them. See *Les juifs et l'Allemagne* (Paris: La Découverte, 1992). In essence, both authors reproach German Jews for not having known about Auschwitz before the Nazis did.

Hitler's stillborn plan to have the Jews hanged one by one on the Marianplatz in Munich is cited by Marc Ferro, *Questions sur la IIe Guerre Mondiale* (Brussels: Castermann, 1993), p. 138. For Himmler's fear of Jewish revenge, see Gordon Wright, *The Ordeal of Total War, 1939-1945* (New York: Harper & Row, 1968), p. 127. Wright, a professor of history at Stanford University, does not seem entirely at home with this question: he devotes over twice as much space to anti-submarine warfare as to the Nazi genocide. For more on the relationship between Christianity and Nazism see Hermann Diem, *Das Rätsel des Antisemitismus* (Munich: Kaiser Verlag, 1960). The author recalls that in 1933, Nazi propagandist Julius Streicher justified the regime's first anti-Jewish measures as punishment for the crucifixion (pp. 5-6).

An insight into Hitler's own religious identity, including his comment to General Engel, can be found in *The Nation* (25 April 1994), 547. The causal connection between Jesus's interpretation of Exodus 21.24 and the slaughter of European Jews was established by Hitler himself in a speech to Nazi militants in the Berlin Sportspalast on 30 January 1942. With over a million Jews already dead, he announced: 'This time and for the first time, the old authentically Jewish law: an eye for an eye and a tooth for a tooth, is being applied.' See Eliahu Ben Elissar, *La diplomatie du IIIe Reich et les juifs* (Paris: Julliard, 1969), p. 473.

Chapter IX

Roosevelt's conversation with Ibn Saud is related by William A. Eddy in his recollections, *F D R Meets Ibn Saud* (New York: American Friends of the Middle East, 1954), p. 34. Colonel Eddy was the first American minister to Saudi Arabia and served as interpreter for the two heads of state. The quotation from Truman on the Jewish vote in the United States also appears in this small volume (p. 37). The Harrison report on conditions in the DP camps can be found in J. C. Hurewitz, ed. *Diplomacy in the Near and Middle East: A Documentary Record* (2 vols.; Princeton, NJ: Van Nostrand, 1956), II, 249-257. Attlee's view that the Jews are purely a religion is cited by Kenneth Harris, in *Attlee* (London: Weidenfeld and Nicolson, 1982), p. 390. His correspondance with Truman about evacuating Jewish DP's to Palestine is contained in Francis Williams, *A Prime Minister Remembers* (London: Heineman, 1961). Attlee blames what he considers to be the immoderate political influence of American Jews for Truman's obstinacy on this point.

A dispassionate study of the Palestine question is presented by Michael J. Cohen, *Palestine and the Great Powers, 1945-1948* (Princeton, NJ: Princeton University Press, 1982). British weariness and American vacillation helped create a power vacuum, which was filled by the Zionists and the King of Jordan. Shut out of this struggle were the Palestinian Arabs. Professor Cohen, who teaches history at Bar-Ilan University in Israel, has written a companion volume entitled *Truman and Israel* (Berkeley: University of California Press, 1990), in which he defines the president's approach as 'refugee Zionism'. Truman attempts to explain his own, often incoherent, policy in volume II of his *Memoirs: Years of Trial and Hope* (New York: Doubleday, 1956). Of particular interest is his assessment of State Department specialists on the Near East, who wanted the United States to continue Britain's policy of cultivating Arab rulers, lest they turn to the Soviet Union for support. Some of these Near East experts were, in Truman's words, 'inclined to be anti-Semitic' (pp. 162-164). The president's anger at being cast in the role of a liar and a double-crosser is recorded in his calendar for 19 March 1948. See Margaret Truman, *Harry S Truman* (New York: Morrow, 1973), p. 388.

For an eyewitness account of the United Nations inquiry into Jewish and Arab claims in Palestine, notably the testimony of the Lebanese foreign minister, see Jorge García-Granados, *The Birth of Israel: The Drama As I Saw It* (New York: Knopf, 1948), pp. 201-202. García-Granados led the delegation of Guatemala at the United

Nations and was largely responsible for his country's being the first to grant the new state *de jure* recognition.

Clark Clifford's plea on 12 May 1948 for American recognition of Israel is documented in *Foreign Relations of the United States, 1948,* V, 976. His comments about Arab oil-producing states are from a memorandum of 8 March 1948 (p. 694). The State Department papers provide conclusive evidence that American policy makers were guided not by domestic political considerations, but by the Palestinian Jews' ability to create facts on the ground. Thus a memorandum of 4 May 1948 by John E. Horner of the United States delegation to the United Nations records 'the inescapable fact that a Zionist State already is in being in Palestine' (p. 899). Horner was regularly attached to the European bureau at the State Department.

A sympathetic approach to Israel's place in Jewish consciousness is shown by Conor Cruise O'Brien in *The Siege: The Saga of Israel and Zionism* (New York: Simon and Schuster, 1986). The author, who was once head of the Irish delegation to the United Nations, justifies Zionism in the light of Western society's inability to guarantee the basic rights of Jews. He does not think that the siege of Israel will be lifted any time soon. The traumatic effect of the Six-day War on the Diaspora can be seen in the writings of Raymond Aron, *De Gaulle, Israël et les juifs* (Paris: Plon, 1968). Alain Finkielkraut has decried the anti-Israel stance of the Western press during the invasion of Lebanon in a series of newspaper articles published under the title *La réprobation d'Israël* (Paris: Denoël/Gonthier, 1983). Since then, the Israelis themselves have largely outgrown their former siege mentality—a trend analyzed by American journalist Glenn Frankel in *Beyond the Promised Land* (New York: Simon and Schuster, 1994). They are increasingly tired of heroics and are inclined to accept the rabbinical adage that a bad peace is better than a good war. There is a moral here for those Diaspora Jews who care to find one.

Chapter X

Joseph Caro's strictures against reading history books are recalled by Lucy S. Dawidowicz in *What Is the Use of Jewish History?* (New

York: Schocken Books, 1994). She holds that Jews tend to abandon critical study of the past when beset by some collective tragedy: only metahistory remains. A more subtle analysis is offered by Yosef Hayim Yerushalmi in his penetrating essay, *Zakhor: Jewish History and Jewish Memory* (New York: Schocken Books, 1989). The author, who has succeeded Salo W. Baron at Columbia, notes that a spate of historical writing—really chronicle—was penned by Sephardic exiles in the early sixteenth century. But these writers founded no new school of thought, and Jews who sought to impart some meaning to their suffering soon turned to mysticism.

To buttress their contention that the coming of the Messiah is imminent, the Lubavitcher Hasidim often resort to historical arguments. Among the most coherent are those put forth by Rabbi Zalman I. Posner of Nashville, Tennessee, 'Moshiach or "Messianic Era"?' in the *Chabad Press* of Montreal (11 Nissan 5746), 21. The repeated instances of man's inhumanity to man since the First World War, he maintains, indicate that there is no progression toward a Messianic age. Only the Messiah in person, acting independently of history, can redeem the human species.

The role of Zionism in promoting Jewish unity in the Diaspora is extolled by Melvin I. Urofsky in *We Are One! American Jewry and Israel* (New York: Doubleday, 1978). That American Jews did not remain united for long can be seen in Jack Wertheimer's critical study, *A People Divided: Judaism in Contemporary America* (New York: Basic Books, 1993). The rise of neo-Orthodoxy and concurrent discomfiture of liberal Judaism are vividly portrayed here. More inspirational in tone but occasionally revealing is Michael Lerner, *Jewish Renewal* (New York: Grosset/Putnam, 1994). The author is troubled by the fact that many Jews are currently leaving the synagogue not because they want less Judaism but because they want more. For an Orthodox viewpoint on the divisions within Judaism, see Reuven P. Bulka, *The Coming Cataclysm: The Orthdox-Reform Rift and the Future of the Jewish People* (Oakville, ON: Mosaic Press, 1984). Rabbi Bulka reveals that some 'reliable Orthodox rabbis' were known to marry Jews after their Gentile spouses had received only a few hours' religious instruction (p. 79).

He insists that such practices have ceased, but urges his colleagues to receive converts lest they seek admittance to Judaism via Reform. Into this mêlée jumps professor Cantor, who, in his conclusion to *The Sacred Chain*, proposes reeducating rabbis, in order to make them more scholarly. In fact, there are quite a few scholarly rabbis around nowadays, some of whose works are cited in these pages. It is just possible that many congregations are not interested in erudition and leave their rabbis with little time to study. For an insight into this problem see Richard L. Rubenstein, 'A Rabbi Dies,' in Jacob Neusner, *American Judaism: Adventure in Modernity* (Englewood Cliffs, NJ: Prentice-Hall, 1972), pp. 46-59. The Reform and Conservative rabbinate is subject to a severe critique in S. Michael Gelber's short book, *The Failure of the American Rabbi* (New York: Twayne Publishers, 1961). The expression 'inverted Marranos' originated with Salo W. Baron (p. 32). Just what he would have thought of the use that was eventually made of it is not known.

Pessimism about the Jewish future is the theme of *Vanishing Diaspora: The Jews in Europe Since 1945* (London: Hamilton, 1996) by Bernard Wasserstein. He bemoans both the increasing rate of intermarriage and the decreasing birthrate among endogamous Jewish couples. Assimilation has replaced anti-Semitism as the main threat to the Jews of Western Europe, who face 'dissolution into a society that killed by kindness' (p. 279). Jewish demography is hardly a new problem. In an article of 1963, 'The Vanishing Jew', Milton Himmelfarb recognized that Jews were not reproducing themselves. His solution: bring in converts to offset the decline. See *The Jews of Modernity*, pp. 120-124.

That Orthodoxy has problems of its own is revealed by the former chief rabbi of Great Britain, Immanuel Jakobovits, in a personal memoir, *If Only My People: Zionism In My Life* (London: Weidenfeld and Nicolson, 1984). The author views the existence of Israel as an encouragement to Jewish piety everywhere. But he strongly opposes attempts by Diaspora rabbis, such as the late Menachem Schneerson of Brooklyn, to dictate Israeli policy (pp. 98-101). In his disputes with Schneerson, Jakobovits recognizes implicitly that the Lubavitch movement is a force to be reckoned with.

The remarkable vigour of contemporary French Judaism has escaped general attention, both in the United States and in Israel. Its importance lies in the fact that France had to endure German military occupation for four years and that a third of its Jewish population perished in Nazi death camps. The French experience is proof that Judaism can thrive in the West even after Auschwitz. Howard M. Sachar refers to a 'demographic revolution' among French Jews in his survey, *Diaspora* (New York: Harper & Row, 1985), but the revolution is more than demographic. Its many facets are explored by Doris Bensimon in *Les juifs de France et leurs relations avec Israël, 1945-1988* (Paris: L'Harmattan, 1989). Israel is hardly mentioned in this book. A lively account of the divisive elements within French Judaism and the rise of militant Orthodoxy is given by Frank Eskenazi and Edouard Waintrop in *Le Talmud et la République* (Paris: Grasset, 1991). The active participation of French Jews in their country's public affairs can be seen in Maurice Szafran, *Les juifs dans la politique française de 1945 à nos jours* (Paris: Flammarion, 1990).

For the power struggle within the French rabbinate and the victory of Joseph Sitruk, see 'Juifs de France: le malaise', *L'Evénement du Jeudi* (19-25 April 1990), 61-62. His reelection as chief rabbi in 1994 did not end discussion on conversions to Judaism, which was soon taken up by the country's leading Jewish periodical. Foremost among those who favoured taking in proselytes was Rabbi Josy Eisenberg, who has presented a weekly television programme on Judaism since 1962. His argument was based on Leviticus 19.33-34: 'You shall love the stranger as yourself'. See 'La question des conversions au judaïsme', *L'Arche* (September 1994), 67-70.

The opposition of Charles Maurras to Hebraic thought is cited by Eugen Weber in *Action Française* (Stanford, CA: Stanford University Press, 1962), p. 8. That fewer and fewer Christians believe in hell is attested to by Pope John Paul II in his recent book, *Crossing the Threshold of Hope* (New York: Knopf, 1994), p. 183. The debate on the Sabbath egg has been used by French Catholic writer Daniel-Rops to belittle Pharisaic Judaism in *La vie quotidienne en Palestine au temps de Jésus* (Paris: Hachette, 1961), pp.

505-506. The author's supporting reference to II Cor. 3.6 ('The letter [of the law] kills, but the spirit gives life.') indicates that the Jewish-Christian argument turns more around Paul than around Jesus. Arnold Toynbee took a more positive approach to Judaism in *Reconsiderations*, volume XII of *A Study of History* (London: Oxford University Press, 1961), pp. 477-517. He soon urged Jews to resume their former missionary vocation. See 'The Future of Judaism in Western Countries', *Issues* (1962-63), VII, 64-77. The fact that he chose to publish this message in the organ of the anti-Zionist American Council for Judaism did little to facilitate its acceptance.

Chapter XI

That the Nazi genocide has had a devastating effect on Jewish thought is self-evident. 'I have never found a way to absolve God of the crime of Auschwitz', writes rabbi and historian Arthur Hertzberg, 'A Lifelong Quarrel with God', in *Jewish Polemics* (New York: Columbia University Press, 1992), p. 243. The problem may not be God, but the rabbinical view of Him. In a seminal essay entitled *The Religious Imagination* (Indianapolis: Bobbs-Merrill, 1968), Richard L. Rubenstein posits 'that the interpretation of Jewish misfortune as the punitive visitation of the Lord of history is disfunctional as a response to Auschwitz' (p. xvii). Rubenstein wrote these words before the Hasidim and their allies incorporated Auschwitz into rabbinical legend by claiming that it was, indeed, divine punishment for the sin of assimilation.

The effect of the tragedy on Christianity has been no less profound: it destroys the traditional Christian apology for Jewish suffering. Whereas rabbinical Judaism held that the Jews were punished for having strayed from the Torah, Christianity claimed that their misfortunes stemmed from being faithful to it. Christian persecutions of Jews in the Middle Ages were a self-fulfilling prophesy, in which only the obstinate were supposed to suffer. Any Jew who wanted to avoid martyrdom could do so, in theory, simply by accepting baptism. Inasmuch as no such possibility existed in the Nazi death camps, one may safely conclude that Jewish obstinacy was not the problem there. In recent years some Christian thinkers have tried to purge Christianity of its anti-Jewish bias. Among the most valiant efforts is that of Rosemary Ruether, *Faith and Fratricide: The Theological Roots of Anti-Semitism* (New York: Seabury Press, 1974). The author would like Christians to learn Jewish history, in particular that of Judaism at the time of Jesus. Franklin H. Littell refers to 'the crisis of faith precipitated by the Holocaust' in *The Crucifixion of the Jews* (New York: Harper & Row, 1975), p. 116. The emphasis here is on Jewish suffering; nothing in this book would encourage a Christian to learn about Judaism. In *Elder and Younger Brothers* (New York: Schocken Books, 1967), A. Roy Eckhardt rejects his fellow Christians' patronizing view of Judaism, which he nonetheless considers a 'mystery'. Eliminating anti-Jewish stereotypes from Christian teaching is the aim of François Houtart and Geneviève Lemercinier in *Les juifs dans la catéchèse* (Brussels: Editions Vie Ouvrière, 1972). The authors are sociologists at the University of Louvain.

To sympathize with Jewish suffering is one thing; to appreciate Judaism is quite another. The failure of even the most benevolent Christians to accept Judaism on its own merits is presented in a series of pregnant articles by American theologian Arthur A. Cohen, *The Myth of the Judeo-Christian Tradition* (New York: Schocken Books, 1971). Christian endeavours to accommodate Jewish sensibilities seem to have reached their limit. The quotations from Karl Barth can be found in his *Church Dogmatics* (4 vols.; Edinburgh: Clark, 1947-56), Vol. II, part 2, pp. 209 and 264; Vol. IV, part 1, p. 671. Israeli philosopher-scientist Yeshayahou Leibowitz comments: 'According to Barth, Christianity cannot endure Judaism, and I think he is right.' See *Israël et judaïsme: ma part de vérité* (Paris: Desclée de Brouwer, 1993), p. 93. More recently, two French priests have published an edition of the New Testament replete with annotations deprecating both Jews and Judaism. A public outcry over this so-called 'anti-Jewish Bible' led the bishop of Versailles to withdraw the *Imprimatur* and his preface to the book. But its publisher continued printing, and the two priests were unrepentant. They held that their edition of the New Testament was entirely consistent with Christian tradition. See *Le Monde*, 10 and 23 March 1995.

The Jewish Challenge 269

The Americanization of the Holocaust is the subject of a perceptive article in *The Economist* (1 May 1993), 94. A telephone call to the Holocaust Memorial in Washington elicited the cheery greeting, 'Holocaust, may I help you?' At the opening ceremonies, the United States Army Band kept playing 'God Bless America'. But the article's author left the exhibition wondering, 'Why, why on earth—why?' Fund raising for the Memorial has been entrusted to a public relations firm which makes one sales pitch to Jews and another to Gentiles. On receiving the Gentile package, John R. MacArthur, publisher of *Harper's Magazine*, exploded with indignation. The material was meant to give recipients a good feeling about their country's role in liberating Europe from Nazism; Jews were hardly mentioned at all. 'This is the cheapening and sanitizing of what I consider the central crime of the 20th century,' writes MacArthur, adding: 'Like *Schindler's List*, the Holocaust Museum Gentile package is a Holocaust story with a happy ending.' See his article, 'The Selling of the Holocaust Museum', *The Globe and Mail* (Toronto), 22 July 1994.

Albert Memmi's proposal to re-open Judaism to the nations can be found in *Juifs et Arabes* (Paris: Gallimard, 1974), p. 183. The study indicating that conversionary marriages enhance the Jewish consciousness of both partners is by Egon Mayer and Carl Sheingold, *Intermarriage and the Jewish Future* (New York: American Jewish Committee, 1979). The authors add that 'in some ways, there is more reason for optimism about Jewish continuity in families where the born-Gentile spouse has converted to Judaism than there is in the typical endogamous family' (p. 30). Their report may be read in conjunction with two works by Jacob Neusner, who has done more than anyone else to revive Jewish learning in the United States. In *History and Torah* (New York: Schocken Books, 1965), he writes that the periods when Jewish inquiry was especially active were 'those in which Jews were most deeply involved in and responsive to the heritage of alien civilizations' (p. 62). He goes on to posit that Jewish consciousness is most intense outside of Jewish society in *Stranger At Home* (Chicago: University of Chicago Press, 1981), p. 195. The future of Judaism would therefore appear to lie more with the Diaspora than with the State of Israel.

Jewish ethnocentrism and nostalgia are dissected by Dow Marmur in *Beyond Survival: Reflections on the Future of Judaism* (London: Darton, Longman & Todd, 1982). 'The trauma of the Holocaust has produced an almost tribal response,' he writes. For Jews, the State of Israel incarnates 'the doctrine of survival as a supra-religious value transcending denominational differences' (p. 43). Rabbi Marmur does not show what may lie beyond Jewish survival, but he recognizes that it can no longer suffice.The great American historian Robert R. Palmer has denounced over-specialization among historians and their growing estrangement from the general reader in 'A Century of French History in America', *French Historical Studies* (Fall 1985), 160-175. 'For us in history the audience is simply ourselves, and it is hard to see what such specialization contributes to the education of the young or the enlightenment of the public' (p. 174). Yet history continues to exert a fascination on non-professionals, such as Rabbi Agus, who may even attempt to find a meaning to it.

INDEX